FROM FRENCH COMMUNITY
TO MISSOURI TOWN

FROM FRENCH COMMUNITY
TO MISSOURI TOWN

Ste. Genevieve in the Nineteenth Century

BONNIE STEPENOFF

UNIVERSITY OF MISSOURI PRESS
COLUMBIA AND LONDON

Library of Congress Cataloging-in-Publication Data

Stepenoff, Bonnie, 1949–
    From French community to Missouri town : Ste. Genevieve in the nineteenth century /
Bonnie Stepenoff.
        p.   cm.
    Summary: "Examines the historical circumstances, legal institutions, and popular customs of
Ste. Genevieve, Missouri's oldest permanent settlement, to discuss how French and Spanish residents, German immigrants, and American settlers compromised on issues of education, religion,
property laws, and women's rights to achieve order and community before and after the Louisiana
Purchase"—Provided by publisher.
    Includes bibliographical references and index.
    ISBN-13: 978-0-8262-1668-7 (hard cover : alk. paper)
    ISBN-13: 978-0-8262-2313-5 (paperback : alk. paper)
    1. Sainte Genevieve (Mo.)—History—19th century.   2. Sainte Genevieve (Mo.)—Social
conditions.   3. Sainte Genevieve (Mo.)—Ethnic relations—History—19th century.   I. Title.
    F474.S135S76   2006
    977.8'692—dc22   2006009568

Typeface: Adobe Garamond

For Nancy

Contents

PREFACE

FOR EIGHT SUMMERS, beginning in 1997, I took Southeast Missouri State University students to Ste. Genevieve to teach them about historic preservation. Every year my students and I followed Professor Hilliard Goldman up the wooden steps to the *galerie* of the Green Tree Tavern. Each summer he would tell us to place our palms against the building's heavy old timbers that stand side by side to form the exterior walls, and after we had followed his instructions, he would tell us that "These logs were here in this wall when George Washington was president of the United States." Ste. Genevieve was not a part of the new American republic at that time; all the territory west of the Mississippi was still under Spanish rule. In the late eighteenth and early nineteenth centuries, Ste. Genevieve's old French families held on to social, economic, and political power. But that would soon change. Or would it?

Time after time, various groups of students and I climbed the bluff above Highway 61 and looked out at the flat expanse of bottom land that stretched for miles along the Mississippi River. Professor Susan Flader told us that the first French settlers in the mid-eighteenth century had built their vertical log houses close to the river banks at the end of long narrow fields that extended from the edge of the water to the rise of the limestone bluffs. We could picture the French, Franco-African, and Native American husbandmen, toiling all day in the fields and then leading their draft animals home to the shelter of the village. They must have walked around the ancient mound left there by farmers of an even earlier civilization known to us now as the Mississippians. In the 1780s, the river overflowed its banks, and the French settlers had to move their houses to the opposite ends of their long lots and into the shelter of the cliffs. But the big agricultural field *(le grand champ)* endured through the centuries, turning amber in fall, brown in winter, yellow gold in spring, and bright green in summer, just as it was when we stood there year after year.

On hot, humid days, my students and I worked with archaeologists, excavating the Delassus-Kern property on Highway 61. In 2003, two students, Jason Moen and Jason Williamson, unearthed a gold ring inscribed with the initials *N. K.* for Nettie Kern. Nettie was a descendant of the German farmer who had acquired the property after an old French family lost control of it. The ring and its inscription created a tangible bond between two twenty-first century students, a nineteenth-century woman, and Pierre Delassus, the hapless French aristocrat who came to Ste. Genevieve to escape the French Revolution.

On one occasion we watched as a dendrochronologist took core borings from some of the old timbers in the Delassus-Kern House. Tree rings tell a story if you know how to interpret them, and the rings on these particular logs indicated that the house had been constructed from timbers cut in 1793. But the rings tell only part of the home's history. To uncover the rest of the story, my students and I took paint samples from hidden places in the walls. We measured, photographed, and delved into the records to piece together the story. But we were never really satisfied. There were never any easy answers.

We gradually realized that easy answers were not the point. Asking questions was the point.

In the summer of 2004, my students and I scrubbed tombstones in the old cemetery in a gentle rain. Some people might have wondered why we cared about the grave markers of people unrelated to us, people who died more than a century ago. But we had no doubt that what we were doing made sense. It was something that mattered.

Those tombstones had something to tell us, but it took us a while to figure that out. The names on the grave markers were French, German, and Anglo-American. We searched for them in probate files and deed books and in the old French archives. We learned something about the people: the ones who died in infancy, the ones who died of cholera in the prime of life, the ones who died in childbirth, and the ones who lived to a ripe old age and owned half the town. We knew they had something to tell us, and I came to believe that it was something important, something about democracy.

That was when I started to write this book.

ACKNOWLEDGMENTS

I WANT TO THANK EVERYONE involved with the Historic Preservation Field School in Ste. Genevieve from 1997 through 2004. Above all, thanks are due to Southeast Missouri State University and the Missouri Department of Natural Resources, the institutional sponsors of the field school. Every year Les Amis and the Foundation for Restoration of Ste. Genevieve provided funding, housing for students, and other valuable assistance, and Jim Baker, B. H. Rucker, Larry Grantham, Kenneth Cole, Stanley Fast, and Kim Dillon shared their knowledge of history, archaeology, and historic preservation with students. Other members of the faculty included Kit Wesler, Carol Morrow, Scott Myers, and Steven Hoffman. Graduate assistants included Debbie Bibb and Michael Morin. Larry and Donna Marler opened their home to students and staunchly supported the field school through eight summers. Hilliard Goldman and Jack Luer showed us the progress they made in restoring the Green Tree Tavern. John Karel provided housing for students and moral support for the program. Special thanks are due to Marge and Royce Wilhauk for long conversational breakfasts and evening swimming parties at the Creole House. Among the many guest speakers were Osmund Overby, Susan Flader, Eric Clements, Pat Huber, Elizabeth Scott, Don Heldman, James M. Denny, Walter Schroeder, Kent Beaulne, and David Cameron. Students in the field school conducted important primary research on the people of Ste. Genevieve, including the free black residents of the town before the Civil War.

Many scholars have studied Ste. Genevieve. Carl Ekberg published several important books on the colonial period. Walter Schroeder explored Ste. Genevieve's connection to the westward movement and the settlement of the Ozarks. Gregory Franzwa and Firmin A. Rozier published fascinating histories of the town. Bill and Patti Naeger and Mark Evans collected important images and created a portrait of the community's past. Osmund Overby and Susan Flader conducted a multiyear study that uncovered important new information about the development of the community, its landscape, and its architecture. Susan Boyle completed a groundbreaking study of French colonial women in Ste. Genevieve. David Denman and Barbara Sanders wrote insightful papers on the social history of the town. Renae Farris penned an exceptional thesis on Marie LaPorte and her experiences in a French colony that became an American town. Carla Jordan tirelessly searched for the roots of a mixed-race family that endured from the colonial period into the twenty-first century. Delilah Tayloe searched for information on Michel Badeau. The University of Missouri–Columbia and the State Historical Society of Missouri worked together to microfilm and index an invaluable collection of Ste. Genevieve Archives.

In writing this book, I have relied upon the advice and assistance of many people. Debbie Bibb helped me gather and analyze data on the white and black populations of the town before the Civil War. Laurel Boeckman and Ara Kaye of the State Historical Society helped uncover information about disease and disaster in nineteenth-century Ste. Genevieve. B. H. Rucker shared information from his meticulous study of the old French cemetery. Kent Beaulne introduced me to the music and folklore of the old French colonies. Jim Baker was always willing to help me find information in the files of Felix Vallè State Historic Site and to share his encyclopedic knowledge of Ste. Genevieve's history. Librarians and archivists at Southeast Missouri State University, the State Historical Society of Missouri, the Missouri Historical Society, and the Sisters of St. Joseph of Carondelet pointed me to the materials I needed. Art Hebrank of Missouri Mines State Historic Site helped me understand the relationship of Ste. Genevieve to the Lead Belt. Sandy Koller helped me find old city ordinances. Susan Flader, Osmund Overby, Jack Luer, Jesse Francis, and many others convinced me that the story of Ste. Genevieve was important enough to be retold in many ways and viewed from many angles. Two peer readers offered suggestions for improving the manuscript. The staff of the University of Missouri Press greeted this project with enthusiasm and professionalism, for which I am very grateful. Susan King edited the manuscript with care and perceptiveness.

And my family helped me in more ways than I can express.

For the spellings of proper names, I have relied upon a variety of primary sources. The surname *Valle* appears in these sources with and without an accent on the final *e* and sometimes with two *ee*'s. The process of Americanization sometimes brought changes, such as the elimination of accents in French names. First names such as Francois eventually changed to American forms such as Frank. Some names appear in official documents in many different forms. For instance, the name *D'Atchurut* is sometimes spelled "D'Atchurutte" or "D'Atcherutte." For the sake of consistency, I have chosen one spelling for each name. In general, the spelling chosen is the one that is most common or the one that appears in the most reliable sources.

Chapter 8 is adapted from a paper by Bonnie Stepenoff, Debbie Bibb, and Carla L. Jordan.

Barbara E. Cohen prepared the index.

FROM FRENCH COMMUNITY
TO MISSOURI TOWN

INTRODUCTION

I have remarked that the maintenance of democratic institutions in the United States is attributable to the circumstances, the laws, and the customs of that country.

Alexis de Tocqueville, *Democracy in America*

WHAT IS THE WELLSPRING of democracy? Is it the landscape, as Frederick Jackson Turner so famously suggested? Was Turner correct when he said, "The existence of an area of free land, its continuous recession, and the advance of American settlement westward, explain American development?"[1] Does liberty spring up on the frontiers of civilization? Does it arise spontaneously from "free land," whatever that may be? Or, more probably and less dramatically, do democratic institutions accumulate through tradition and habit? Is democracy embodied in the land or in the law? Can governments or regimes present it as a gift to the people? Or does it abide in the people themselves, in their everyday behavior and attitudes? Is there something peculiarly "American" about it, as Americans, encouraged by Turner, have tended to believe?

Observing life in the United States in 1830, an aristocratic Frenchman named Alexis de Tocqueville concluded that three factors made it possible for democratic institutions to take hold and thrive in America. Circumstances, including the physical environment, natural resources, and population of the country, provided the basis for the prosperity and mobility that characterized the new republic. The Constitution, the legal system, and the operation of the courts allocated power and protected individual

1. Frederick Jackson Turner, *The Frontier in American History*, 1.

I

liberty, although threats to liberty remained. Far more important, in Tocqueville's view, than either the landscape or the laws were the customs of the people, who lived, died, and prepared new generations for democratic life.[2]

Although he was French, Tocqueville credited Anglo-Americans with a special gift for democracy. During his nine-month sojourn in America, he paid little attention to the French communities in the middle Mississippi River valley. His itinerary took him to New York, Buffalo, the Great Lakes region, Wisconsin, Michigan, Canada, Boston, Philadelphia, and Baltimore. Then he traveled west to Pittsburgh, Cincinnati, Nashville, and Memphis. When he encountered the great Mississippi north of Memphis, the river was frozen, so he went south and never came close to Ste. Genevieve. He traveled to New Orleans and then headed east to Washington, D.C., and New York. No one can guess what he might have learned from studying a small but thriving west bank village that became officially "American" in 1803.

Ste. Genevieve was a frontier town, and its people exhibited some of the democratic spirit that Turner extolled. But most of its inhabitants were French and had lived for several decades in the Spanish colonial empire. Did these French roots and Spanish legal systems leave a permanent mark on the character of Ste. Genevieve's inhabitants? Or did the old European traditions vanish with the unfurling of the American flag?[3] By becoming an American town, did Ste. Genevieve become more democratic, and if so, what specifically did that mean? How did the process of Americanization alter the customs and behavior of the people? Perhaps more important, how did the habits and traditions of the people of Ste. Genevieve support or undermine the development of American institutions?

Carl Ekberg wrote extensively and authoritatively about colonial Ste. Genevieve, but his histories ended with the Louisiana Purchase in 1803.[4] Firmin Rozier, Francis Yealy, and Gregory Franzwa chronicled the town's history after 1803, but their work did not delve deeply into the social and

---

2. Alexis de Tocqueville, *Democracy in America*, 1:319–30.

3. A preliminary treatment of this subject is in Stuart Banner, *Legal Systems in Conflict: Property and Sovereignty in Missouri, 1750–1860*.

4. See especially Carl J. Ekberg, *Colonial Ste. Genevieve: An Adventure on the Mississippi Frontier*.

political changes resulting from Americanization.[5] Geographer Walter Schroeder published an important volume on the westward migration through Ste. Genevieve and its environs into the Ozark highlands. As Schroeder pointed out, however, the dramatic intermingling of French, African, Anglo-American, and German families in Ste. Genevieve after the French and Spanish periods is a story that still needs to be told.[6]

This book explores the complex transformation of a French village to an American small town. Taking a cue from Tocqueville, the chapters that follow examine the landscape, legal institutions, and the customs of the people of Ste. Genevieve with one objective: a better understanding of how democracy works. Chapter 1 presents a portrait of the town at the historical moment when Meriwether Lewis and William Clark traveled up the Mississippi River toward St. Louis at the outset of their journey through the Louisiana Territory.

Lewis and Clark paid scant attention to the town directly across the river from the east bank settlement of Kaskaskia. At the time, however, with approximately three thousand residents, Ste. Genevieve was about the same size as St. Louis.[7] Most of the inhabitants were French. Others were slaves or free people of African descent or Native Americans. The community encompassed wealthy landowners, busy merchants, fur traders, carpenters, blacksmiths, boatmen, farmers, housewives, laborers, slaves, adventurers, and ne'er-do-wells.

The people of Ste. Genevieve built the walls of their houses with logs upended from holes in the ground *(poteaux en terre)* or mounted on heavy timber sills *(poteaux sur solles)* in a manner reminiscent of homes in medieval Normandy or in colonial Quebec.[8] These vertical log houses visually signaled the differences between French settlers and their Anglo-American counterparts, who laid the logs horizontally one on top of the

5. Gregory Franzwa, *The Story of Old Ste. Genevieve;* Firmin Rozier, *Rozier's History of the Early Settlement of the Mississippi Valley;* and Francis Joseph Yealy, *Sainte Genevieve: The Story of Missouri's Oldest Settlement.*

6. Walter A. Schroeder, *Opening the Ozarks: A Historical Geography of Missouri's Ste. Genevieve District, 1760–1830,* 20.

7. Ibid., 15–16.

8. See Charles E. Peterson, "Early Ste. Genevieve and its Architecture"; and Melburn D. Thurman, *Building a House in Eighteenth Century Ste. Genevieve.*

other. The farmers of Ste. Genevieve laid out their croplands in long narrow lots that stretched from the river to the bluffs in a pattern that differed dramatically from the checkerboard or crazy-quilt land claims of the
Anglo-Americans.[9] The houses and stores of Ste. Genevieve clustered
around the Catholic Church, which was in many ways the heart of the
community. There was no courthouse, but there were several taverns.

No one would have called the town a democracy. In fact, several prominent citizens came to the area seeking refuge from the democratizing
thrust of the French Revolution. Landed patriarchs (seigneurs) made decisions for the community, mediated disputes, and presided over legal proceedings. Henry Brackenridge, who came to Ste. Genevieve at the end of
the colonial period, observed that ordinary citizens gave little thought to
politics because the local "commandants" made all the decisions.[10] Even in
the Spanish colony, however, ordinary people exercised the right to sue
for damages or bring their grievances to the attention of local officials. By
living on the frontier, the residents of Ste. Genevieve gained some prepa-
ration for democracy. As chapter 2 reveals, some of the old French aristocrats failed to adapt to their backwoods environment, but others embraced
the American system and seized opportunities for economic advancement.[11]

After the Louisiana Purchase, Anglo-Americans descended upon Ste.
Genevieve. Some came to stay; others stopped briefly on their way to
points farther west. Some were typical frontiersmen, struggling to establish small self-sustaining farms, or speculators, hoping to make a fortune
from mining or land acquisition. Others were doctors and lawyers, seeking professional opportunities, or merchants, wanting to tap into the
lucrative river trade or to outfit the wagons heading west. Many Anglo-
Americans who settled in the town came from tobacco or cotton-producing
states in the South, and many owned slaves. They may have been democrats, but they did not believe in equality. Some of them rose in the social
system by forming business alliances with the old French families; others

9. Schroeder, *Opening the Ozarks*, 242–43.

10. H. M. Brackenridge, *Recollections of Persons and Places in the West*, 20–22.

11. For two fascinating studies of prominent old French families, see Carl J. Ekberg's *François Vallé and His World: Upper Louisiana before Lewis and Clark* and *Louis Bolduc: His Family and His House*.

achieved prominence in the rough and tumble politics of the new American republic.

Chapter 4 documents how German immigrants, who trickled in after the American takeover and poured in during the 1840s, helped stabilize the growing community. Most of the Germans who migrated to Ste. Genevieve were Catholics from Baden. They came in family groups and quickly joined the local Catholic Church. By the third quarter of the nineteenth century, these immigrants had established themselves as merchants, tradesmen, and pillars of the local community, but they retained their separate ethnic identity. The French and the Anglo-Americans viewed them as outlanders but also lived with them as neighbors. By the 1880s, the character of Ste. Genevieve had changed. French vertical log houses still dotted the landscape, but mingled among them were horizontal log houses and gabled stone residences of Anglo-Americans and typical German American dwellings of timber and brick with tall symmetrical facades set close to the street.[12]

Ste. Genevieve's history as an American town began officially in 1808, when local leaders defined its boundaries, filed papers of incorporation, and passed ordinances outlining the responsibilities of citizens. The roster of elected officials included Anglo-American, French, and German names. As chapter 5 makes clear, the new American order brought some important changes. Participatory democracy replaced the old seigniorial system, but only white males could participate. Black people and women gained little from the change and, perhaps, lost some of the protections they enjoyed in a paternalistic community. American antagonism toward native peoples inspired strict regulation of the free and easy French trade with the Indians.[13]

In any emerging democracy, there must be a certain amount of chaos. As chapter 6 demonstrates, Ste. Genevieve had its share of thugs, desperadoes, guns, knives, and general mayhem. White male southerners brought with them a social code that glorified the use of firearms in defense of personal honor.[14] The steamboats that arrived after 1817 carried gamblers,

12. See Robyn Burnett and Ken Luebbering, *German Settlement in Missouri: New Land, Old Ways.*
13. *Goodspeed's History of Southeast Missouri,* 405–6.
14. See Dick Steward, *Duels and the Roots of Violence in Missouri.*

tipplers, tricksters, and con artists looking for action on every landing. Professional methods of law enforcement had not reached the trans-Mississippi West; justice in Ste. Genevieve was frontier justice. Sheriffs sometimes behaved as badly as outlaws. Cold-blooded killers stared down frightened juries, while other miscreants—more guilty or less intimidating—hung by the neck on gallows hill.

Women had to fight for equality in the new republic. In an important study of women in colonial Ste. Genevieve published in the 1980s, Susan Boyle argued that French laws and customs, as well as the peculiar conditions of life in Ste. Genevieve, gave local women an unusual degree of economic independence. French inheritance laws allowed daughters to inherit a portion of their father's estate, giving many women property and wealth of their own and reducing their dependence on their husbands. The wives of traders and trappers had to maintain households, farms, and businesses because their husbands were absent most of the time.[15] American practices, based on English common law, transferred a woman's property to her husband; therefore women did not necessarily benefit from Americanization. As chapter 7 illustrates, however, women in Ste. Genevieve continued to exercise some economic power and to speak up for themselves in courts of law.

Chapter 8 examines the impact of Americanization on the precarious legal and social position of persons of color. Under French and Spanish rule, a substantial number of free blacks lived, married, worked, and owned property in Ste. Genevieve. When Missouri joined the Union as a slave state in 1821, the position of free blacks became tenuous. The new legislature nearly passed a bill forbidding blacks from living as free persons in the state. Instead, lawmakers passed a bill requiring each free black individual to post a bond and obtain a license from the county clerk.[16] As America moved toward civil war, Ste. Genevieve's free black residents presented themselves and received licenses, but even that did not guarantee them the right to continue living as citizens of the community. The Fugi-

15. Susan C. Boyle, "Did She Generally Decide: Women in Ste. Genevieve, 1750–1805," 775–89.

16. See Lorenzo Greene, Gary R. Kremer, and Antonio Holland, *Missouri's Black Heritage;* Donnie D. Bellamy, "Free Blacks in Antebellum Missouri, 1820–1860."

tive Slave Law of 1850 and the *Dred Scott* decision of 1857 denied them any protection in federal courts. Several black men from Ste. Genevieve joined the Union army during the Civil War, but even the Union victory did not guarantee them all the rights and privileges of citizens. Racism and discrimination continued to make their lives difficult.

Frontier life and changes in the legal system had an impact on democracy in Ste. Genevieve. But, as Tocqueville argued, the customs, beliefs, and behavior of the people, from day to day, year to year, and generation to generation, are far more important. In all places and times, work and family are the central realities of life. Chapter 9 illuminates the struggles of the rich, not-so-rich, and poorer folk of the community, who tried to make it in a land that promised opportunity for anyone, or at least any white man, with capital, courage, shrewdness, or a strong back. Individual effort, in most cases, did not suffice. Family ties and interpersonal connections often made the difference between success and stagnation in the Americanizing town.

Rearing the next generation was, perhaps, the most important task of the citizens of the new republic. Democracy could not survive or develop to a higher level without concerned and committed people to serve in public office, exercise the electoral franchise, and hold the community together. Chapter 10 focuses on home, church, and school, the three fundamental institutions that work, more or less in concert, to educate the young and perpetuate the values of a society aspiring toward democratic ideals.

In any society, hope rests in new generations because life is unpredictable and brief. Chapter 11 examines life, death, and remembrance in Ste. Genevieve. Early death haunted the streets of this small town, and every year the river washed unidentified corpses onto the landing. In 1832 and 1849, deadly cholera epidemics traveled up- and downstream on the steamboats. Ste. Genevieve had no shortage of doctors, but their medical knowledge was limited. Women died in childbirth, children died of common contagious diseases, and men died violently in duels, knife fights, and wars. The tombstones in the old French cemetery recorded these losses and reflected the growing diversity of the town.

Holidays, festivals, and celebrations renew the joy of living and connect people to one another through the generations. Chapter 12 reveals that in Ste. Genevieve, old French customs, such as the New Year's *Guillonee,* survived and became as American as the Fourth of July. Through the decades, the community celebrated its shared history that included the creation of the French colony as well as the advent of the new republic. In 1885, residents splurged on a festival commemorating the year of the big waters and the movement of the settlers from the old town to New Ste. Genevieve at a safer distance from the Mississippi River. By 1885, the town had changed in significant ways but retained much of its old French character. Advances had been made, particularly in education and the creation of a free press. But Americanization had not obliterated the French colonial past. Nor had it given birth to unfettered freedom or equality.

The history of Ste. Genevieve challenges some common beliefs about democracy in America. Tocqueville assumed that freedom could not survive in the presence of a landed aristocracy. But several old French families retained large landholdings and high status well into the nineteenth century, and yet democratic institutions took hold in Ste. Genevieve. Tocqueville viewed democracy as somehow quintessentially Anglo-American in character, and yet the French, German, and African residents of Ste. Genevieve maintained the basic tenets of democracy by participating in communal life and standing up for their rights. Their experiences cast doubt on the notion that democracy originates in federal mandates, judicial decrees, or military action. In certain instances, governmental authorities can intervene to protect the rights of the people, but the people also have to demand protection of their rights. To paraphrase a cliché, all democracy is local. It may be untidy and uncertain, but freedom can survive only if people are willing to embrace it as their own.

Tocqueville correctly asserted that democracy depends less on physical circumstances, laws, and government than it does on the customs and habits of the people. Traditions evolve incrementally. Habits take root through endless repetition and daily affirmations of faith. No earthly power can impose or create them in a moment of idealism or an act of will. Those who would attempt to export American democracy to other cultures and societies should keep this simple truth in mind.

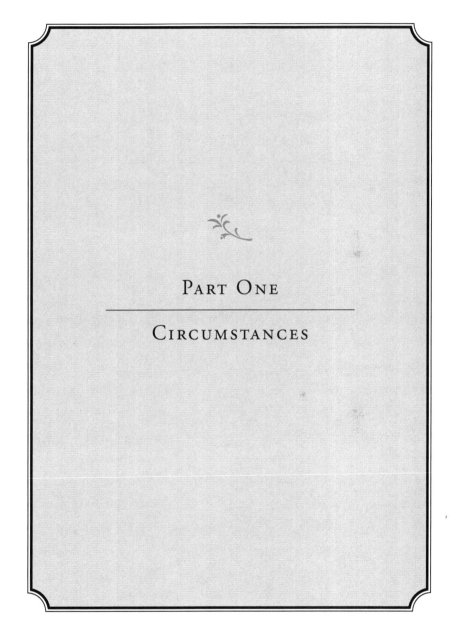

PART ONE

CIRCUMSTANCES

CHAPTER ONE

Ste. Genevieve in 1803

Set out this morning before Sunrise, at ¾ of a mile passed the mouth of a Small Creek Called Gabia [Gabouri], at the mouth of this Creek is the landing place for the Tradeing Boats of St Genevieve, a Small town Situated on the Spurs of the high land at ¾ of a mile distant nearly South This Village contains (as I am informed) about 120 families, principally French, . . .

Journals of the Lewis and Clark Expedition,
December 4, 1803

LEWIS AND CLARK never set foot in Ste. Genevieve, but the explorers noted from a vantage point on a bluff across the river that a French settlement existed on the banks of a creek between the wide river and a line of craggy limestone cliffs.[1] Other Americans showed more interest in the community, either because of the mineral wealth in the surrounding hills or the challenges of creating a new form of government in the former French colony. Mining tycoon Moses Austin cast a sharp eye on the area even before the Louisiana Purchase. Henry Brackenridge observed the American takeover from a unique perspective, coming to the French community as a boy and returning to the American town as a grown man. Amos Stoddard, a United States government official, wrote a revealing analysis of local society and politics.

There were actually two towns in this French settlement: Ste. Genevieve, nestled between the branches of the Gabouri Creek, and New Bourbon,

1. *Journals of the Lewis and Clark Expedition,* 2:123. The explorers underestimated the population, which apparently approached three thousand, as Walter Schroeder and others have calculated.

perched on a promontory overlooking the vast tilled field along the river. Ste. Genevieve, the lowland village, would survive into the twenty-first century, and New Bourbon would fade away. Their histories are linked with each other's and with the spread of the new American republic across the Mississippi to the western sea.

Frederick Jackson Turner might have viewed the stories of these towns in terms of the ever-expanding frontier, and in truth they were frontier outposts. But their inhabitants were not typical backwoodsmen in the American mold. New Bourbon sheltered a nobleman, who intended to create a refuge for himself and for his peers, fleeing the French Revolution. Ste. Genevieve boasted its own aristocratic families, who had long maintained a dominant social position within the compact village at the edge of a huge cultivated field. To outsiders, Ste. Genevieve may have seemed more like a medieval manor than a collection of hardscrabble farms.

Surviving French houses and landscapes have made it possible for modern-day travelers to imagine Ste. Genevieve and its environs at the time of the Louisiana Purchase. Perhaps the most amazing survival of all was the big common field *(le grand champ)* that stretches fertile and flat for miles along the banks of the Mississippi. In the nineteenth-century railroad tracks intruded upon it, and in the twentieth century earthen levees altered its contours to hold back floods. But the big field remained an agricultural landscape, substantially undeveloped for hundreds of years.

Centuries before Columbus made his famous voyages, Native American farmers cultivated the dark, flood-enriched soil of the big field. Archaeological evidence indicates that these ancient people grew maize and made stone weapons and tools, but that they had no metals, draft animals, or wheels. They created sophisticated ceramic pottery and jewelry, embellishing many items with human or animal effigies. In the absence of written records, archaeologists have called these people Mississippians, because remnants of their civilization studded the banks of the river. Most prominent among these were the earthen mounds, which the Mississippians built to elevate their temples, plazas, fortifications, and burial sites. Sometime before Columbus, the Mississippians abandoned their villages and disappeared or dispersed. Their fate remains a mystery. French settlers, who divided the big field into long lots and tilled it in the eighteenth century, did not disturb the Mississippian mounds, which remained visible in the twenty-first century.

After the Mississippian civilization declined, a succession of peoples lived or hunted in the creek bottoms and hills along the western banks of the Mississippi River. The Missouri and Osage tribes were accomplished hunters, who carried on a lively trade with European explorers, adventurers, and settlers who came to North America after Columbus. By 1800, however, the Missouri had moved farther west. The Osage remained in the area but became increasingly hostile toward the European intruders.[2]

In the eighteenth century, three powerful European nations competed for control of North America. Spain sent soldiers, priests, adventurers, and traders to Florida, California, and the Southwest. England funded boatloads of settlers, who built communities along the Eastern seaboard. France sent relatively small numbers of colonists to Canada, the Great Lakes region, and the Mississippi River valley, which pierced the center of the continent. A series of colonial wars culminated in the French and Indian War, which began in 1754 and ended badly for France in 1763. After this conflict, England dominated the eastern half of the continent, and Spain took over the territory west of the Mississippi.

Because of this turmoil, the French settlements in the Mississippi valley struggled without much help or interference from the mother country. French residents occupied Cahokia (Prairie du Rocher) on the eastern side of the river as early as 1698. Kaskaskia, established in 1703, suffered from periodic floods. Emigrants from this community crossed to the west side of the river and began farming the rich bottomlands sometime in the middle of the eighteenth century. No one bothered to record the year in which the first permanent residents established themselves in the Point Basse, the alluvial plain directly across the river from Kaskaskia. This migration might have occurred as early as the 1730s, but it almost certainly had happened by the late 1740s. The earliest official records of the town's existence date from the 1750s.[3]

By 1752, the first town of Ste. Genevieve had begun to take shape.

2. Carl H. Chapman and Eleanor F. Chapman, *Indians and Archaeology of Missouri*, 120.
3. Schroeder, *Opening the Ozarks*, 225; Ekberg, *Colonial Ste. Genevieve*, 22–23.

According to Walter Schroeder, the west bank settlers had partitioned Point Basse into long lots, mirroring those of Kaskaskia, and by 1766 most of the lots had been sold to private owners. The long lots *(terres)* were perpendicular to the riverbank and to a line of limestone bluffs. A single fence enclosed all the terres to form the big common field, even though it was divided into private plots. At the edges of the big field, farmers shared open lands for grazing. Altogether, the big field extended across more than eleven square miles of bottomland. In the early years, villagers built their houses close to the river at the ends of the long lots, forming a linear settlement. They probably had to cross the river to Kaskaskia to attend church.[4]

In the 1760s, the settlers built a church in a central location, but their houses remained scattered along the riverbank. Contemporary observers noted that the seventy households in the village stretched across one full mile of terrain. Archaeological studies in the 1980s located house sites at a distance of 180 feet apart. At the time, Spanish officials worried that because the residents were separated by such great distances, they would not be able to defend the town.[5]

During the American Revolution, the English occupied Fort de Chartres on the east side of the river, and a French exodus to the west bank began. The French Revolution and a slave uprising in the French colony of San Domingue (Haiti) spurred more immigration to the little town in the Mississippi river bottoms. Between 1772 and 1803, the population of Ste. Genevieve grew from less than seven hundred to more than two thousand.[6] These were tumultuous times, and the linear village was defenseless against attacks by English soldiers and hostile tribes, such as the Osage.

After the American Revolution, new populations of Native Americans crossed into Spanish territory. Remnants of the Illinois tribe left the east bank to escape oppression under British and American rule. A group of Peoria settled in New Ste. Genevieve, and one hundred of their tribesmen established a village in the Bois Brule bottom south of the town.[7] In 1789,

4. Schroeder, *Opening the Ozarks*, 227.
5. Ibid., 228.
6. Peterson, "Early Ste. Genevieve and its Architecture," 210–11.
7. Schroeder, *Opening the Ozarks*, 213, 371, 377.

the Spanish government invited groups of Delaware and Shawnee people, enemies of the Osage, to settle on the Apple and the Shawnee creeks south of the Peoria village. These groups occupied agricultural villages with enclosed gardens and fields, domesticated animals, and horizontal log buildings in the Anglo-American style. For the Shawnee, the west bank was not a tranquil place because of harassment by the Osage.[8]

Life on the frontier could be precarious, but the real threat to Ste. Genevieve came from the unpredictable Mississippi River. Every year the river ate away at its banks, causing a series of cave-ins. Floods represented a constant peril to crops, livestock, and the log houses along the river. After major overflows in 1785, the year of the big waters (l'annee des grandes eaux), the French villagers pulled up stakes and rebuilt their homes in a new location in the shelter of the limestone bluffs at the landward edge of the big field.

The new town differed from the old in that it was much more compact and less linear in form. Some of the settlers chose to build their houses in a line along the road to the salt springs (La Saline) south of Ste. Genevieve and along the bluff line below the South Gabouri Creek. But most of the residents established their homes in the central village at a break in the bluffs between the North and South Gabouri. Dirt streets divided the town into blocks that were each roughly four hundred feet square. These blocks were divided into quarters of more or less equal size. The streets were not quite straight, and cross streets met at some approximation of ninety-degree angles, but the intention to create a grid was obvious.[9] Without a professional surveyor, the settlers did their best.

At the center of the village, French residents laid out a public square on which they built a chapel. By 1793, they moved the church from Old Ste. Genevieve and reassembled it in the central square. Historians have speculated about the origins of the town plan of Ste. Genevieve. French towns such as Kaskaskia often followed a grid pattern; Spanish traditions prescribed a compact layout around a central plaza. Both St. Louis and New Orleans exemplified Spanish town-planning ideals. Local leaders such as

8. Chapman and Chapman, *Indians and Archaeology of Missouri*, 120.
9. Schroeder, *Opening the Ozarks*, 236–37.

Francois Vallé would have been aware of this and might have consciously emulated the larger cities.[10]

Even in New Ste. Genevieve, the French liked to build their houses far apart. Wealthy citizens might own and occupy an entire four hundred square foot block in addition to owning land in the common field. The houses themselves, even those belonging to the wealthy, were small by modern American standards. Residents ate, slept, socialized, and often conducted trading business in three rooms that were laid out side by side, with no hallways and with little concern for privacy. Most houses were one story with hip roofs supported by heavy truss work and exterior walls made of hand-hewn timbers that were palisaded. To fill the openings between the rough-hewn vertical logs, the villagers used *bousillage* (soil, horsehair, and clay) or *pierrotage* (rocks, soil, and horsehair). In most cases, they covered the walls with whitewash. For relief from summer heat, villagers built covered porches *(galeries),* sometimes on all four sides of the houses, giving the dwellings a Caribbean appearance. Stone fireplaces and chimneys might be centrally placed or located at each end of the building.

House lots often were bounded by log fences for privacy, protection, or to keep out free-ranging livestock.[11] Outbuildings were numerous. Privies served an obvious need. Kitchens also were separate from the main house because of heat and the danger of fire from cooking hearths. Other outbuildings might include slave quarters, barns, stables, henhouses, and corncribs. Gardens served both utilitarian and aesthetic purposes, producing vegetables, herbs, fruit, and flowers. Wealthy families, who could afford slaves to tend them, sometimes had elaborate formal gardens with geometric walks and well-trimmed shrubbery.

As New Ste. Genevieve developed and grew in the 1790s, a French aristocrat acquired land on the river bluffs and planned another settlement, which he called New Bourbon. Arriving in the area in 1793, Count Pierre Delassus DeLuzieres intended to establish a haven for monarchists fleeing the French Revolution. Delassus' landholdings included a large tract of farmland that became New Bourbon's big common field. He also owned

10. Ibid., 238–39.
11. Peterson, "Early Ste. Genevieve and its Architecture," 213–14.

rights to mineral lands, which he intended to exploit. In 1796, he published a pamphlet extolling the beauty and natural resources of the area, but his fellow aristocrats failed to respond to his solicitations. A small number of settlers, mostly farmers and tradesmen, did build houses in New Bourbon.[12]

Nicolas de Finiels, a French cartographer employed by Spain, visited Ste. Genevieve and New Bourbon in 1801 and observed the count's situation. Like Delassus, the geographer raved about the beauty and productivity of the area. He mentioned La Saline and noted that local residents shipped salt from the region to the rest of Spanish Louisiana. He described Point Basse, the big field, which produced huge harvests, except when the river flooded. Despite the constant peril, farmers returned season after season to plant crops in the incomparably rich soil.[13]

According to Finiels, the residents of New Bourbon included farmers from Ste. Genevieve and a few American families, which was not precisely what the count had in mind. But the population was substantial, Finiels reported, with 460 to 480 inhabitants, black and white, slave and free. The site was attractive because of its location on a hilltop with a spectacular view of the fields, the river, and the woods and rock formations on the east bank. Monsieur Delassus' house at a high spot in the hills commanded a view of the full panorama of field, river, woods, and cliffs.[14] Reporting back to the Spanish crown, Finiels tried to put a good face on the situation at New Bourbon, but the village faced serious problems. The count and his wife had arrived unprepared for life in the American wilderness. Their fellow countrymen had altered the land to reflect their own memories and traditions, but the transformation was far from complete.

American entrepreneur Moses Austin also reported on Delassus' predicament. Austin came to the west bank after reading Delassus' glowing account of the mineral wealth of the area. According to Delassus, the country

---

12. Pierre Charles Delassus De Luzières, *An Official Account of the Situation, Soil, Produce, and etc., of that Part of Louisiana Which Lies between the Mouth of the Missouri and New Madrid, or L'Anse à la Graise, and on the West Side of the Mississippi, Together with an Abstract of the Spanish Government, and etc.*

13. Nicolas de Finiels, *An Account of Upper Louisiana*, 42–43.

14. Ibid., 46–47.

around New Bourbon contained "a great quantity of iron, lead and copper ores, and of stone coal; lead ore in particular is so very abundant, that where they work it, they are generally at no other pains than to pick it up on the surface of the ground."[15] In late January 1797, Austin arrived in Ste. Genevieve, where Francois Vallé provided him with horses for the forty mile trip to the lead-rich area known as Mine a Breton (in present-day Washington County). There he discovered twenty stone furnaces already in operation, smelting lead from crude ore. Delassus had been telling the truth; large pieces of ore were lying in plain sight on the ground. Almost immediately, Austin asked for a large Spanish land grant for the production of lead in sheets, shot, and rolls. For two decades, he successfully mined the land. By 1820, however, he was hit hard during an economic downtown and was ruined financially. Six years later, he died.[16]

In 1797, Austin painted a melancholy portrait of Delassus and his wife, Domitille. After a visit to their home, the American guest reported that their circumstances in New Bourbon compared very unfavorably to their previous life in France. Their new vertical log house may have had a beautiful view, but Domitille missed the pageantry and luxury that accompanied her status in their native land. Austin touched a nerve when he admired a painting on the wall of her bedchamber depicting a great parade of nobles in Paris. "She came to me," he wrote, "And putting her finger on the Picture pointing out a Coach, 'There said she was I on that Happy Day. My situation is now strangly Chang'd.'"[17]

The relatively small number of Anglo-Americans who came to Ste. Genevieve before the Louisiana Purchase tended to view the local culture as exotic and somewhat mysterious. For the young Brackenridge, the adjustment must have been difficult. As the son of Pennsylvania writer and lawyer Hugh Henry Brackenridge, he had a privileged but difficult childhood. His mother died when he was only eighteen months old, and his father had some unusual ideas about education. In 1793, because he wanted his son to learn the French language, he arranged to place Henry in the

15. David B. Gracy, *Moses Austin: His Life,* 53.
16. Ruby Johnson Swartzlow, "The Early History of Lead Mining in Missouri, Part 4: The Austin Period, 1800–1820," 111–14; Gracy, *Moses Austin,* 60–64 .
17. George P. Garrison, ed., "Moses Austin: the Journal," 541.

home of a French family hundreds of miles from home.[18] This was a peculiar decision because Ste. Genevieve had no organized educational system. There were only itinerant schoolmasters and the Catholic Church.[19]

Young Henry lived with the family of Vital St. Gemme Beauvais, studied with an unidentified schoolmaster, and later wrote an often-quoted narrative of his experience. As he remembered it, not one person in town, except for the priest, understood a word of English. The young newcomer spoke almost no French, but he quickly made friends with the local boys. They played, he reported, in the street, "or rather highway, for the houses were far apart, a large space being occupied for yards and gardens by each." As he recalled, the boys treated him politely instead of ridiculing him, as he had learned to expect from the boys in Pennsylvania.[20]

Brackenridge contrasted life in the French settlement with the life he had experienced in American towns. The Beauvais home appeared long and low in contrast to the taller gabled houses of Anglo-Americans. Madame Beauvais' garden impressed him and so did the substantial palisade that enclosed it. As a young boy, he seemed amazed that she could cook vegetables that he willingly ate, implying that he had been used to eating mostly meat. He observed the big field and enjoyed watching farmers return from their work each evening with their draft animals, carts, and plows. It surprised him that so little money changed hands; pelts and furs were the medium of exchange. Perhaps most important, he noticed that the people rarely or never discussed politics. There was no participation in government, as he said, "the commandant took care of all that sort of thing."[21] By "commandant," he meant Francois Vallé.

In 1810, Brackenridge returned to Ste. Genevieve, hoping to make a living as a lawyer. Failing in that objective, he wrote and published descriptive essays and journals about life in the trans-Mississippi West. His *Views of Louisiana,* first published in 1814, contained a long discourse on the reaction of the French to the change of government in the Missouri Territory. He described the local people as tranquil and amiable, fond of cards, billiards,

18. Claude Milton Newlin, *The Life and Writings of Hugh Henry Brackenridge,* 110–11.
19. Ekberg, *Colonial Ste. Genevieve,* 276–77.
20. Brackenridge, *Recollections of Persons and Places,* 19–20.
21. Ibid., 20–22.

and dancing, and not interested in politics. Then he went on to explain that the change in government had brought about a more general, pervasive change in the local culture. "Upon the whole," he observed, "The American manners, and even language begin to predominate."[22]

Brackenridge noted that the old French families continued to hold power in the new republic. Men with French surnames received military commissions as generals, colonels, majors, and captains in the militia. They also served in the civil government as judges, jurors, and magistrates. On the other hand, these powerful men changed their behavior to fit the American mold. For instance, according to Brackenridge, they gave up some of their gentle and relaxed habits in favor of a new "industry and spirit of enterprise."[23]

Trial by jury was an Anglo-American innovation, which the French at first found uncomfortable. According to Brackenridge, they had been accustomed to speedy, simple justice, meted out by the local commandant. But they also recognized that some cases languished in the old system and never received a hearing. Gradually, Brackenridge predicted, they would come to agree that the American system provided more access to justice in a complex and economically expansive society.[24]

Positive results of Americanization included improvements in education. Many prominent families sent their sons to academies and seminaries around the nation or in Canada. Others instructed their sons at home or sent them to local schoolmasters. Even girls received the benefits of this new interest in education. Brackenridge noted that "the females are also instructed with more care, and the sound of the Piano is now heard in their dwellings for the first time."[25]

Ironically, according to Brackenridge, the birth of the new republic gave rise to a new taste for luxury and more obvious distinctions among economic classes. The American spirit of enterprise spawned great fortunes and helped some people join the middle class. But for the least affluent

22. H. M. Brackenridge, *Views of Louisiana: Together with a Journal of a Voyage up the Missouri River, in 1811*, bk. 2, 139.
    23. Ibid., 144–45.
    24. Ibid.
    25. Ibid., 140.

members of society, life became more precarious. American farmers purchased or rented some of the areas in the common field that had previously belonged to the working poor. Day laborers who hauled lead from the mines made less than subsistence wages. Some families became squatters on public lands, but the rush of settlement and speculation constantly threatened their economic survival.[26]

The American takeover also put pressure on Native Americans. According to Brackenridge, the French and Spanish regimes had treated local tribes, including the Osage, with "impolitic lenity." Native American raiding parties sometimes stole horses or other items from townspeople but rarely committed violence against them. Before the Louisiana Purchase, no one had pursued these raiders back to their villages. After the territory was acquired, however, the Americans followed them zealously and forced them to surrender. Within a few years after the American takeover, most of the tribes had disappeared from the area.[27]

Were the people of Ste. Genevieve happier under the new regime? Brackenridge found that question difficult to answer. He believed they were glad to be free of Indian raiding parties. But he detected some resentment for the American government and some nostalgia for Spanish rule. The wealthiest citizens expressed great anxiety about the settlement of land claims; many of them stood to lose large concessions they had received from the Spanish crown. Middle-class people, generally, could expect to hold on to their modest claims. For them, the American system presented a host of new hopes and opportunities. As for the poor, Brackenridge noted that "they are of late observed to become fond of intoxicating liquors."[28] This may have been an elliptical way of saying that they had become more discontented.

Major Amos Stoddard, the military leader who presided over the transfer of power in Upper Louisiana, also observed that many people in the territory used or abused alcohol. He blamed it on the heat, maintaining that the "men in our warm climates, especially of the laborious classes, are attached to stimulating liquors." Alcohol claimed more victims, he argued,

26. Ibid., 140–41.
27. Ibid., 141–42.
28. Ibid., 143–44.

than the Indians' tomahawks and knives. He doubted, however, that any civil or legal authority could curtail its consumption.[29]

Stoddard remarked that the Spanish authorities had done little to stimulate learning. Before the Louisiana Purchase, there were no laws compelling the inhabitants to maintain schools, and there were no funds forthcoming from the Spanish treasury. In Ste. Genevieve, local schoolmasters occasionally offered private instruction. As Brackenridge documented, some of the prominent families sent their sons to seminaries.[30] But most children received no systematic formal education before the American takeover. After that momentous event, support for education increased, but decades would pass before a regular system of public schools would come into existence.

To reconcile the French colonists to the American regime, Stoddard proposed "an academy, under the direction of the government." This, he believed, "would gradually introduce the English language among the French, without the destruction of their own, and awaken a spirit of enquiry and investigation." Anglo-Americans would also benefit because most of them could not afford to send their children to seminaries elsewhere. The goal, as he saw it, was to assimilate the French, educate the Americans, and create a more homogeneous local culture. "The best way to secure the affections of these people," he argued, "Is gradually to change their modes of thinking; and the only way to attach them to our republican systems, is to enlighten their minds by a more general diffusion of knowledge among them."[31] Stoddard was an idealist.

What were the prospects for establishing a democratic republic in a French and Spanish colony? According to Tocqueville, it would depend on three factors: circumstances, laws, and customs. The circumstances, in general, seemed favorable. In 1803, the landscape around Ste. Genevieve and New Bourbon showed great promise for economic development. The big field, with its rich river-saturated soil, produced wheat and other crops. A few miles south of New Bourbon, a salt spring contained great quantities of

29. Amos Stoddard, *Sketches Historical and Descriptive of Louisiana*, 305–6.
30. Ibid., 309–10; Brackenridge, *Views of Louisiana*, 140.
31. Stoddard, *Sketches Historical and Descriptive of Louisiana*, 311.

a staple product needed for preserving food in a time without refrigeration. The hills to the west and north contained valuable lead deposits, which the French were busily engaged in mining with both free and slave labor. Hunters and trappers roamed the nearby woods in search of beaver, fox, rabbits, deer, and other animals whose furs and pelts were as valuable as cash and provided the basic medium of exchange.

Probably the most important resource flowed between shifting banks, bringing traders, entrepreneurs, speculators, and gamblers from as far north as Canada and as far south as New Orleans. Hopeful men worked their way up and down the Mississippi valley, loading and unloading cargo and providing the muscle that propelled the boats upstream. Steamboats had not yet arrived on the scene, but when they did, the river became an engine of progress, perpetually in motion, consuming the timber from the nearby forests, belching smoke, and turning the wheels of commerce. The port of Ste. Genevieve became a portal to the West, and local merchants were in a position to supply the growing demand for blankets, provisions, and ready-made clothes for migrants heading for the Ozarks, the Great Plains, Texas, or California.

Laws and governmental institutions gradually evolved. By 1803, after decades of turmoil, the French towns had accommodated themselves to Spanish rule. Those who held authority in colonial Louisiana were the governor general in New Orleans, the lieutenant governor in St. Louis, and the local commandants. During the transitional decade from 1794 to 1804, Pierre Delassus was commandant of New Bourbon, and Francois Vallé II was commandant of Ste. Genevieve. Delassus' son Charles (Carlos) de Hault Delassus served in St. Louis as the last Spanish lieutenant governor of Upper Louisiana from 1799 to 1804.[32]

Theoretically, the general laws of Spain, which were based on Roman law, applied in the colonies. Unfortunately, few public officials, except those in New Orleans, knew and understood the laws, most of which were never published. Lacking legal knowledge, the local commandants acted independently and decided many cases according to their own ideas of

32. Ekberg, *Colonial Ste. Genevieve*, 356, 448.

justice.[33] This led to many disagreements between the Spanish governors and the commandants.

Colonial Ste. Genevieve and New Bourbon operated under a confusing and inconsistent combination of French customs and statutes, Spanish decrees, and ordinances issued by the local commandants. For the most part, the two communities observed French rules on inheritance and the distribution of property. Spanish authorities reaffirmed the Black Code, which governed the enslavement of people of color in French colonies. Decrees of the Spanish governor in St. Louis were posted on the church door, and there was no attempt to separate church and state. There was also no separation of governmental powers: local commandants could make laws, enforce them, and act as judges. But criminal cases occurred rarely and were usually referred to higher authority.[34]

Despite living under an authoritarian regime, the people of New Bourbon and Ste. Genevieve frequently engaged in lawsuits or legal disputes. In the early days, there were no lawyers, but notaries could help people prepare petitions for the court. People from all walks of life showed a willingness to stand up and insist they had been wronged. Literacy, or the lack of it, did not seem to be a stumbling block for petitioners. The commandants referred some cases to St. Louis but decided many issues locally.[35]

One particularly revealing case was that of Elizabeth D'Atchurut, a free black woman, who sued a prominent white man in New Bourbon. Although she occupied a lowly position in the social hierarchy, she had the courage to air her grievance against Antoine Aubuchon, the son of one of Ste. Genevieve's earliest French residents. Aubuchon probably purchased Elizabeth as a concubine, perhaps from the D'Atchurut family. They apparently had a long-term sexual relationship, which began in the early 1780s. On the 1787 Ste. Genevieve census, Elizabeth was enumerated as a free person of color, and it was reported that she had two young sons.[36] Aubuchon most likely granted Elizabeth her freedom, perhaps because

33. Stoddard, *Sketches Historical and Descriptive of Louisiana*, 273.
34. Ekberg, *Colonial Ste. Genevieve*, 360–64.
35. Ibid., 366–67.
36. *Spanish Census of Ste. Genevieve, Missouri, 1787*, Census Collection, 1732–1980, Missouri Historical Society.

she was the mother of his children. After his death in 1798 she filed suit against his estate claiming that he had fathered her ten children.[37] She won her suit. As judge, Pierre Delassus awarded her thirty-five minots of wheat, ten minots of maize, a carbine, and a rifle to settle the claim.[38]

When there are no opportunities to participate in the daily business of governing the community, people seek other ways of making their voices heard. Open rebellion is one possibility. Mobs can take to the streets, and crowds can loudly demand their rights. Organized groups can circulate petitions, and individuals can take their cases to court. In New Bourbon and Ste. Genevieve, residents learned to use the judicial process to their advantage and continued to do so in the American courts.

For the people of Ste. Genevieve and New Bourbon, these were revolutionary times. The concepts of liberty and equality resonated in recent French, as well as American, history: most of the local residents could remember both the American and the French revolutions. Some of their neighbors had fled from Illinois or emigrated from France during these upheavals. At least one resident, Jacques Guibourd, fled to Ste. Genevieve from San Domingue after the slave uprising there.[39] Many, like Delassus, would have taken the conservative or monarchist position. But even those who wanted to preserve the old order could not deny the power of the revolutionary ideals. Americans such as Moses Austin and Amos Stoddard represented the advance guard of the new order for the citizens of two small towns, poised for political and social change, on the west bank of the Mississippi River.

---

37. Ekberg, *Colonial Ste. Genevieve,* 226–27.

38. *Elizabeth D'Atcherutte v. Heirs of Antoine Aubuchon, 1798,* folder 317, Ste. Genevieve Archives, 1756–1930, Western Historical Manuscript Collection, State Historical Society, University of Missouri–Columbia.

39. See Bill Naeger, Patti Naeger, and Mark Evans, *Ste. Genevieve: A Leisurely Stroll through History.*

CHAPTER TWO

The Old French Aristocracy

> But a few years ago one of those patriarchs could be seen in the city of
> Ste. Genevieve leaning on the staff of old age with ease and grace, his
> head bleached with the snows of nearly a hundred years. This re-
> markable man was Jean-Baptiste Vallé, the last commandant of the post
> of Ste. Genevieve.
>
> Firmin A. Rozier, *Rozier's History of the Early
> Settlement of the Mississippi Valley*

AMERICAN DEMOCRACY did not eliminate landed aristocrats, but it
changed the conditions under which they could exist. Some of them played
leading roles in the new order; others faded into the background. The
Vallés of Ste. Genevieve sustained and increased their political, social,
and economic power through many generations. Their neighbors, the
Delassus of New Bourbon, struggled for decades and failed to retain their
land and wealth. The causes of their downfall included unfortunate circumstances, individual character traits, and the vagaries of life in the emerging
American republic.

Before the Louisiana Purchase, Finiels described Ste. Genevieve and
New Bourbon as traditional communities ruled by benign patriarchs. In
his view, the residents lived together as members of an extended family,
bound by complex ties of kinship and affection, sharing pain and hardship as well as joy. Francois Vallé in Ste. Genevieve and Pierre Delassus in
New Bourbon ruled their small fiefdoms without much interference from
a higher authority and without much participation from the people under
their administration. Nevertheless, according to Finiels, the people did not
feel oppressed.

Finiels especially romanticized the figure of Francois Vallé II as a kindly father, adored by the townspeople. As Finiels noted,

> Monsieur François Vallé, commandant of Ste. Genevieve is head of the principal family of these two villages [i.e., Ste. Genevieve and New Bourbon]. His contribution to the sweet harmony, which is so hard to find elsewhere, is not insignificant. He is loved and esteemed like a father; his wife is modest, unaffected, and always as caring as a mother. How could they not be loved?—they both conduct themselves as if all the good people here were their own children.[1]

Finiels did not include Pierre Delassus in this glowing description. The financially troubled count and his homesick wife hardly lived up to this wholesome image. But the Vallés also must have occasionally revealed the harsher sides of their characters. The Vallé patriarch, Francois I, built an economic empire that included lead mines, sawmills, farms, and stores and that relied on slave labor. His sons inherited and expanded these enterprises in a competitive marketplace. Loyalty and affection might have solidified the Vallés' position in the community, but shrewdness, ambition, and a certain degree of ruthlessness had to underpin their business enterprises.

Both the Vallé and Delassus families figured dramatically in the transfer of power that occurred with the Louisiana Purchase. Francois Vallé I died in 1783; and his heir, Francois II, passed away a few days before the official American takeover in 1804. His brother Jean-Baptiste served briefly as the community's last commandant. When the American flag rose over Ste. Genevieve, Jean-Baptiste relinquished the outmoded title but maintained his stature as a civic leader. Under his management, the family's enterprises grew and prospered. His son Felix became the town's unofficial patriarch and his daughter-in-law, Odile (née Pratte) became the town's most beloved benefactor. Odile attached the Vallé name to churches, schools, and a cemetery, ensuring its place in history.

Pierre Delassus' son Charles did not accept historical change with such grace. A soldier in the Spanish army, he came to America to be closer to his parents after they settled in New Bourbon. In 1799, he became lieutenant

---

1. Finiels, *Account of Upper Louisiana*, 50–51.

governor of Upper Louisiana. When Lewis and Clark arrived in the west in advance of their famous journey, Charles behaved like a military man and refused to let them into Spanish territory without approval from his superiors in New Orleans. Although France and America had already agreed to the Louisiana Purchase, Spain had not officially relinquished its control over the area. As a result, the explorers had to make their winter camp on the east side of the Mississippi at Wood River (La Riviere du Bois). In February 1804, Charles Delassus received orders to transfer authority to the United States government. At that point, he became more accommodating and invited Lewis and Clark to join Spanish officials for a tour of the local fortifications.[2]

A few weeks later, he informed several local commandants, including his own father, Pierre Delassus of New Bourbon, and Jean-Baptiste Vallé of Ste. Genevieve, about the change in his status. On March 9, Charles presided over the transfer of power from Spain to France, and on the next day, from France to the United States. This must have been a painful moment for him. He had lost his position of authority under the Spanish regime. His own landholdings might be in question, and he might not be able to protect his father's troubled household in New Bourbon.[3]

The Delassus family's experience in America had been disappointing. Charles's parents left France in August of 1790 along with their two youngest children (Jeanne Felicite Odile and Phillippe Francois Camille) to escape the French Revolution. They arrived in America in 1791 and settled in Gallipolis, which is located in present-day Ohio. Sometime in 1792, Pierre made his way to the Upper Louisiana Territory. In the spring of 1793 he traveled to New Orleans and requested that his longtime friend, the Baron de Carondelet (who was then serving as governor of Spanish Louisiana), support his desire to found a new community approximately two to three miles south of Ste. Genevieve.[4]

2. William E. Foley, "Friends and Partners: William Clark, Meriwether Lewis, and Mid-America's French Creoles," 272.

3. Robert R. Archibald, "Honor and Family: The Career of Lt. Gov. Carlos de Hault de Lassus," 32–33.

4. Paul Auguste St. Vrain, "Genealogy of the Family of Delassus and Saint Vrain, 1944," Delassus-St. Vrain Collection, Missouri Historical Society; Ekberg, *Colonial Ste. Genevieve,* 446; Archibald, "Honor and Family," 33–34;

Delassus returned to the Ste. Genevieve District in August 1793 with grand visions for his settlement overlooking the Mississippi River. He not only expected to bring his family to Upper Louisiana, along with large numbers of settlers from both Gallipolis and France, but he anticipated making the area productive through agriculture, the development of lead mines, and the construction of water and flour mills. Pierre received several land grants for his enterprises, but his dreams did not come true. New Bourbon never grew or thrived as Pierre had thought it would. Other than the commandant's house, the town had no public buildings. Villagers had to walk two and a half miles to Ste. Genevieve to attend mass. New Bourbon developed no mills, no mercantile establishments, and no trade with the Indians.[5]

By 1794 Pierre was ill, most likely suffering from either yellow fever or malaria, and had become destitute. That same year, he and his wife promised their land, house, furnishings, and one-half of all their slaves and animals to their youngest son, Camille, with the understanding that he would "never ever leave or abandon them for the duration of their lives." The despondent count also sent a letter to his son Charles, who was serving in the Spanish King's Royal Guard in Madrid, asking him to come to Upper Louisiana to help the family. Charles beseeched the king of Spain to transfer him to a regiment there, and the king obliged.[6]

For the next two years, Charles engaged in trading ventures, which he hoped would alleviate his family's financial difficulties. Political connections helped Charles become civil and military commandant of New Madrid in 1796 and lieutenant governor of the territory in 1799. While taking on these public responsibilities, Charles did what he could to ease his family's burden. Although he utilized his official powers to issue land grants and accrue favors, he also amassed large debts of his own by trying to pay his parents' mounting bills and by helping other family members

5. Kit W. Wesler, Bonnie Stepenoff, N. Renae Farris, and Carol A. Morrow, "Archaeological Test Excavations at the Delassus-Kern House, Ste. Geneveive, Missouri," 69; Ekberg, *Colonial Ste. Genevieve,* 446; Archibald, "Honor and Family," 34; Schroeder, *Opening the Ozarks,* 253.

6. Deed transferring property from Pierre and Domitille Delassus to their son Camille, 1794, folder 43, Ste. Geneveive Archives; Archibald, "Honor and Family," 36; Gertrude Beauford, "De Luziere, De Lassus, St. Vrain, and Derbigny," 689.

and friends. Unfortunately, his good will was never reciprocated and he remained deeply in debt. By 1801, Pierre and Domitille mortgaged most of their possessions to Charles to cover a large indebtedness.[7]

Charles and his siblings had to fight to keep the family's land in New Bourbon. This proved to be an exhausting legal battle as American officials tried to sort out the complex web of poorly documented and inadequately surveyed Spanish land concessions. As soon as people learned that the United States intended to acquire Louisiana, speculators rushed to secure new land grants or enlarge existing ones by legal or illegal means. Within a year after the purchase of the Louisiana Territory, Jefferson appointed a Board of Land Commissioners to investigate all land grants and separate legitimate from fraudulent claims.[8]

American authorities had trouble mapping and recording Pierre Delassus' enormous landholdings. A confusing body of records indicates that in 1795 he received a grant of 7,056 arpents (one square league) of land, on which he planned to mine lead. Three years later, he received three additional concessions—one of 1,000 arpents, one of 810 arpents, and one of 100 arpents (roughly, but not exactly, equivalent to 100 acres).[9] The majority of Pierre's land grants were formally surveyed by 1800, and his tract of 810 arpents was subdivided into two sections of 500 and 310 arpents each. Somewhere on the 810-arpent tract, he built his house, but the specific location remains in question. Finiels drew a map that placed it on a bluff overlooking the big field and the river. Modern-day archaeologists have not been able to pinpoint the site.[10]

7. Archibald, "Honor and Family," 35; Bill of sale: Sale of Slave by Chas. De Luzieres to His Son Chas. De Hault De Lassus 1801, folder 405; and Mortgage: Pierre Delassus Deluzieres to Charles Delassus 1801, folder 100, both in Ste. Genevieve Archives.

8. Frederick Bates, *The Life and Papers of Frederick Bates*, 1:29.

9. One French arpent was a linear measure, roughly equivalent to 192 English feet or 64 English yards. A square plot of land measuring one arpent (64 linear yards) on each side would measure 4,096 square yards; one acre equals 4,840 square yards. The number of arpents usually represented the smaller dimension of a French long lot, so that one arpent of land could actually be larger than 4,096 square yards in area. An arpent could vary in size but, generally, nearly equaled an acre.

10. *Charles Dehault Delassus, appellant v. the United States*, 34 U.S. 117 (1835). For more on this topic, see Bonnie Stepenoff and Debbie Bibb, *Ste. Genevieve Historic Preservation Field School 2000 and 2001: The Delassus-Kern House*. Large grants of one square league (or

To defend his claims, Delassus had to prove that he had developed and improved the land. In 1806 Israel Dodge gave fascinating, albeit ambiguous, testimony on the count's behalf. Dodge alleged that a "cabin" was built on the 310-arpent portion of land in 1798, and that a free black woman had continuously occupied it for approximately five to six years. In a 1797 census, Delassus listed only one free black woman living in New Bourbon. He gave her name as Lisette and reported that she farmed and raised livestock. One year later he awarded damages to Elizabeth D'Atchurut in her case against Antoine Aubuchon. Lisette is a French pet name for Elizabeth, and it seems plausible that Elizabeth D'Atchurut is the Lisette noted in the 1797 census and, perhaps, the woman who occupied the cabin on the Delassus property.[11]

Pierre and Domitille both died in 1806, with the land claims still unsettled. Their son Camille and family friend Marie Philippe Leduc, who administered their estate, had little luck with the Board of Land Commissioners. Between 1805 and 1812, the board reviewed more than three thousand claims and confirmed about thirteen hundred of them (about two out of five). In the Ste. Genevieve District, which included New Bourbon, the board confirmed 169 claims but not those of the Delassus family. After investigating documents and hearing testimony, the commission denied the family's claims in 1810 and 1811. The family did not give up: they went to court to validate their landholdings.[12]

When Camille passed away in 1812, Pierre's remaining heirs in the United States were his son Charles, his daughter Jeanne Felicite Odile, his son Jacques, and Camille's widow, Mathilde Vallé Villars Delassus, and her young children. Marie Philippe Leduc was left as the surviving administrator. Because funds had been insufficient to pay Pierre's debts of more than forty-eight thousand dollars, Leduc petitioned the courts for permission

7,056 arpents) were common under the Spanish regime (Walter Lowrie, ed., *Early Settlers of Missouri as Taken from Land Claims in the Missouri Territory*, 467, 472, 556).

11. Wesler, Stepenoff, Farris, and Morrow, "Archaeological Test Excavations," 69; "Land Claims in the Missouri Territory," *American State Papers: 8, Public Lands*, 2:564–65 and 3:339; Greene, Kremer, and Holland, *Missouri's Black Heritage*, 16; Debbie Bibb, "Lisette," 4–6.

12. Archibald, "Honor and Family," 38–40; Schroeder, *Opening the Ozarks*, 146; Lowrie, ed., *Early Settlers of Missouri*, 467–68; *Charles Dehault Delassus, appellant v. the United States*.

to sell Delassus' property at auction. This sale finally took place in February 1819, and Pierre's loyal son Charles was the highest bidder. For the sum of $11,835 he purchased claims to six separate tracts of land, allowing the property to remain in the family.[13]

The following day, February 5, 1819, Charles deeded his parents' property to his late brother Camille's minor children: Odile, Ceran, and Marie Louise. Their mother had remarried in April of 1818; her new husband was Joseph Vital Beauvais.[14] One might speculate that Charles transferred ownership of the family property to his nieces and nephews for their financial support and to prevent it from being seized by their new stepfather's family.

Several land disputes continued long after Camille's death, leaving his estate in legal limbo. In May of 1824, the U.S. Congress gave federal courts the authority to rule on cases pertaining to any French or Spanish land concession, warrant, or order of survey that had been issued before March 10, 1804. In the late 1820s, Charles Delassus filed a petition in the Federal District Court for the Eastern Division of Missouri to have his family's claim of 7,056 arpents declared legitimate, but the request was denied. By 1833, a blanket confirmation was issued for many claims, including some of the Delassus property; finally, a ruling from the U.S. Supreme Court in 1835 validated these claims. But debts, illnesses, marriages, and deaths had attenuated the estate. By the time Charles died in 1843, family members had sold much of the property to Anglo-American settlers.[15]

What became of the old commandant's house with its spectacular view of the big field and the river? Did it survive in modified form and take on

13. St. Vrain, "Genealogy of the Family of Delassus and Saint Vrain, 1944," Delassus-St. Vrain Collection; Ste. Genevieve County, deed book C, pp. 166, 167, 168.

14. Odile, married and widowed twice, became a nun; Ceran eventually married Eleanor Beauvais; and Marie Louise married Peter Pratte. Ste. Genevieve County, deed book C, pp. 168, 169, 170; St. Vrain, "Genealogy of the Family of Delassus and Saint Vrain, 1944," Delassus-St. Vrain Collection; Mary Rozier Sharp and Louis J. Sharp III, *Between the Gabouri: A History of Ferdinand Rozier and "Nearly" All His Descendants,*, 258–60.

15. Statement of the Situation of the Estate of Camille Delassus, March 20, 1824, file 59–0084, Franz Papers, Missouri Historical Society; *Charles Dehault Delassus, appellant v. the United States;* Archibald, "Honor and Family," 40.

the appearance of a typical nineteenth-century Missouri farmhouse? Did Camille's heirs or the buyers of his property dismantle it and reuse the heavy old timbers? Or did the house simply rot in place and vanish from the landscape? The answer may be lost in a blur of land transactions beginning in 1834. By this time Camille's children were adults; one of them had passed away, and two had spouses and families of their own. In April of that year, Odile Delassus, Ceran and Eleanor Delassus, Leon Delassus, and Peter Pratte (widower of Marie Louise Delassus) arranged to draw lots to determine who would receive various portions of the Delassus landholdings.[16]

Peter Pratte, represented in the transaction by a colleague named Martin Sweek, received lot number one, the part of the property on which a poteaux sur solle house survived in dramatically altered form in the twentieth century. There is no conclusive evidence that this house had belonged to Pierre and Domitille, although some scholars believe that it did. But this house was located on low ground, not high on a hill as the count's house was supposed to be. In March of 1836, Pratte sold this property to Martin Sweek for two hundred dollars. Sweek, in turn, sold the property to a physician and farmer named Ichabod Sargent for twelve hundred dollars in July of 1837.[17]

Sargent owned the property throughout the 1830s and 1840s. Local records indicate that he improved one or more of his landholdings between 1846 and 1848, although it is uncertain exactly which property might have been involved. Either Sweek or Sargent could have salvaged old timbers and used them to build a farmhouse. In the twentieth century, tree-ring dating and archaeological excavations supported the conclusion that the house that still stood on the Pratte-Sweek-Sargent tract contained eighteenth-

16. This was the research question that occupied faculty and students in the field school from 1997 to 2001; no definitive answer was found. For a summary of the research, see Stepenoff and Bibb, *Ste. Genevieve Historic Preservation Field School,* and Wesler, Stepenoff, Farris, and Morrow, "Archaeological Test Excavations." The property transfer was recorded in Ste. Genevieve County, deed book E, pp. 71 and 72.

17. Ste. Genevieve County, deed book E, pp. 8, 9, 10, 71, 72, and 124. See also Stepenoff and Bibb, *Ste. Genevieve Historic Preservation Field School,* and Wesler, Stepenoff, Farris, and Morrow, "Archaeological Test Excavations."

century timbers and the contention that the house had been erected some-time after 1830.[18]

A German farmer named John D. Kern bought the property from Sar-gent's estate for one thousand dollars in 1855. Sometime between 1895 and 1900, he added a second story to the existing vertical log house. Kern had a large family, and his farm was a bustling place. Both a vegetable and flower garden existed on the property, as well as a small orchard and grape-vines for producing wine. The hardworking German family raised chickens and mules as well. Descendants of John Kern occupied the farm until the early 1980s.[19]

Generations of Kerns proudly told visitors that their farm had once be-longed to a member of the French nobility. According to family tradition, John Kern often pointed to a spot in an orchard, high on a bluff, with a spectacular view of the river. On this spot, Kern said, the French aristocrat had built a house. This family story seemed to confirm Finiels's placement of the house on high ground with a commanding view of the river. But that house—the fabled house on the hill—had vanished from the landscape.[20]

Although they had not retained most of their family estate, the descen-dants of Pierre Delassus played a role in Ste. Genevieve's history. Camille

18. Regarding the Sargent estate, see Probate Records, Circuit Court Clerk's office, Ste. Genevieve County Courthouse, drawer 4, packet 62, 1852. For a summary of dendro-chronolgy and archaeology, see Wesler, Stepenoff, Farris, and Morrow, "Archaeological Test Excavations."

19. The property transaction is recorded in Ste. Genevieve County, deed book I, p. 587. A photograph of the house, dated *ca.* 1894, shows a one-story house. The second story must have been added soon after that date (Shirley Kern, interview with Cathy Grove, Summer 2001).

20. Shirley Kern related this family story in her 2001 interview with Cathy Grove. It seems that although the Kern family knew they lived on the French nobleman's land, they never believed they had actually occupied the old count's house. Scholars are still debating whether the house, known as the Delassus-Kern House, was the house built by Pierre De-lassus in the late eighteenth century. The documentary evidence is inconclusive. Archaeo-logical excavations support the conclusion that the Delassus-Kern House was not erected on its present site until sometime after 1830 (for more about the Kern family and the house, see chapter 4). In the spring of 2001, Southwest Missouri State University's Center for Archaeological Research conducted excavations on the property of Joe Hecker and uncovered part of a stone foundation high on a bluff in what was once New Bourbon (Mark A. Rees and Neal H. Lopinot, *Archaeological Survey and Testing of the De Lassus De Luzieres-Hecker Site [23SG176], Ste. Genevieve County, Missouri*).

served in governmental posts after the American takeover. His children and their children kept a connection with the town; one daughter in particular supported the development of the local parochial schools. Ironically, by the time Odile Delassus gave some of her family's money to the town's educational system, she had married and been widowed twice and her surname was Vallé. Interestingly, two Odiles, one born a Delassus and another born a Pratte, married into the Vallé family and made contributions to the town.

The Vallé family dominated Ste. Genevieve before and after the Louisiana Purchase. The family's roots ran very deep in North America. The patriarch, Francois Vallé, was born in Canada in 1716. His parents and grandparents did not belong to French nobility but to the middle class. Francois was shrewd, hardworking, and uneducated. He did not inherit a fortune, he made one. By 1739, he had arrived in Kaskaskia, where he made handsome profits as a merchant, trading lead and furs for luxury items in New Orleans. By the 1750s, he had established a residence in Ste. Genevieve and owned several slaves. When he died in 1783, his estate included farmland in the big field, large tracts in town, a house, outbuildings, furniture, a substantial amount of silverware, and seventy slaves. His wealth dwarfed that of anyone else in Ste. Genevieve.[21]

Francois Vallé I extracted and smelted lead at Mine la Motte in Madison County, west of Ste. Genevieve, as early as the 1740s, when the Osage Indians still inhabited the area. On April 7, 1774, an Osage raiding party killed six people, including Joseph Vallé, Francois' twenty-one-year-old son.[22] Despite this loss, the family continued mining lead, using slave labor to do the backbreaking work of digging and hauling the ore. Just one year before the Louisiana Purchase, Jean B. Pratte, Jean Baptiste St. Gemme Beauvais, Jean-Baptiste Vallé, and Francois Vallé II petitioned the Spanish crown to confirm their title to an immense tract of land on which they were operating smelters.[23]

Francois Vallé I fathered six children: five with his wife Marianne

21. Kristen Kalen Morrow, "Ste. Genevieve's First Family. . . a Chronicle of the Vallès," 25, 26, 28; Ekberg, *François Vallé and His World*, 21, 24, 36, 255–75.

22. Ekberg, *François Vallé and His World*, 23.

23. John Rothensteiner, "Earliest History of Mine La Motte," 211.

Billeron de las Fatigue, and one illegitimate daughter. Between 1751 and 1753, Marianne gave birth to Charles, Marie-Louise, and Joseph. Francois II was born in 1758, and Jean-Baptiste followed in 1760. Marie-Louise married and moved to New Orleans. Marguerite, Francois' younger, illegitimate daughter, married a local man and bore eleven children. Of the sons, the eldest, Charles, lived a dissolute life. Joseph's violent death at Mine la Motte left Francois' youngest sons, Francois II and Jean-Baptiste, to carry on his legacy.[24]

Unlike their father, they inherited a great fortune and did not have to earn it, but they were ready and willing to put their energy into running the family's various enterprises. Francois Vallé II invested in lead mining, agriculture, land speculation, milling, and trading. In 1787, at the age of twenty-nine, he headed a household that included his wife, Marie Carpentier, several children, and thirty-nine slaves. Before his untimely death in 1804, he and Jean-Baptiste cooperated in numerous ventures, including lead mining.[25] Jean-Baptiste expanded these businesses enormously, while participating in the civic life of the new American community. At the end of his long life he was a familiar figure in town and had earned the title "Pere Vallé."

As a young man, Jean-Baptiste engaged in a wide variety of business activities. By the age of twenty-two he was co-owner of a saltworks on La Saline, a saltwater creek south of New Bourbon. He also owned farmland, which he used thirty-seven slaves to cultivate. Auguste Chouteau, the founder of St. Louis, relied on him to provide corn and lead, which Jean-Baptiste traded for sugar and coffee from New Orleans. During the 1790s, he worked side by side with his brother in a rough and tumble struggle for control of lead mining resources at Mine la Motte. By 1800, the Vallé family had a near monopoly on local mining, bolstered by generous claims from the Spanish crown.[26]

After the American takeover, Jean-Baptiste had to defend the family's land claims. In some cases, the legal wrangling dragged on for more than

24. Morrow, "Ste. Genevieve's First Family," 29–30; Ekberg, *François Vallé and His World,* 119–21.
25. Morrow, "Ste. Genevieve's First Family," 30–31.
26. Ibid., 30, 32.

twenty years. During this period, the family continued to manage its enterprises at Mine La Motte, sawmills near New Bourbon, and various tracts of farmland. In 1826, the heirs of Francois Vallé received a favorable ruling on their title to a huge tract, two leagues square (more than 24,000 acres) at Mine La Motte. Seven years later Congress confirmed the family's rights to 7,056 arpents of land nine miles southeast of New Bourbon on La Saline.[27] The Vallés also retained possession of numerous smaller tracts.

Apparently, Jean-Baptiste knew how to ingratiate himself with the American authorities. After Francois died, the American military commander Amos Stoddard quickly appointed Jean-Baptiste to serve as commandant until a replacement could be found. In July 1804, Stoddard informed him that Major James Bruff would take over the military command of the Ste. Genevieve District. Jean-Baptiste retained some civil power, however, as a justice of the peace. In this capacity in 1805, he built Ste. Genevieve's jail. As an official of the Court of Quarter Sessions, he helped define the boundaries of Ste. Genevieve, which also encompassed New Bourbon, when the town was incorporated in 1808. He served on the town's first board of trustees.[28]

In 1817, he organized the trading firm of Menard and Valle with his cousin Pierre Menard of Kaskaskia. Jean-Baptiste Vallé and his wife, Jeanne Barbeau, had four sons, Jean-Baptiste, Francois, Louis, and Felix, who helped run the business. Their youngest son, Felix, went to Bardstown, Kentucky, for his education, but he returned to Ste. Genevieve in the 1820s and joined the family firm. In 1824, the elder Vallé purchased a stone building from a merchant named Jacob Philipson. Felix, his wife Odile (née Pratte), and their infant son Louis Felix moved into the building, using part of it as a residence and part of it as a store.[29] Felix became the sole owner of the family's enterprises after the deaths of his brothers, Louis in

27. "Land Claim in Missouri," bill no. 497, February 15, 1826, *American State Papers: 8, Public Lands*, 4:534–41 and 6:758–61.

28. Morrow, "Ste. Genevieve's First Family," 32; *Goodspeed's History of Southeast Missouri*, 405, 810.

29. M. Colleen Hamilton, "French Colonial Land Use: The Felix Valle House State Historic Site," 29.

1833, Jean-Baptiste *fils* in 1837, and Francois in 1851. Jean-Baptiste *pere* died in 1849.[30]

By the middle of the nineteenth century, long after Moses Austin lost his Missouri holdings because of financial problems,[31] the Vallé family's mines remained at the forefront of the state's lead mining industry. In 1824, Joseph Schuts had discovered a huge lead deposit, called the Big Lode, on land belonging to the Valle Mining Company near the St. Francois-Jefferson County line north of Ste. Genevieve. In partnership with Felix Rozier, Felix Vallé continued to operate this mine for the next fifty years. Before the Civil War, the company used slave labor; after the war, Rozier and Vallé employed free African Americans along with white miners. The town of Valle Mines was established near the Big Lode and continued to exist in the twenty-first century.[32]

At the time of his death in 1877, Felix Vallé was the wealthiest man in Ste. Genevieve, and his widow inherited hundreds of thousands of dollars in cash and real estate. A bank failure reduced her assets, as did her own generosity. Before her death in 1894, she contributed large sums of money to the local Catholic Church and donated land for parks, a cemetery, and schools—called the Valle schools. Local citizens remembered her as "Mama Vallé."[33]

The Vallé family left an indelible imprint on the land. Three of their houses still stood in the twenty-first century. The houses of the two brothers, Francois Vallé II and Jean-Baptiste Vallé, remained from the colonial period. The Francois Vallé II house, constructed in New Ste. Genevieve in the 1790s, underwent significant alterations over the years; the vertical log walls remained intact, but the truss work and all other colonial vestiges disappeared. Succeeding generations took better care of the Jean-Baptiste Vallé house, constructed in 1794 near the central plaza in New Ste. Genevieve. The family of the last commandant owned the home until 1865,

30. Ekberg, *François Vallé and His World,* 290.

31. Swartzlow, "Early History of Lead Mining in Missouri," 110.

32. G. C. Swallow, *First and Second Annual Reports of the Geological Survey of Missouri,* 35–36; Steve Frazier, "Lost History of Valles Mines"; Valle Mines Company store books are housed at the Missouri Mines State Historic Site in Park Hills, Missouri.

33. Ekberg, *François Vallé and His World,* 294–95; Naeger, Naeger, and Evans, *Ste. Genevieve: A Leisurely Stroll,* 94.

Jean-Baptiste Vallé House preserved in its 1860s form. Photograph courtesy of the State Historical Society of Missouri, Columbia.

when it was purchased by Leon Vion of France. Vion updated the home to reflect the standards of the time but kept much of the original structure intact. His great-granddaughter Vion Pepin and her husband, Bernard Schram, bought the house and restored it a century later. Perhaps the most significant feature of this property was the formal garden, which retained its graceful outlines from the colonial period.[34]

The most interesting surviving structure was the Felix Vallé house, which became the Felix Vallé State Historic Site. This was not a French house but a federal-style stone house, built by Jacob Philipson, an American Jew, in 1818. He sold it to the Menard and Valle mercantile firm in the 1820s. Felix Vallé continued to reside there long after the store closed. Until her death in 1894, his widow, Odile, frequently stood on the porch throwing dimes to the children as they walked home from school. In the 1970s, the state of Missouri returned the house and store to their 1830s appearance and opened them to the public.[35]

Without a doubt, the Vallés were the premier family of Ste. Genevieve in the eighteenth and nineteenth centuries. Did they qualify as landed

34. Naeger, Naeger, and Evans, *Ste. Genevieve: A Leisurely Stroll,* 74–75.
35. Ibid., 94–95.

aristocrats? Clearly, the answer is yes. While the patriarch Francois could not claim noble birth, he did acquire large tracts of land in the Illinois Country, in Ste. Genevieve, and in the lead mining region of Missouri, and he did own slaves. He passed down his great wealth to his sons and grandsons, who augmented the family holdings with large grants from the Spanish crown. Under Spanish auspices, the family gained not only wealth but power. As commandants of Ste. Genevieve, Francois, Francois II, and Jean-Baptiste Vallé acted as civil and military rulers of a district in which there was no representative government, no electoral process, and no formal participation by the citizens in their own governmental affairs. The commandants were legislators, chief executives, and judges in Ste. Genevieve, and the title of commandant passed from father to son.

Did their status change with the American takeover? Most certainly, it did. They had to defend their land claims in American courts. The cases dragged on for years, and some of their claims were denied. But the family managed to retain enormous mining interests and huge tracts of farmland, on which they utilized slave labor. They kept their interest in other lucrative enterprises, including sawmills and saltworks, and they made significant amounts of money in trade. The Vallés continued to outstrip their neighbors in wealth and economic influence, but they had to share their political power with other men, many of whom were newcomers to the region. After Jean-Baptiste surrendered the title of commandant, he became a justice of the peace in an American court system. When Ste. Genevieve incorporated as an American town, he served as a member of its board of trustees.

Unlike the Delassus family, the Vallés prospered under the new regime. Pierre Delassus was a born aristocrat, who lived a life of coaches, pageantry, and luxury in France before the nasty shock of the French Revolution. He did not have solid roots in North America. Although he planned to engage in lead mining, milling, and other enterprises in his settlement at New Bourbon, he lacked the business experience and frontier shrewdness of Francois Vallé. Pierre's son Charles at first showed contempt for the new American regime. When the takeover became official, he relinquished his power gracefully and began the desperate struggle to save the family's landholdings. In this effort he had some success, but he could never get out from under the family's debts. For a brief period, his brother Camille served as a justice of the peace under the American regime, but the family did not play a prominent role in the development of the town in the new republic.

According to Tocqueville, the establishment of a democracy required the elimination of a landed aristocracy. Ste. Genevieve's history offers an interesting test of this hypothesis. The United States government made an effort to break up the huge holdings that had been awarded to families such as the Vallés and Delassus by the French and Spanish monarchies. Ultimately, the American courts denied more than half of the claims brought before them for validation. Many men died before their claims could be settled. To retain their holdings, families had to remain united and continue the fight in the courts. Saddled with debts, the Delassus heirs divided the family's holdings, which eventually passed into American and German American hands. The Vallé family stayed strong through decades of hard work, sharp dealing, and legal battles, even as older generations faded away.

The dominant position of the Vallés and the community's acceptance of their largesse seem to contradict Tocqueville's hypothesis. Did the people of Ste. Genevieve develop democratic institutions while under the sway of a wealthy and beneficent family? If so, how did they do it? How did newcomers who arrived after the Louisiana Purchase adapt to this community with its entrenched European patriarchy? What did the American settlers think about the social arrangements in this old French town? What kind of people were they? And what kind of society did they create?

CHAPTER THREE

Americans in a French Community

Such for the most part is the district of Ste. Genevieve; tho' it must be confessed that there are several agreeable settlements of American Emigrants, who have chosen to establish themselves in this quarter of the country, for the purpose of uniting mineral with agricultural pursuits. Those of them, who emigrated prior to the acquisition are, with few exceptions industrious, intriguing, turbulent, and avaricious. Mean and fawning when it suits their purposes, and insolent Bravos when they drop the mask, on a disappointment of their hopes.

Frederick Bates, *Life and Papers*

THE FRONTIERSMAN HAS become a stock character in American fiction and movies. His virtues and failings are well known. The popular media has portrayed him as brave, hardworking, persistent, and honest to a fault. Nevertheless, any school child would probably tell you that frontiersmen were also hot-tempered, quick on the trigger, stubborn, intemperate, and not particularly responsive to the influences of art and literature. This stereotypical image may apply in some respects to the Anglo-American settlers who came to Ste. Genevieve after the Louisiana Purchase, but like all stereotypes, it has barely more than a grain of truth.

Lawyers, doctors, craftsmen, businessmen, and farmers were among the newcomers to Ste. Genevieve. Not all the newcomers were Anglo-Americans. In 1805, an educated German man named Otto Schrader arrived in the area and became a judge in local courts. Unfortunately, he died in 1811. But other Germans also immigrated to Ste. Genevieve. Michel Badeau, a carpenter, emigrated from the French island of Saint Domingue, married a young woman of color, and raised his family in the town. A young Frenchman named John James Audubon came to Ste. Genevieve in 1811. After trying his hand at business and hating it, he moved on and many years later won international fame as a painter of mammals and birds. Audubon's traveling companion and business partner, Ferdinand Rozier, liked Ste. Genevieve and remained there for the rest of his life.

In the 1830s, after he had become famous, Audubon published his impressions of the frontiersmen who settled in the Mississippi valley. Instead of the word *frontiersmen,* he used the term *squatters.* According to Audubon, most of these people moved from other parts of the United States where land prices were too high. In general, he said, they were "persons who, having a family of strong and hardy children, [were] anxious to enable them to provide for themselves." In the Mississippi valley, they hoped to settle on public land, pay nothing in rent, hold onto a tract for a few years, and eventually make it their own.[1]

For most of these squatters, he said, the first season in the Mississippi valley was arduous. Many suffered from fevers because of the marshy terrain, mosquitoes, and humid climate. But after they became acclimated, most of the newcomers were able to make a living, either from the lush timber, rich soil, or abundant game. By building a raft or some other form of watercraft, they could ship their goods to market in New Orleans. Every year they added to their profits, and after ten or twenty years, they could legally claim their land, either by purchase or through a government grant. The squatters formed bonds with their neighbors, married their sons and daughters to neighbors' children, built houses, barns, warehouses, workshops, and stores. They grew old and earned the right to "live respected and in due time die regretted, by all who knew them."[2]

In its broad outlines, this was an accurate picture of the settlers who came to Ste. Genevieve after the American takeover. Many arrived with few economic resources. As a group, they were hardworking and ambitious. Many were able to obtain land, and most participated in the river trade.

1. John James Audubon, *Delineations of American Scenery and Character,* 137.
2. Ibid., 140–42.

Many settlers prospered; some even became wealthy. Most were heads of families and had sons and daughters who would carry on the family farm or business. Of course, there were many variations on this overall pattern.

Some newcomers allied themselves with the powerful old French families of Ste. Genevieve. As men like Jean-Baptiste Vallé struggled to hold onto their huge Spanish land grants, they won the allegiance of a group of ambitious young American lawyers.[3] Ste. Genevieve's first lawyer, John Scott, came from a Virginia family with sufficient means to send him to Princeton College. He graduated in 1802 and moved to Ste. Genevieve in 1804. He arrived in town at a crucial time, when wealthy local families needed legal assistance to defend their land claims.[4]

Scott earned a reputation as a flamboyant character. Short in stature, quick-witted, and fast-talking, he liked to wear baggy pants and a cloth cap pulled down over his forehead. He frequently argued cases in territorial and federal courts, and when he did so, he traveled on horseback with saddlebags full of books and papers. In and out of court, he carried a knife and a pistol and thus fit the image of a gun-toting frontiersman.[5] He was considered to be an effective speaker and won the respect of prominent men not only in Ste. Genevieve but also in St. Louis. He and another young lawyer, Thomas Hart Benton, became the protégés of a group of wealthy French families, including the Chouteaus and the Gratiots, who headed a political faction called "the St. Louis junto."[6]

After the U.S. Congress organized the Missouri Territory, Scott represented the Ste. Genevieve District in the territory's legislative council.[7] In 1816, the St. Louis junto backed Scott as the territorial delegate to Congress in a race against the incumbent, Rufus Easton. This was a furiously contested election, in which a raucous group of land speculators threw their support to Easton with the backing of the *St. Louis Missouri Gazette*. Scott campaigned hard. In March 1816, he issued a pamphlet in which he

3. William E. Foley, *History of Missouri, Volume I: 1673–1820*, 198–99.

4. Alan S. Weiner, "John Scott, Thomas Hart Benton, David Barton and the 1824 Presidential Election: A Case Study in Pressure Politics," 461–62.

5. Ibid., 462.

6. Foley, *A History of Missouri*, 198–99.

7. Rozier, *History of the Early Settlement of the Mississippi Valley*, 253–55.

laid out his political program. He wanted to end the government's monopoly of lead mining and salt production, abolish government-owned Indian trading posts, press for Missouri statehood, remove squatters from public lands, push for the sale of public lands at low prices, support public schools, and build roads.[8]

The campaign became very ugly. Scott's opponents accused him of being a trash-talking gambler and of cheating an orphan out of two thousand dollars.[9] In response to these attacks, Scott challenged a young adversary named Charles Lucas to a duel. Several of Lucas's influential friends, including Frederick Bates, intervened to prevent bloodshed.[10] Lucas's friends should have intervened again in the summer of 1817, when he questioned whether Thomas Hart Benton had paid his poll taxes. Benton responded by calling Lucas a "puppy." Lucas had already withdrawn from one duel with Benton, but this time the antagonists met in combat on a Mississippi river sandbar known as Bloody Island. Benton shot Lucas in the left arm. Lucas forgave his adversary and then died.[11]

Territorial governor William Clark declared Scott the winner of the election by fifteen votes. Easton cried foul. In a second election conducted in 1817, Scott won by a significant margin. Easton protested again, but this time Scott officially took office. Two years later, Scott acted as the spokesman for Missouri's petition to become a state. As the delegate to Congress from the Missouri Territorial Legislature, he reported a bill "To authorize the people of the Missouri Territory to form a Constitution and State Government, on an equal footing with the original States." The bill passed on December 19, 1819.[12]

In the summer of 1820, Scott attended Missouri's constitutional convention in St. Louis, where he, Benton, and another political ally, David Barton, all supported Missouri's entrance into the Union as a slave state. Missouri entered the Union after heated congressional debate over slavery.

8. Foley, *History of Missouri,* 200.

9. John Scott to Charles Lucas, August 10, 1816, in "Correspondence between Mr. Scott and Mr. Lucas, St. Louis, August 10-September 20, 1816," Missouri Historical Society.

10. Frederick Bates's statement in "Correspondence between Mr. Scott and Mr. Lucas."

11. Foley, *History of Missouri,* 204.

12. Rozier, *History of the Early Settlement of the Mississippi Valley,* 259.

At stake was the balance of power between states that had abolished slavery and states that permitted it. According to the Missouri Compromise, Maine joined the Union as a free state, and Missouri as a slave state. Slavery was prohibited in any new states north of 36 degrees 30 minutes latitude in the land comprising the Louisiana Purchase (with the exception of Missouri). Scott became Missouri's first congressman; Benton and Barton, the state's first two senators.[13]

Scott's political career ended abruptly in 1826. His troubles began with the 1824 presidential election. Initially, he, Barton, and Benton all supported the candidacy of Henry Clay in a four-man race against Andrew Jackson, John Quincy Adams, and William Crawford. Missouri's voters agreed with them. On Election Day in Missouri, Clay came away with 1,401 votes; Jackson, with 987 votes; and John Quincy Adams, with 311 votes. William Crawford, who had suffered a stroke during the campaign, won no votes. The numbers were small because only adult white males, a minority of Missouri's population, qualified as voters. In the rest of the nation, Jackson won more than 40 percent of the vote, with Adams running second, and Crawford, third, eliminating Clay from consideration for the presidency. Since no candidate won a majority of the electoral votes, according to the Constitution, the House of Representatives had to choose among the top three candidates, with each state casting one vote. Scott was Missouri's only representative.[14]

When the state legislature failed to give clear instructions to its congressman, Scott learned a costly lesson in American politics. His friend Benton embraced Jackson's candidacy as the wave of the future. Jackson represented the rough and tumble men of the West, and he had come in second to Clay and beaten Adams in Missouri's popular vote. Clay personally pressured Scott to vote for Adams as the person most likely to preserve the status quo. Barton also advised him to give his support to Adams, the patrician son of a former president and the most likely person to get the nod from Congress.[15]

13. Weiner, "John Scott, Thomas Hart Benton, David Barton and the 1824 Presidential Election," 466.

14. Ibid., 460, 474–75.

15. Ibid., 481–87.

With an eye to obtaining favors for Missouri, Scott cast his vote for Adams, the eastern Whig, against Jackson, the frontier Democrat. Adams won, but for Scott this turned out to be a fatal political error. Newspapers all across the state denounced Scott's action as undemocratic: editorial writers insisted that he should have followed the will of the people and backed the man who had won more votes in his state. He defended himself by arguing that he had protected Missouri's interests by backing a winner. But his popularity melted away, Benton deserted him, and Scott lost his bid for re-election in 1826.[16]

A political pariah, Scott returned to Ste. Genevieve and continued to practice law. In 1830, he defended the notorious adventurer John Smith T on a charge of murder. This famous case proved that Scott had not lost his power to sway a jury. He never lost his frontier swagger, and even as an elderly man, he carried an elaborately carved knife and a pistol. After his death at the age of eighty in 1861, his neighbors remembered him as an old man with long white hair that flowed past his shoulders.[17]

Scott exemplified many of the qualities of a typical frontiersman. He was fiery, profane, stubborn, ambitious, persistent, and brave. But he was never a poor man, and he became a United States congressman with the help of powerful friends. His support came not only from Anglo-Americans, including Thomas Hart Benton, but also from members of the old French aristocracy, including the Chouteaus and Gratiots of St. Louis. His fall, as stunning as his ascent, resulted from misreading the democratic trend that would elevate another frontiersman, Andrew Jackson, to the highest office in the land.

Perhaps another man, Ichabod Sargent, provides a more typical example of the Anglo-Americans who flocked to Ste. Genevieve in its early years. Sargent, a doctor, came to Ste. Genevieve in 1822, when he was thirty years old. There was no shortage of physicians in the community—at least three other doctors, Walter Fenwick, Benjamin Shaw, and Lewis F. Linn,[18] offered medical services—but there was also no shortage of patients.

16. Ibid., 494.

17. Rozier, *History of the Early Settlement of the Mississippi Valley*, 253–58.

18. Lewis F. Linn began practicing medicine in Ste. Genevieve in 1815. In the 1830s he was appointed to the United States Senate (see Louis Houck, *A History of Missouri*, 3:54, 82).

The problem seemed to be inducing patients to pay. Sargent filed suit on at least twenty occasions attempting to collect debts owed to him individually or to him and Dr. Shaw.[19] Like his French counterparts, Sargent was a litigious fellow, who made many appearances in court.

He was also a very busy man. In addition to practicing medicine, Sargent bought a farm and speculated in land. His name appeared twenty-one times in Ste. Genevieve's index of deeds. In 1837, he purchased the property in the river bottoms at New Bourbon that had once belonged to Count Delassus. It appears that he rented this property to a farmer, who shared the profits with him. At the time of his death he still owned a house in Ste. Genevieve, the farm at New Bourbon, and ten other pieces of property.[20]

Sargent was a family man. On October 6, 1824, he married Anstes Brown in Randolph County, Illinois. She moved with him to Ste. Genevieve and was baptized there in the Catholic Church.[21] The couple's only son, John Ichabod, died in childhood. They also had four daughters: Isabelle, Jeanne Elizabeth, Emily Ann, and Susanne Jeanne Elisabeth. Isabelle married Jules Vallé and thus became part of Ste. Genevieve's most prominent French family. Jeanne Elizabeth married Felix St. Gemme, and Emily Ann married Henri Pernot.[22] If Susanne married, the local Catholic Church did not record it, but three of Sargent's four daughters married into French families.

The inventory of his estate, which was recorded at the time of his death, indicates that Sargent was also a slave owner. Listed among his possessions were one black boy named Bat, age about seven years; one negro woman

19. Folders 931, 933, 943, 962 (containing records of several law suits), 975, 1000, 1001, 1004, Ste. Genevieve Archives. Thanks are due to Richard Jackson for careful research in the archives.

20. "Last Will and Testament of Ichabod Sargent," Ste. Genevieve County, deed book H, p. 118. See also probate records and inventory, Circuit Court Clerk's office, Ste. Genevieve County Courthouse.

21. According to church baptismal records, Anstes Brown was baptized on April 29, 1833 (Ste. Genevieve Catholic Church, Parish Center, Baptisms and Marriage records, 1760–1860).

22. Ste. Genevieve Catholic Church, Parish Center, Baptisms and Marriage records, 1760–1860, bk. A, pp. 67, 77, 145.

named Malinda, age twenty-five years; one negro woman named Ellen, age twenty years; one negro woman Sarah, age fifteen, and Sarah's child; and one negro girl named May, age twelve. The inventory also listed one gray horse, three cows and calves, one hog, a cart and harness, one gig, running gear for a carriage, two old ploughs, a grindstone, surgical instruments, a bookcase and books, one rifle, one pistol, and other miscellaneous items. At the time of his death in 1848, the total value of Sargent's estate exceeded ten thousand dollars. He was a wealthy man.[23]

The Americans certainly did not bring equality to Ste. Genevieve. Like their French predecessors, they practiced racial slavery. Many observers, including Frederick Bates, noted that the Americans tended to be more ambitious and aggressive than the French—more prone to social climbing. Brackenridge remarked that class distinctions increased with the coming of the new republic, something that he found paradoxical.[24] This seeming contradiction actually made perfect sense, however, in terms of American ideology.

Before the American Revolution, Benjamin Franklin unabashedly announced that ordinary men had the right to, and would be foolish not to, strive for worldly success. Posing as "Poor" Richard Saunders, between 1733 and 1758, he reached out to the "common folk" with terse homilies on life, sex, drink, thrift, and hard work.[25] To men hungering for fame and fortune, he warned, "No man e'er was glorious, who was not laborious."[26] If life seemed arduous, he comforted, "Hope of gain/Lessens pain."[27] For those who trusted too completely in Providence, he had these words: "God helps them that help themselves."[28] In case anyone doubted the value of financial rewards, he insisted, "Nothing but Money/Is sweeter than Honey," and "A light purse is a heavy Curse."[29]

23. Ichabod Sargent, probate records and inventory, Circuit Court Clerk's office, Ste. Genevieve County Courthouse.

24. Bates, *Life and Papers*, 1:238; Brackenridge, *Views of Louisiana*, 140–41.

25. Benjamin Franklin, *The Autobiography of Benjamin Franklin*, 120.

26. Benjamin Franklin, "Poor Richard's Almanack," in *Benjamin Franklin: Writings*, 1191.

27. Ibid.

28. Ibid., 1201.

29. Ibid., 1197, 1235.

As a printer, inventor, writer, and businessman, Franklin acquired not only wealth but also international fame, which allowed him to rub shoulders—gleefully—with titled and leisurely European aristocrats. In the fall of 1776, he left the rebellious colonies for a diplomatic mission in France, and he loved it there. By the time of the Constitutional Convention in 1787, he had returned to America as an elder statesman. With the publication of his autobiography in the 1790s, he came to symbolize the self-made businessman, who worked hard and rose from humble circumstances to wealth and fame. In this way, he personified what Gordon Wood has called "the bumptious capitalism of the early republic," or, in other words, the American dream.[30]

In the 1830s, Tocqueville observed that Americans fiercely pursued economic advancement as the key to self-respect. In a democratic society, honor and dignity no longer came as a birthright, through family connections, aristocratic roots, or a settled place in a traditional hierarchy. According to Tocqueville, "In a democratic society like that of the United States, where fortunes are scanty and insecure, everybody works, and work opens the way to everything; this has changed the point of honor quite around and has turned it against idleness."[31] The French writer contrasted aristocratic men in France, who chose idleness and privation to maintain their self-esteem, with wealthy Americans, who worked in a profession to retain the respect of their peers.

American ideology led not to equality but to fierce competition for advancement in the social hierarchy. In Bates's view, this could result in some rather nasty behavior. Americans, as he saw them, could be conniving sycophants, who could easily become dangerous when thwarted in their ambitions. To be fair, he was also not fond of the French and seemed to take a dim view of human nature in general. A more tolerant man might have viewed the Americans as hardworking optimists, intent on bettering themselves and providing a better life for their families. The truth was somewhere between these two extremes.

American settlers came to Ste. Genevieve in pursuit of economic gain.

---

30. Gordon S. Wood, *The Americanization of Benjamin Franklin,* 207, 230, 246.
31. Tocqueville, *Democracy in America,* 1:237.

William Shannon, for example, migrated from Tennessee to Ste. Genevieve in 1804. He became one of the leading merchants in the community and sold goods in partnership with Samuel Perry in St. Louis. Like Ichabod Sargent, he speculated in land, and he bought a sizable tract from Moses Austin in 1811. The tract contained a large house, a kitchen, a stable, and a garden. He and his wife, Susan, lived here with their ten children. One daughter, Josephine, died in 1818 when she was just eighteen months old. In addition to this farm, located on the road to New Bourbon, the Shannon family owned a lot in town and several other properties.[32]

William Shannon also owned slaves. Probate records dated February 25, 1836, indicate that Shannon owned five slaves: Eliza (Elizabeth, Liz), age forty-two or forty-three, valued at $350; William, age nine, valued at $250; Mary, age eight, valued at $200; Eliza, age six, valued at $175; and Louisa, age two, valued at $150. Three years later, a second appraisal of the estate revised the list to include Amy, age twenty-six, and a child, valued at $700; Louis, age seventeen, valued at $700; Bill (William), age twelve, valued at $400; Mary, age ten, valued at $250; Eliza, age seven, valued at $200; and Liz (Eliza, Elizabeth), age forty-four or forty-five, valued at $325; and Emily, age twenty-five, valued at $550.[33]

Elizabeth almost certainly was the mother of four of the Shannon slaves and possibly of all of them. The local Catholic Church recorded the baptisms of Elizabeth's children. In the church records, Elizabeth's name appears sometimes as Elizabeth and sometimes as "Louise, Negress of William Shannon." The church recorded the birth of her son Louis on March 31, 1822, and his baptism on May 19 of the same year. A second son, Louis Felix Adolph, was born on April 20 and baptized on May 2, 1824; burial records indicate that Louis died at the age of three. Bill, or William, was born in 1827, but there is no baptismal record for him. Mary Jane was born on December 12, 1828, and baptized on January 1, 1829. Eliza was born on May 17, 1831, and baptized "Susanne Eliza" on June 5 of that

32. Ste. Genevieve County, deed book A, p. 53; deed book B, p. 136: deed book D, pp. 147, 281; and deed book F, p. 252. Mary Christina Manning, "Elizabeth Shannon: A Freed Slave and Her Family."

33. William Shannon, Probate Records, Circuit Court Clerk's office, Ste. Genevieve County Courthouse.

year. Amy, who may have been Elizabeth's eldest daughter, had her own child, Emelie Louise, on May 15, 1836.[34]

After William Shannon's death, his slaves were sold to various owners. Elizabeth continued to live as a slave in the household of Shannon's widow, Susan, until 1839. In that year, Francis Durand of Ste. Genevieve County sold her to Augustus Gregoire of Wisconsin for the sum of $327. Records identified her as "a certain Negro slave named Elisabeth or Lizi formerly owned by William Shannon deceased and sold at an administration sale of the Estate of the said Shannon." With the sale to Gregoire, Elizabeth contracted herself to serve a three-year term in the Wisconsin Territory. At the end of that term, Gregoire declared her "Free and at liberty to act for herself during the remainder of her life."[35] At the time, she was about forty-eight years old.

As soon as she obtained her freedom, Elizabeth made arrangements to purchase three of her daughters from their owners. On March 24, 1845, she purchased her twenty-four-year-old daughter, Mary Jane Jackson, from Thomas C. Fassett of Iowa. Five days later, she purchased her twenty-year-old daughter, Eliza Catherine Jackson, from Susan Shannon and secured the freedom of Emily from William Myers of the Iowa Territory. With her daughters, she returned to Ste. Genevieve.[36]

On May 24, 1845, Elizabeth Shannon purchased farm property that had once belonged to William Shannon. She and her daughters operated this farm on which they had previously been slaves. On April 17, 1854, she emancipated Eliza Catherine, Mary Jane, and Mary Jane's daughter, Eliza. Why she waited so long to give them their freedom remains a mystery. Her daughter Emily had been free since 1845. In 1857, Elizabeth sold the farm, and it appears that she and her family left Ste. Genevieve.[37]

34. Ste. Genevieve Catholic Church, Parish Center, Baptisms and Marriage records, 1760–1860, baptismal register for the years 1820–1843, pp. 23, 51, 114, 150, 244.

35. Ste. Genevieve County, deed book E, p. 559.

36. Registry of Free Black Persons, Office of the County Clerk, Ste. Genevieve County Courthouse. See also "Registry of Free Blacks and Mulattoes, Ste. Genevieve County, Missouri," Missouri State Archives, Jefferson City, Missouri.

37. Mary Christina Manning traced Elizabeth Shannon's life through church records, deed and probate records, and U.S. census records for Ste. Genevieve County (see "Elizabeth Shannon," typescript).

Because Ste. Genevieve was a frontier community, people came and went frequently. For instance, Michel Badeau first appeared in local records in 1813, after his father, Francois, passed away and left him an estate worth about one hundred dollars.[38] Census records subsequently listed his birthplace as Port au Prince (Saint Domingue, later Haiti). His family may have fled the West Indies during the turmoil in the late eighteenth century. Badeau may have been a white man, but he married a free woman of color named Caroline Cavelier in 1818. Local records identified their eight sons, variously, as black or mulatto.[39]

Michel Badeau, who was also known as Joseph, worked as a carpenter. Six of his eight sons lived to adulthood, and three of them, Henri Eli, Israel, and Michel Jules, appear in census records and other documents as following their father's trade. Apparently, Badeau succeeded in this line of work. In 1862, he filed a lien on a property, indicating that he was owed four hundred dollars, a significant sum, for his services. He also owned real estate in his own name: federal records in 1822 confirmed his claim to a tract of 240 acres.[40] In 1850, he purchased cropland in the big field. His son Henri, at age twenty-eight, owned property worth one hundred dollars, according to the 1850 census. While not wealthy, the Badeaus were substantial citizens of Ste. Genevieve for half a century.[41]

Tragedy struck the family in 1860, when Michel's wife, Caroline, and several of their grandchildren died of cholera. Michel, his sons, their wives, and their children must have pulled up stakes within the next few years. In 1876, Michel Badeau passed away in St. Louis. An obituary in the *St. Louis Republic* read: "Michel Badeau born San Domingo 1770 died in St. Louis August 4, 1876, spent a couple of years learning the trade of

38. March 11, 1813, Orphan's Court Records, Ste. Genevieve County Courthouse. Thanks are due to Delilah Tayloe for her careful research on Michel Badeau in primary sources.

39. The Ste. Genevieve Catholic Church recorded his marriage to Caroline Cavelier on June 13, 1818, and his children are listed in the U.S. Bureau of the Census, *Seventh Census: 1850, Population Schedule: Ste. Genevieve County, Missouri,* NARA microfilm, M432, reel #413.

40. Land deeds, box 8, Federal Land Certificate #258, Missouri Historical Society.

41. Delilah Tayloe, Carla Jordan, Richard Taylor, Jason Moen, and Jason Williamson traced the Badeau and Cavelier/Louison families through the U.S. census population schedules for Ste, Genevieve County, 1840, 1850, 1860, 1870, and 1880.

carpenter and house builder in Philadelphia as a boy, then moved to Ste. Genevieve and Kaskaskia until he came to St. Louis shortly before his death."[42]

The life stories of Elizabeth Shannon and Michel Badeau demonstrate that lines of race and class remained somewhat fluid in Ste. Genevieve after the American takeover. As time went on, however, the United States experienced deep divisions on the issue of slavery, and racial lines hardened. Even in Ste. Genevieve, people began to fear slave uprisings, and the town passed an ordinance in 1842 stipulating that "no negroes or mulattoes over the age of fourteen years, shall be permitted to assemble within the limits of said Corporation to the number of five or more, and remain so assembled for the space of thirty minutes" without written permission.[43] This ordinance applied not only to slaves but also to free people of color. Perhaps the Shannon and Badeau families left Ste. Genevieve in search of a place where they could be more secure in their freedom. Just why they left the area may never be known.

Ste. Genevieve both gained and lost when the Americans came. The greatest gain was the chance to participate in a representative form of government, although the opportunity was open to white males only. By all accounts, the men of Ste. Genevieve took advantage of this opportunity. Ichabod Sargent, William Shannon, and John Scott all took part in civic life, helping to create political institutions and schools that would make it possible for democracy to flourish. Gender and race kept the Shannons and the Badeaus from participating fully in the life of the community. As many historians have pointed out, the full benefits of democracy in the early years of the republic were available only to a small percentage of the American people. In Ste. Genevieve and in the rest of the Missouri Territory only a small elite engaged actively in political life.[44]

Perhaps the greatest loss to Ste. Genevieve resulted from the Americans' hatred of Native Americans. Within twenty years of the Louisiana

42. *St. Louis Republic,* August 5, 1876.
43. Ordinances Passed by the Trustees of the Town of Ste. Genevieve, Missouri, 1842, booklet, Missouri Historical Society.
44. Foley, *History of Missouri,* 204.

Purchase, the Peoria, the Shawnee, and the Delaware tribes had lost their lands on the west bank, leaving their villages deserted. Immediately after the American takeover, some of these people moved into settlements along Wilson's Creek, the James Fork, and the Current and the White rivers in Osage territory. Under the terms of a treaty in 1808, the Osage gave up all their lands in the Missouri, opening them for white settlement. The War of 1812 brought turmoil, with Indian tribes fighting for and against the British.[45] After the war, American settlers pressed the Shawnee and Delaware into smaller and smaller pockets of land in the Ozark hills.

As Missouri's delegate to Congress in 1820, John Scott proposed the removal of the Indians to reservations in the West. Voicing the sentiments of most Anglo-Americans, he argued that conflicts between Indians and whites over land ownership and grazing rights posed a threat to the territory. He urged Congress to resolve the disputes by forcing the Shawnee and Delaware to exchange their land in Missouri for land in Indian Territory. By this time, the federal government had already begun the process of finding new lands for the Indians, and the Indians, facing inevitable displacement, had abandoned many of their villages. Treaties in the late 1820s and early 1830s recognized what had already occurred.[46] After statehood, the Native Americans who had walked the streets and conducted business at the trading posts of Ste. Genevieve during the French and Spanish periods no longer made an appearance in the town.

Racial divisions haunted American democracy. In the 1830s Tocqueville clearly saw this as a threat to the republic. Like most Europeans of his time, he divided mankind into three groups: whites, blacks, and "savages." He did not question the hierarchy that placed whites, or European people, on a plane above all people of color. Although he deplored the cruelty and misery of forced migrations from their homeland, he calmly predicted the extinction of the Indian tribes and the supremacy of white people on the North American continent. More troubling, in his view, was the enslavement of African Americans. "The Indians," he wrote, "Will perish in

---

45. Chapman and Chapman, *Indians and Archaeology of Missouri,* 120.
46. Schroeder, *Opening the Ozarks,* 378–81.

the same isolated condition in which they have lived, but the destiny of the Negroes is in some measure interwoven with that of the Europeans. These two races are fastened to each other without intermingling; and they are alike unable to separate entirely or combine." In his view, this posed the single greatest threat to the survival of the nation.[47]

Tocqueville was mistaken: the Native American tribes did not disappear. Throughout the nineteenth century, western tribes fought valiantly against the encroachment of the United States. In the late twentieth century, the American Indian Movement (AIM) stridently insisted that the tribes and Indian cultures, languages, and ways of life had survived and would persist in the face of industrialization, modernization, and every possible form of oppression. If Tocqueville had been alive at the beginning of the twenty-first century, he would have been astonished to discover that millions of Americans traced their roots to tribal groups, which proudly celebrated ancient rituals and customs and reclaimed their heritage.

Tocqueville was also wrong about African Americans. Although he condemned slavery, he succumbed to the slave owners' prejudices and described black people in terms of commonly held stereotypes. He was correct in perceiving slavery as a "calamity" that would ultimately threaten the survival of the democratic republic. Slavery had existed in ancient cultures, but it had faded away in the Christian era. Racial slavery was a relatively modern concept that persisted only in certain parts of America. When the slave and his master were of the same race, the slave could become a free man by a simple revision of his legal status, but ending racial slavery would be much more difficult. Not only the law, but the customs and prejudices of the people would have to change. This, he feared, might prove impossible. He held a deep conviction that African Americans would not adapt well to freedom and that white Americans would never grant it. In light of this double dilemma, he questioned the fate of the Union.[48]

To some extent, Tocqueville's dismal predictions did come true: the Union foundered on the issue of slavery, and only a bloody Civil War

47. Tocqueville, *Democracy in America*, 1:338, 339, 356.
48. Ibid., 357, 381.

brought an end to the institution. But in Ste. Genevieve, before and after that war, the people would be more resilient, more adaptable, and more diverse than Tocqueville had predicted. New populations would come to town. The fate of democracy, and not just the Union, would rest in their hands.

Chapter Four

German Influx

No European, unless he belongs to the lowest classes, will be able to refrain from considering the moral implications of slavery when he arrives with plans for settlement beyond the Allegheny Mountains. The decision as to whether or not one wants to keep slaves has such an influence on the choice of the state, on the place within that chosen state, and on all one's arrangements, that every settler should make up his mind on the subject before he crosses the ocean.

Gottfried Duden, *Report on a Journey to the Western States of North America and a Stay of Several Years along the Missouri during the Years 1824, 1825, 1826, and 1827*

IN THE 1820s, Gottfried Duden traveled through Missouri, sending letters and reports home to his countrymen in Germany that extolled the beauty and bounty of the state. Missouri's acceptance of slavery troubled prospective immigrants. Duden condoned the practice of racial slavery but cautioned Germans to consider carefully whether their consciences could abide it.[1] After 1830, many German immigrants came to Ste. Genevieve seeking economic prosperity and political freedom. In general, they eschewed the practice of slavery, but a few became slave owners. Like most immigrants, they adapted to the mores of their adopted country, while clinging to important aspects of their ethnic heritage.

German Americans played a significant role in shaping the community after the Louisiana Purchase. Otto Schrader, for example, organized the

---

1. Gottfried Duden, *Report on a Journey to the Western States of North America and a Stay of Several Years along the Missouri during the Years 1824, 1825, 1826, and 1827*, 106.

first Masonic lodge in Ste. Genevieve, and indeed in the Missouri Territory, in 1807. The German-born Schrader held the title of grand master. Dr. Aaron Elliott, an Anglo-American, and Joseph Hertich, a native of Switzerland, served the order as wardens. After Schrader's death in 1811, Henry Dodge succeeded him as grand master, but the lodge stopped meeting by 1817.[2]

Another early German settler in Ste. Genevieve was Albert Bisch. Born in 1779 in Frankenthal, he immigrated to the United States in 1802, stopping first in Philadelphia and then migrating to Ste. Genevieve in 1816. He and his wife, Hannah, had a business relationship with two merchants in town, Henry Keil and Edmund Roberts. Both Albert and Hannah signed documents dissolving the partnership in 1821.[3] Bisch and his four sons owned and operated farms.

When he died in 1845, Bisch left a substantial estate, including two slaves. According to the terms of Albert's will, Hannah received $4250 in cash, one-fifth of his real estate and two mulatto slave "girls," valued at $200. Five years earlier, the 1840 census had listed two slaves in his household: a female less than ten years of age and another female age thirty-six to fifty-five. The remainder of his estate was divided equally among the four sons.[4]

Before 1830, only a few Germans, including the Bisch family, lived in Ste. Genevieve. After that, German immigration to the United States increased dramatically, reaching a peak in the 1850s, when Germans accounted for more than 35 percent of all immigrants to America. This trend had an enormous impact on Ste. Genevieve: the number of German-born residents increased steadily until the 1880s, and German Americans accounted for nearly half of the local population.[5]

Typical of these newcomers were John Dominic Kern and his wife, Regina, who emigrated from Baden in the late 1830s, along with John's brother Matthew. The Kern brothers became naturalized American citizens in 1844. They were ambitious and enterprising men, who actively

---

2. *Ste. Genevieve Plaindealer,* March 9, 1860.

3. Indenture, Ste. Genevieve County, deed book C, p. 461, December 11, 1821. Thanks are due to Adrianna Salazar and Olivia Starr for research in the primary sources.

4. Ste. Genevieve County, deed book F, p. 242.

5. See Barbara Sanders, "The Germans of Ste. Genevieve, 1830–1890."

participated in building their community. Matthew opened the Landing Hotel and operated an omnibus to carry visitors from the riverfront to the town. By the 1860s, he had built another hotel and established a carriage line conveying passengers from Ste. Genevieve to Farmington three times a week. He also worked as a bookkeeper for the *Ste. Genevieve Plaindealer,* a Democratic newspaper published during the crisis of the Union in the 1850s and 1860s.[6]

John Dominic Kern made a living as a farmer with the help of his large family. Kern, his wife, and their three young children first appeared on the Ste. Genevieve census in 1840. During the next two decades, the Kerns brought up eight children: Wilhelmina, John Edward, Mary, Charles, William, Josephine, August, and Julia. In June of 1855, Kern invested in four city blocks of land, which he and several partners developed as part of the town of Ste. Genevieve. The section containing Roberts Road became known as Kern's Addition. On July 26, 1855, John purchased a seventy-five acre farm from the estate of Ichabod Sargent for one thousand dollars.[7]

The Kern family did not own slaves. John Kern worked the farm himself with the help of his sons Charles and John Edward and his daughter Wilhelmina's husband, Benjamin Etter. The Etters and their two children, Charles and Louise, lived on the farm, as did a hired hand named Benedict Severman, a native of Switzerland. In addition to livestock, the family raised vegetables and fruit. In the 1860s, Kern planted grapevines on three acres of land and started making wine, which he fermented in barrels in the basement of his house.[8]

Between 1867 and 1870, he and his family must have suffered from various diseases because he paid numerous bills for medicine and for treat-

6. Thanks are due to Terri Foley, Cheryl Nagle, Laura Myers, Cathy Grove, and others for primary research on the Kern family. Sources include U.S. Department of Justice, Naturalization Records, housed in the county clerk's office, Ste. Genevieve County Courthouse; and the *Ste. Genevieve Plaindealer,* March 29, 1861.

7. Ste. Genevieve County, deed book I, pp. 563–64 and 587.

8. This information was gleaned from the U.S. Bureau of the Census, *Seventh Census: 1850, Population Schedule,* NARA microfilm, M432; *Eighth Census: 1860, Population Schedule: Ste. Genevieve County, Missouri,* NARA microfilm, M653; and John D. Kern, Probate Records, Circuit Court Clerk's office, Ste. Genevieve County Courthouse, drawer 42, packet 1012.

ment from a local physician, F. T. Bernays. Kern paid in cash some of the time, but sometimes he paid in produce. The old system of barter had not yet given way to the cash economy in Ste. Genevieve. The family's medical bills mounted in the late 1860s. For instance, on July 4, 1867, Bernays accepted one gallon of wine as payment for ringworm medicine and other medical services. In August of that year, the doctor accepted three gallons of wine in return for fever medicine for "Madame Kern." During the following summer, the doctor came to the farm and performed hemorrhoid surgery: he charged three dollars for the visit and five dollars for the operation. In the fall, there was another bill for fever medicine for Mr. Kern and the children. Mr. Kern apparently paid these charges with an unspecified amount of rhubarb and thirty heads of cabbage.

The Kern family's health deteriorated in 1869 and 1870. During those two years, Dr. Bernays made at least twenty-five visits to the household. On some visits he brought medicine for Madame Kern. Once he extracted a tooth for one of the Kern sons. Several times he gave fever medicine to various members of the family. In the winter of 1869, Mr. Kern's problems became acute. He suffered from rheumatism, and in December the doctor had to make a "*visite* at night Pleurisy Mr. Kern." He was still suffering from this ailment in the spring of 1870. The doctor's records show that Kern paid his mounting bills with rhubarb, a bushel of pecans, two geese, and five gallons of wine.[9]

Kern passed away on August 16, 1871, leaving a substantial estate to his wife and children. In addition to his farm and other tracts of land, his personal property included five hundred gallons of wine, one two-horse wagon, a plow, a mower and reaper, seven horses, three mules, twenty-one cows and calves, more than one hundred hogs and pigs, eight cords of wood, and various household items and furnishings. After his debts had been settled, his estate was valued at more than twenty-five hundred dollars.[10]

    9. Account records of F. T. Bernays, in John D. Kern, Probate Records, Circuit Court Clerk's office, Ste. Genevieve County Courthouse, drawer 42, packet 1012.

    10. John D. Kern estate inventory, filed October 4, 1871, Probate Records, Circuit Court Clerk's office, Ste. Genevieve County Courthouse, drawer 42, packet 1012; Ste. Genevieve County, deed book A, p. 194.

Kern's children continued his farming and winemaking enterprises. In 1873, John Edward Kern ran afoul of Missouri's state laws against selling liquor on a Sunday. He reportedly sold a variety of spirits, including whiskey, brandy, rum, gin, wine, beer, and ale, to Ignatius Layton. Kern was arrested on November 11 and indicted on May 9, 1873, for "keeping open a grocery on Sunday." The court fined him five cents for each pint sold.[11]

Descendants of John Kern owned and operated the farm until the final decades of the twentieth century. In 1875, John Edward, William, and August purchased most of their father's possessions from their mother and other heirs for two thousand dollars. When John Edward passed away, his widow attempted to sell her portion of the estate, and William and August took their sister-in-law to court to prevent the sale. A judge ruled that the land could not be divided without injury to other parties and ordered the entire property sold at auction on the courthouse steps. William and August bid five hundred dollars for the farm on February 12, 1878, and kept it in the family. Later that year, William sold his share to August, making him the sole owner of the farm.[12]

August Kern and his wife, Sarah, had nine children: Frederick August, Rachel, Catherine, Nettie, Nicholas, Filmore and Hilber (twins), Charles, and Edna. With the help of his large family and an African American man called Brother Jim, August kept the farm going through the 1930s. August frequently let passersby drink from the well or come into the house for something to eat. In 1909, a band of gypsies came through and camped out near a spring across the road. August invited them over for dinner, and they gave the family a bouquet of flowers made from dyed feathers. The gift remained in the family into the twenty-first century.[13]

According to family lore, August once had an encounter with a famous outlaw. A stranger stopped in the front yard to get a drink from the well. He asked Kern if he could put up his horse in the barn for the night. Kern told the stranger no, because the barn was full of mules, but explained that if the stranger went south to the bluffs, he could shelter his horses

11. John D. Kern, Probate Records, Circuit Court Clerk's office, Ste. Genevieve County Courthouse, packet 1012.

12. Ste. Genevieve County, deed book 26, pp. 469; and deed book 30, pp. 458–60.

13. Kern, interview.

there. The stranger went south and did not reappear. The next day the bank was robbed, and it was rumored that the bandit Jesse James had committed the crime.[14]

When August died in 1939, he left the farm to his children. At the time of his death, his unmarried daughters, Nettie, Rachel, Edna, and his son Filmore (Phil) were still living at home. None of them ever married, and they remained at the farm for the rest of their lives. Nettie was the cook of the household, Rachel was the gardener, Edna was the driver, and Phil farmed the land. After Phil's death, the three sisters were the last occupants of the house. In 1955, Nicholas Kern's son August W. (Gus) Kern and his wife, Shirley, purchased the farm from the sisters but allowed them to continue living in the house for the rest of their lives.[15]

In 1985, architectural historians investigated the Kern House and discovered that it contained a mystery. Under the clapboard siding of the two-story farmhouse were the old vertical log walls of a one-story French colonial house. By eighteenth-century standards, it would have been a very large house with six rooms across the front and six across the back, and it stood on property once owned by Pierre Delassus. Osmund Overby and Toni Prawl documented the house for the Historic American Buildings Survey in 1987. When a dendrochronologist took samples and determined a felling date of 1793 for the logs used to construct the house, scholars reasoned that this must have been the old count's home. An anonymous benefactor purchased the property and donated it to the state of Missouri for use as a historic site.[16]

In the 1990s, archaeological investigations cast doubt on the Delassus' connection. Although the logs dated from 1793, excavations around the foundation and in the yard of the property uncovered no artifacts from the eighteenth century. There were plenty of nineteenth-century bottles, buttons, and pottery shards and even a ring with the initials "N. K." for Nettie Kern. Archaeologists found projectile points and other remnants

14. Ibid.
15. Ibid.
16. Overby and Prawl, "Pierre Delassus De Luziere House," HABS No. Mo-1283, January 1987, Historic American Buildings Survey Collection, Library of Congress; B. H. Rucker, preface to Stepenoff and Bibb, *Ste. Genevieve Historic Preservation Field School.*

of the Mississippian period but found nothing from the 1790s. Other than the prehistoric artifacts, there was nothing that dated before the 1830s.[17] Scholars debated the issue and wondered about the historical significance of the property.

All this speculation about the Kern House casts a strange light on the way Americans view their history. Scholars strained to establish a link between the German American farmhouse and the eighteenth-century French nobleman. When that effort faltered, the historical value of the house came into question. But why should it have? Why should Americans give special consideration to a person's or a home's aristocratic origins? Why should a brief and tenuous link to a wealthy Frenchman outweigh more than a century of occupancy by a hardworking German American family?

Whether or not Pierre Delassus ever slept under its roof, the Kern House represented important trends in Ste. Genevieve's history. In the 1830s, someone salvaged logs from an old house and erected a new dwelling in the traditional French manner. It might have been the children or grandchildren of Pierre Delassus, or it might have been the Anglo-Americans who purchased the property from them. Almost certainly the house was there when John D. Kern purchased the farm in the 1850s. Photographs from the 1890s show members of the Kern family standing in front of a one-story house. Sometime after that August Kern added a second story to the house to accommodate his extended family. When he did so, he created a typical German American house with a high profile, a steeply pitched gable roof, decorative vents in the gables, and white clapboard siding. His children lived in the house and preserved it until the final decades of the twentieth century, leaving an important, albeit complicated, legacy. The story it tells is not about a displaced French count but about a family who migrated from Germany and became American citizens.

John and August Kern are excellent examples of the ways in which German immigrants shaped the culture of Ste. Genevieve. John Kern came to Missouri as part of a mass migration in the 1830s and 1840s, when political turmoil in Germany caused thousands of people to seek refuge from oppression. Duden and others urged their countrymen to

17. Wesler, Stepenoff, Farris, and Morrow, "Archaeological Test Excavations," 86–87.

establish ethnic enclaves on the American frontier.[18] Emigration societies encouraged the creation of "pure" German communities such as those in Hermann and Marthasville along the Missouri River.[19] But many German immigrants settled in cities, such as St. Louis, where other ethnic groups predominated. Several towns on the west bank of the Mississippi River, such as New Madrid, Cape Girardeau, and Ste. Genevieve, attracted substantial numbers of German immigrants.[20]

Many German immigrants came to Missouri in search of religious freedom. For example, a group of Old Order Lutherans from Saxony immigrated to St. Louis in 1838 and subsequently settled in Perry County, just south of Ste. Genevieve. They wanted to escape from the new doctrines being promulgated from German pulpits and in German classrooms and to cling to the teachings of Martin Luther. Families and individuals who were not affiliated with such an organized group sought out communities where they could practice their faith.[21] The Bisch family, the Kern family, and many of the other Germans who came to Ste. Genevieve were Catholics, who soon became active members of the local parish church.

German settlers conformed to, and challenged, American social and cultural norms. A nineteenth-century American traveler in the Mississippi valley praised German immigrants for their thriftiness and industriousness but criticized their intemperance. In the 1820s, Timothy Flint noted that German farmers tended to build sturdy houses, barns, fences, and gates. They planted orchards and raised horses and cattle, and their farming operations generally prospered. According to Flint, the Germans were religious and loved to discuss theology. But Flint faulted them because they also raised grapes and distilled grain to make alcohol and because they loved to sample their own products.[22] Whether or not John Kern liked to discuss theology, he was Catholic. He did build a substantial

18. Adolf Schroeder, "German Folklore and Traditional Practices in the Mississippi Valley," 156–57.

19. Steven Rowan, *Germans for a Free Missouri: Translations from the St. Louis Radical Press, 1857–1862,* 25.

20. Burnett and Luebbering, *German Settlement in Missouri,* 58.

21. Schroeder, "German Folklore," 158.

22. Timothy Flint, *Recollections of the Last Ten Years in the Valley of the Mississippi,* 169–72.

house and outbuildings; he did raise grapes and make wine. His son offended the American authorities by selling these products on a Sunday, and it seems likely that he sampled his own products.

By the time the Kerns came to Ste. Genevieve, clearly identifiable German American enclaves had developed in Missouri. Earlier German immigrants, such as the Bisch family, who came to Ste. Genevieve in small numbers, tended to blend more completely into existing local culture. With the waves of immigration in the 1830s, 1840s, and 1850s, Germans in Ste. Genevieve formed a community within a community, sharing a common language, customs, and attitudes. They also had access to the German-language newspapers issued in St. Louis. By the 1850s and early 1860s, these publications had become stridently antislavery and pro-Union. With a few exceptions, the German residents of Ste. Genevieve rejected the mores of the slaveholders. Matthew Kern worked for the *Plaindealer,* a southern-sympathizing newspaper, but other local German residents clearly expressed their support for the Union.

On February 28, 1862, the *Plaindealer* accused some local Germans of pro-Union rowdyism. An editorial identified the disturbers of the peace as "Teutons" and listed some of their names as "August Wilder, Small, Eikelop, Jokerst." The writer accused the participants of riding riotously through town, brandishing American flags, cursing and insulting law-abiding citizens, and scaring little old ladies. He also played upon ethnic stereotypes by blaming the incidents on "whiskey and beer," insinuating that German Americans had a special vulnerability to the effects of liquor.

The editorial read,

> The slumbers of this quiet old town were considerably disturbed on last Tuesday by a wagonload of obstreperous men and boys. What started the noisy Teutons, we know not; whether whiskey, beer, Washington's Birthday, or the victory in Kentucky, it does not appear clear; except as to the whiskey and beer, they without doubt were the principle and inspiring cause....
>
> The programme appeared to be about thus. A two-horse wagon, three or four small U.S. flags, a few drinks a piece, and the party consisting of August Wilder, Small, Eikelop, Jokerst, and a few small boys mounted the wagon. Hip, Hurrah it went around the squares, halting . . . at some favorite beer house and then off again, shaking their flags in the faces of

the citizens who happened to pass—and cursing and insulting them, pretty indiscriminately, without regard to age sex, or condition.[23]

This odd incident reveals a great deal about ethnic divisions in Ste. Genevieve during the Civil War. In spite of the bloody collapse of the Union, Ste. Genevieve remained a "quiet old town." The loyalties of the old French and Anglo-American residents remained with the slaveholding South. German newcomers, apparently, kept their sentiments to themselves, until alcohol weakened their inhibitions. Under its influence, some of the younger men and boys could not resist flaunting their Union sympathies. Angry local residents, "insulted" by this behavior, indulged in anti-German epithets. But the incident ended without escalating into violence.

After the war, the divisions continued. Joseph A. Ernst, who settled in Ste. Genevieve in the 1870s, stridently expressed the German, and Republican, point of view. In his newspaper the *Ste. Genevieve Herald,* he railed against "Bourbonism," which he linked not only to the old French aristocracy but also to the postwar Democratic Party. In an editorial in September 1882, he accused local political leaders of "thoroughbred mossback intolerance." Paraphrasing Alexander Stephens, Ernst defined *Bourbon* as "a man who believes that, if the Democracy succeeds, confederate money and bonds will be at par, and that every white man may wollop a 'nigger' whenever he feels so disposed, as in the good old anti-bellum days." He believed local Democrats fit that description.[24]

Ernst was born in Westphalia in 1836, immigrated to the United States in the late 1850s, and married Adeline Hechinger of Cincinnati, Ohio, in 1865. The couple had nine children, but only two sons and a daughter would outlive their mother, who passed away in 1901. In 1875, the family bought property on the plank road between Ste. Genevieve and Farmington. Joseph Ernst, who had received a classical education in Germany, taught school and served as a school principal in Ste. Genevieve before he founded his newspaper in May 1882.[25]

23. *Ste. Genevieve Plaindealer,* February 28, 1862.
24. *Ste. Genevieve Herald,* September 23, 1882.
25. Ste. Genevieve Catholic Church, parish records; *Ste. Genevieve Herald,* May 6, 1882, and October 12, 1901; Ste. Genevieve County, deed book 26, p. 205, and deed book 27, p. 49; Sanders, "Germans of Ste. Genevieve," 10.

The *Herald,* printed in both English and German, was not the first German-language paper in the community. In the mid-1870s, Ernst had some association with the *Freie Presse* (Free Press), another newspaper that was published in both German and English. Apparently no issues of this newspaper have survived. S. Henry Smith, the publisher of a rival newspaper, the *Ste. Genevieve Fair Play,* ranted in print about the radical republican sympathies of the German American paper. In 1876, the owners of the *Fair Play* bought the English-language version of the *Freie Presse* and discontinued it. The German version continued for a brief period before it was replaced by another German-language paper, the *Beobachter.*[26]

In his "Salutary" message in the first issue of the *Herald* on May 6, 1882, Ernst explained that the untimely death of J. G. Rudolph had caused the suspension of publication of the *Ste. Genevieve Beobachter.*[27] Friends had urged him, Ernst said, to produce an independent paper, "which was controlled neither by party nor clique, independent of even the personal associations of politics, a free, frank and fearless herald of news." He decided to print this new paper in both English and German, "for the great majority of the German people speak and read the English language, the young generation having received almost none but an English education. Besides, the American population of this county is as much in need of an independent paper as the German."[28] Interestingly, he distinguished the "American" population from the German and the French.

Ernst believed in democracy, but he insisted that a political elite, entrenched within the Democratic Party, unfairly kept Germans and Republicans from holding local and county offices. By using the word *Bourbon,* he implied that old French families dominated this clique. He reinforced this idea by repeatedly using the word *thoroughbreds* to describe and insult the local aristocracy. Nevertheless, he believed the American system of government provided a way for the common people to unseat the elites. Again and again, he urged German Americans to vote.

In the spirit of democracy and Americanization, his newspaper announced, in glowing terms, plans for celebrations on the Fourth of July.

26. *Ste. Genevieve Fair Play,* March 2, 1876.
27. It appears that no issues of this newspaper have survived.
28. *Ste. Genevieve Herald,* May 6, 1882.

On June 17, 1882, the paper urged all citizens to attend "a grand turnout procession" on Independence Day. "George Sexauer," the paper said, "is making active preparations for a grand picnic on the 4th of July which shall eclipse everything that was offered in this line before." Clearly, the editor wanted German Americans to take part in commemorating the birth of the republic.[29]

Although Ernst placed great faith in the electoral franchise, he did not advocate voting rights for women. In his paper, he linked women's rights to the temperance movement, which he strongly opposed. Throughout the country in the late nineteenth century, the Woman's Christian Temperance Union (WCTU) loudly called for action to curtail the sale and consumption of alcohol. In Ste. Genevieve, local officials irked Ernst by enforcing state laws that required licenses for saloons and prohibited Sunday sales of liquor. Ernst connected this local form of oppression with the growing stridency of American women. In Ernst's view, women's rights and the temperance crusade marched hand in hand.[30]

As he saw it, the temperance movement, liquor licensing laws, and Sunday closing laws abridged personal liberty and threatened the livelihood of many German immigrants. German Americans owned most of the saloons and dram shops in Ste. Genevieve. Licensing laws, enacted in the early 1880s, forced these businessmen to pay high fees to the government. Sunday closing laws restricted not only their profits but also the social life of the German community. Ernst roundly condemned the prosecuting attorneys who filed charges against saloon keepers for selling on Sundays, and although he cited the Constitution, he couched his protest in the language of the Declaration of Independence.

Invoking the Founding Fathers, he asserted a natural right to consume alcohol any day of the week. "We do not believe," he wrote,

> That the people of this county desire to see the saloons closed on Sunday. We believe it to be one of the inalienable rights guaranteed by the Constitution of the United States that a man has a right to drink a glass

29. Ibid., June 17, 1882, and September 23, 1882; Sanders, "Germans in Ste. Genevieve," 11.
30. Sanders, "Germans in Ste. Genevieve," 15–16.

of beer on Sunday as well as on any other day of the week, and that the practice of indicting and fining $5.00 as done in this county, can not advance the cause of justice or morality, as the Prosecuting Attorney is the only one benefited by doing so.[31]

In one terse editorial, he managed to invoke the highest principles of human freedom and take a cheap shot at a local official.

Behind his public crusading, Ernst apparently faced some private demons. In 1896, he took the unusual step of conveying all his real and personal property to his wife. In a document filed with Ste. Genevieve County's recorder of deeds he stated that he owed Adeline a debt of five thousand dollars, which he had taken from her and invested under his own name. He publicly apologized for his actions and declared that in payment of this debt and in recognition of other wrongs he had done her, he "freely and absolutely" granted "unto the said Adeline M. Ernst, my wife, all and all manner of goods, chattels, debts, money and all other things, of me the said Joseph A. Ernst, whatsoever, as well real as personal, of what kind, nature or quality whatsoever, particularly my lot on Second street bounded North by lot of the said Adeline M. Ernst, my wife, as also the property known as the Ste. Genevieve Herald."[32]

Joseph gave her everything, including his newspaper, to settle a debt he owed her. But what kind of a debt? What had he done? It appears that he had taken her money and invested it foolishly. Records filed in the Ste. Genevieve County Courthouse indicate that Ernst became involved in numerous property transactions and held mortgages on several properties. If he lost money on these ventures, he might simply have wanted to repay what he thought he owed to his wife. Or he might have betrayed her in a more personal way, resulting in a pressing need to make amends. In any case, from 1896 until her death in 1901, she held the purse strings in the family. After her death, Ernst sold or gave most of his property, including the newspaper, to his sons John and Frank.

---

31. Ibid., 21; *Ste. Genevieve Herald,* May 6, 1882.
32. Entry dated April 11, 1896, Ste. Genevieve County, deed book 50, pp. 226–27.

For many years Adeline suffered with "bronchial consumption, grown out of chronic catarrh aggravated by la grippe."[33] Her husband outlived her by nearly twenty years: he passed away at the age of eighty-four on February 29, 1920. Ernst and his wife belonged to the Catholic Church, although according to church records, Ernst had not practiced his faith for a long time before his death. Both received the last sacraments from the church and were buried at Valle Spring Cemetery. The *Ste. Genevieve Herald,* published by Frank Ernst, carried only a brief death notice for the newspaper's founder.[34]

By the time Ernst died, the United States had accepted two innovations that were anathema to him: women's suffrage and Prohibition. As the antiliquor movement gained power, his staunchly "wet" position placed him out of the American mainstream. But he fearlessly expressed his views in his newspaper, which outlasted him and continued its run for more than a century. He guarded his First Amendment rights by stridently exercising them. In the process, he gave a voice to the growing German American community in Ste. Genevieve.

As a newspaper editor, he represented a community that differed in significant ways from the French and Anglo-American populations. During his lifetime, Ste. Genevieve's German citizens upset the town's Confederate-leaning sensibilities by embracing the Republican Party and the Union. In the late nineteenth century, they came into conflict with the growing temperance movement. Anti-German sentiment inspired some Americans to support Prohibition, especially during World War I. In the aftermath of this war, Missouri ratified the Eighteenth Amendment, providing the legal basis for a nationwide ban on alcohol.

Nevertheless, in important respects, German Americans blended into the Ste. Genevieve community. Like their French and Anglo-American neighbors, they held traditional views of marriage and the family. Most of them joined the local Catholic Church; others formed a Lutheran congregation. Through the generations, they adopted English as their primary

33. *Ste. Genevieve Herald,* October 12, 1901.
34. Ibid., March 5, 1920; Ste. Genevieve Catholic Church, parish records.

language. They contributed to the economy by investing in businesses and farms, and they actively participated in social and civic life. Otto Schrader introduced Masonry to Ste. Genevieve. Matthew Kern operated hotels and transportation services. John and Regina Kern maintained a busy and productive farm that they passed on to future generations. Joseph Ernst established a newspaper that affirmed the principles embodied in the Declaration of Independence, the Constitution, and the Bill of Rights.

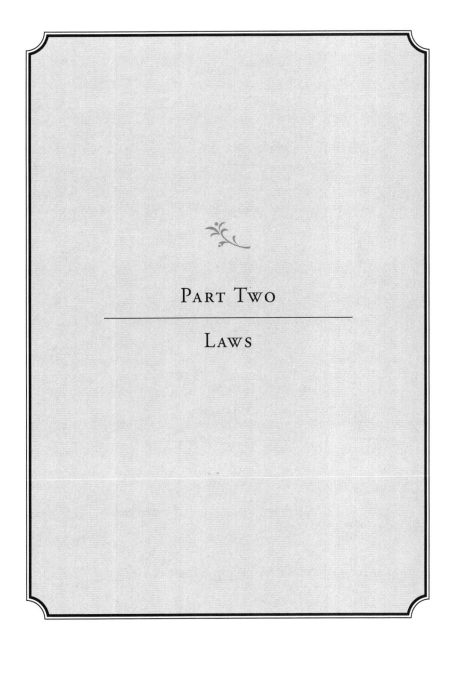

PART TWO

LAWS

CHAPTER FIVE

Becoming an American Town

We must not forget that the nation possesses a life, a reason, a conscience, an individuality of its own. It has a spiritual as well as a material, a moral as well as a physical existence. As such, the nation is sovereign.

Felix Janis, speaking at Union Hall in
Ste. Genevieve, April 12, 1883

WHILE THE RESIDENTS of Old Ste. Genevieve moved their households from the linear settlement on the banks of the Mississippi River to the new town with its central plaza between the Gabouri creeks, a group of elite white men met in Philadelphia to create a government, combining a diverse group of states in a permanent union. These men identified themselves as representatives of "the people," but they used the term in an abstract sense to denote the locus of power in a democratic republic. Real people did not exist as isolated units or as an undifferentiated mass. They lived in backwoods outposts, rural hamlets, market villages, county seats, and growing cities, where they met one another face-to-face, formed lifelong bonds, engaged in business, quarreled, dueled, and tried to operate under certain agreed upon, albeit frequently broken, rules. Each of these communities became a laboratory in which people tested the principles of government established under the United States Constitution.

Under the new federal system, local communities retained substantial autonomy. The framers of the Constitution recognized the existence of a three-tiered system of authority. At the bottom were thousands of local units that functioned on a very personal level through the bonds of kinship, friendship, and day-to-day familiarity. Above these were an expanding number of states, which brought together the representatives of these

Street scene in nineteenth-century Ste. Genevieve. Photograph courtesy of the State Historical Society of Missouri, Columbia.

localities but operated on a more abstract and formal level. At the top, the Constitution created a contractual authority that relied on a specific enumeration of powers and responsibilities, strictly limited by the rights of the states and the people (as articulated in the Bill of Rights). According to historian Thomas Bender, in the early years of the republic these levels remained separate and discrete. "The degree of interpenetration was minimal; a doctrine of spheres seemed to have prevailed."[1] Under the federal system of government, local elites continued to dominate politics in villages and towns and to serve as representatives to the state and national governments.

America's local communities nurtured political leaders and helped to shape the nation's destiny. Historian Rowland Berthoff argued that economic development, immigration, and mobility weakened the social fabric of small towns and cities, creating a disorderly society of self-interested individuals. In his view, the inhabitants of the expanding republic learned to identify themselves as Americans, but he argued that they had lost

1. Thomas Bender, *Community and Social Change in America,* 84.

their connection to local communities as they moved from place to place in search of economic gain.[2] Ste. Genevieve served as a stopover for many ambitious people, who stayed for a time and then moved on to pursue opportunities elsewhere. But the town also had a core group of long-term residents, who valued French traditions but also embraced the ideals of the new republic.

Despite the arrival of new Anglo-American residents, the town of Ste. Genevieve did not grow and New Bourbon actually declined in population between 1804 and 1819. The lead mining region, the Ozarks, and the Far West lured adventurous people away from the old French communities. Many individuals and families headed for rapidly growing American towns such as Potosi and Fredericktown; others were drawn to the fertile fields of the Bellevue valley or the game-rich Ozark hills. New Bourbon eventually disappeared; Ste Genevieve remained a small town on the river but was eclipsed by the growing city of St. Louis.[3]

Ste. Genevieve lost its prominent position among towns on the west bank of the Mississippi River. Under Spanish rule, the town had served as the administrative center for a district that extended from the Mississippi River in the east to the Ozark highlands in the west and from Apple Creek in the south to the Meramec River in the north. Initially, after the Louisiana Purchase, the United States government chose to accept the same district boundaries, officially reuniting Ste. Genevieve and New Bourbon. In 1812, when the federal government organized the Missouri Territory, the Ste. Genevieve District became Ste. Genevieve County.[4] Subsequent population growth and migration resulted in the partition of the area into several counties, and Ste. Genevieve lost its authority over the mining lands in the west, the agricultural lands in the south, and the timbered hills of the southeastern Ozarks.[5]

In December 1807, Frederick Bates wrote a long letter describing the state of affairs in America's new land on the west bank. From his headquarters

2. Rowland Berthoff, *An Unsettled People: Social Order and Disorder in American History,* 218–19.

3. Schroeder, *Opening the Ozarks,* 410–14.

4. Marian M. Ohman, "Missouri County Organization, 1812–1876," 261.

5. Schroeder, *Opening the Ozarks,* 409.

in St. Louis, he described the people of Ste. Genevieve as a motley assemblage of "turbulent" Americans and "insolent" creoles, who resisted republican ideals and failed to grasp the concept of liberty. By contrast, he believed the people of St. Louis exhibited a "proud, aristocratic spirit" that would improve and profit from a "leavening of democracy."[6] Bates viewed St. Louis as a forward-looking city, and Ste. Genevieve as a backwater town that would be left behind in the inevitable march of the new republic.

Territorial government, according to Bates, hardly reflected the principles of democracy. He stated flatly that western "territorial Governments are *executive* and *arbitrary* emanations from the general Government in Washington. The People have no share in legislation. The Governor and the Judges *make* the Laws, as they *adopt* them in the territories east of the Mississippi." Although he recognized the irony of such a form of government in a supposed republic, he believed it was necessary because of the unruliness and "irregular habits of those adventurous People who are commonly found on a frontier."[7]

Within the territorial government, there were three levels of authority. The governor and three superior court judges represented the top level: the governor enforced the laws and the superior court judges, appointed by the president, acted as legislators as well as adjudicators. The superior, or territorial, court held sessions twice yearly, once in St. Louis and once in Ste. Genevieve. On the second level were three to five judges, appointed by the governor, who held three court sessions annually in each district. On the bottom level were the justices of the peace. These justices were also appointed by the governor, and they decided minor cases in their chambers in various communities. Appeals could be made from the lower courts to the superior court. Attorneys could practice in the territory even if they had not been admitted to the bar or passed an examination.[8]

The first Court of Quarter Sessions of the justices of the peace for the Ste. Genevieve District met at the house of Andrew Buat on December 11, 1804. Governor William Henry Harrison had appointed five justices:

6. Bates, *Life and Papers,* 1:237–39.
7. Ibid., 1:246.
8. Ibid., 1:246–47.

Moses Austin, Jacques Guibourd, Benjamin Strother, John Hawkins, and Jean-Baptiste Vallé. No federal attorney attended the session, so the justices of the peace asked William C. Carr to act as prosecutor. The court appointed constables to police various parts of the district: Peter Leural, Ste. Genevieve; Andrew Morris, New Bourbon; Joseph Tucker, the Saline; Thomas Donohoe, between the Saline and Cape Girardeau; John Paul, Belleview; and Bernard Foster, Mine a Burton. A grand jury of fifteen citizens, including Camille Delassus, returned no indictments. Anticipating a future need, however, the court requested proposals for the construction of a jail, twenty-five by fifteen feet in area with heavy timber walls in-filled with rocks. Jean-Baptiste Vallé submitted the successful bid, and his workmen completed the jail in 1805.[9]

New judges were frequently appointed. In 1805, the judges were St. Gemme Beauvais, P. Detchmendy, Camille Delassus, Charles Smith, Andrew Henry, and J. Donohue. The following year a new cadre of judges included John Smith T, John Hawkins, Jean-Baptiste Vallé, Nathaniel Cook, John Callaway, Isidore Moore, Amos Bird, John Perry, and William James. Before 1821, there was no courthouse, and court convened in various residences and taverns, including the establishment owned by John Price, known as the "Old Brick House," which survived into the twenty-first century. Elite white males, both French and Anglo-American, rotated through the various local offices with dizzying speed. Providing some stability was Joseph D. Grafton, who served as a clerk of the courts from 1804 to 1842. He had an important job, explaining the proceedings and preparing petitions for illiterate citizens.[10]

In 1812, Governor Benjamin Howard divided the newly organized Missouri Territory into four counties: St. Charles, St. Louis, Ste. Genevieve, and New Madrid. One year later, the territorial authorities disbanded the Courts of Quarter Sessions and created a Court of Common Pleas for each county. In the years before statehood, the political boundaries kept changing. By 1820, there were fifteen counties in the territory. When Missouri became a state in 1821, there were twenty-five counties, including

9. *Goodspeed's History of Southeast Missouri*, 310.
10. Ibid., 310–14.

Ste. Genevieve County, which had been reduced to its modern-day boundaries. By 1861, Missouri had 114 counties.[11]

Based on the traditional English shire system, the county structure provided for local control of law enforcement and legal proceedings. After
statehood, Missouri's constitution required every county to maintain courts
for civil and criminal cases, justices of the peace to settle disputes and attend to minor legal matters, a sheriff to enforce the law, and a coroner to
investigate suspicious deaths. The counties, combined into districts, also
became the basis of the electoral system for choosing representatives for
the territorial, and later the state, legislature. In 1821, the citizens of Ste.
Genevieve erected a county courthouse on the public square in close
proximity to the Catholic Church. Some residents objected to placing a
governmental building so close to a religious institution, but their objec-
tions did not prevail.[12] The courthouse with its decorative cupola became
a prominent symbol of the new American order.

During this formative period, elections could be raucous and even
deadly. In August 1816, Auguste De Mun and William McArthur competed for a place in the territorial legislature. De Mun smeared McArthur
by alleging that he fraternized with known criminals. When McArthur
challenged De Mun to a duel, De Mun refused on the grounds that his
opponent was not a gentleman. This infuriated McArthur, who called his
adversary a coward.

On August 28, 1816, De Mun and his brother met McArthur and
McArthur's brother-in-law, Dr. Lewis Fields Linn, in Ste. Genevieve's central plaza. John Scott, a witness, later testified that McArthur and Linn
shot first; others insisted that De Mun started the shooting. After the first
volley, McArthur took refuge in a nearby tavern, and De Mun ran after
him. There were more shots. McArthur survived unharmed, but De Mun
later died of his wounds. McArthur was not charged with any crime.[13] Scott
won a place as a territorial delegate to the U.S. Congress in 1817 and later
became a congressman. In 1833, Linn became a senator.

11. Marian M. Ohman, *History of Missouri's Counties, County Seats, and Courthouse
Squares*, 4–11.
12. Ibid., 4–25.
13. Steward, *Duels and the Roots of Violence in Missouri*, 48–49.

Many public officials seemed more interested in pursuing their own personal adventures than in performing their civic duties. Ste. Genevieve's first sheriff died shortly after taking office; his successor became embroiled in a variety of conflicts that must have distracted him from his duties. This was unfortunate because the sheriff performed important functions in the community. First among these duties was law enforcement, which must have been difficult enough in a frontier town with a shifting population and a generous supply of guns. In addition, the sheriff acted as financial officer, assessor, and treasurer for the district and later for the county.

Ste. Genevieve's first sheriff was Israel Dodge, a veteran of the American Revolution. In the 1790s Dodge had migrated from Connecticut to New Bourbon, where he received a large Spanish land grant. Pierre Delassus supported Dodge's claim to the tract, and Dodge erected mills, breweries, and distilleries on the land. He also engaged in salt making and lead mining with the help of slave labor. In March 1804, he watched the American flag replace the French banner in a ceremony at St. Louis. Several months later, Governor Harrison appointed him sheriff of the Ste. Genevieve District. His son Henry, born in 1782, served as his deputy. After Israel's death in 1806 at the age of forty-seven, Henry took over his duties as sheriff. Between 1814 and 1821, the Court of Quarter Sessions met in Dodge's home.[14]

Soon after becoming sheriff, Henry Dodge took off on a strange adventure that underscored the instability of the new republic, especially in the West. After the Louisiana Purchase, territorial governor James Wilkinson engaged in complicated and questionable dealings with the Spanish government in the Southwest. Wilkinson, a hero of the American Revolution, removed the Spanish garrison from Natchez, Mississippi, in 1798 and presided over the transfer of the Louisiana Territory to the Americans in New Orleans in 1803. One year later, he renewed his relationship with Spanish authorities and provided them with information for which he received handsome payment.[15]

14. Louis Pelzer, *Henry Dodge,* 9–18.
15. Isaac Joslin Cox, "General Wilkinson and His Later Intrigues with the Spaniards," 794–95.

During that same year, General Wilkinson rekindled his old friendship with Vice President Aaron Burr. In 1800, Burr narrowly lost the presidency to Thomas Jefferson. Burr served as vice president in Jefferson's administration, but the two Decmocratic-Republicans became bitter enemies. Alexander Hamilton, a Federalist and an old rival, also incurred Burr's wrath and died after a duel with him in 1804. Vilified by the American public and hated by the president, Burr began secretly drawing maps, with Wilkinson's help, of Mexico and the Southwest.[16]

Wilkinson has gone down in history as a scheming double agent for selling his country's secrets for Spanish gold. In the spring of 1805, the unscrupulous governor met with Burr to discuss the probability of war with Spain and the possibility of equipping an army to go to Mexico to foment a revolution. The object of all this remained unclear. Perhaps Burr planned to conquer Mexico and annex it to the United States. Or perhaps he intended to create his own military empire in the Southwest.[17]

In 1806, word spread to Ste. Genevieve that Burr had called for volunteers to join an expedition against the Spanish. Many frontiersmen, including Andrew Jackson, supported the idea of annexing territory in the Southwest. Two Ste. Genevieve men, Henry Dodge and a strange character named John Smith T, became "Burrites." Smith's real name did not suit him, so he had added the *T* for Tennessee. When he left his home state in the late 1790s, Smith T purchased land grants in the lead mining regions. Within a few years, he laid claim to some land in the Ste. Genevieve District at Mine Shibboleth that had originally belonged to James St. Vrain. Insatiably ambitious and always spoiling for a fight, Smith T competed with mining titan Moses Austin. Smith T was just the type of man to heed the call for a big adventure in the West.[18]

Hearing that the former vice president planned to gather forces in New Madrid, Dodge and Smith T procured canoes and headed down the river. Unfortunately, Wilkinson had decided to curry favor with Jefferson by exposing Burr's treacherous conspiracy. On November 27, 1806, the president

16. Ibid., 801.
17. Bates, *Life and Papers,* 1:25.
18. For a book-length treatment of Smith T's strange career, see Dick Steward, *Frontier Swashbuckler: The Life and Legend of John Smith T.*

issued a proclamation denouncing the plot and ordered the War Department to take measures to stop it.[19]

When they arrived in New Madrid, Dodge and Smith T heard about the president's proclamation, which placed them on the wrong side of the law. Realizing the danger of their position, the two adventurers sold their canoes, bought horses, and headed back to Ste. Genevieve. In the meantime, Burr landed on the eastern bank of the Mississippi River near the town of Natchez with a flotilla of nine boats and one hundred men. He surrendered to authorities in Mississippi, but uncertainties about the facts of his case, questions of jurisdiction, and Burr's failure to appear at several hearings delayed legal action for two months.[20]

By the time Dodge and Smith T returned to Ste. Genevieve, a grand jury had already indicted them for treason. Smith T apparently threatened to shoot Otto Schrader, who had come to his house to arrest him. Dodge surrendered to the authorities, paid his bail, and appeared in court, although he subsequently intimidated the jurors so completely that they refused to take action against him. The illustrious and disreputable Burr eventually stood trial for treason; a cadre of eminent lawyers defended him, and the jury found him not guilty.[21]

President Jefferson removed Wilkinson, the star witness against Burr, from the governorship but retained him as a military official. Frederick Bates, the territorial secretary, became acting governor. On May 1, 1807, Bates stripped Smith T of all his public offices, including his commission as a lieutenant colonel in the militia and his position as a judge of the Court of Quarter Sessions, and he charged him with resisting arrest. In his letter to Smith T, the acting governor stated:

> It is not to excite your sensibilities but to convince you of my justice
> in this Proceeding, that I must be permitted to make one remark: you
> have resisted a public officer in the legal and proper discharge of his
> duties; your menaces and the intimidations you have thrown forth have

19. Cox, "General Wilkinson," 803; Thomas Perkins Abernethy, "Aaron Burr in Mississippi," 9.
20. Abernethy, "Aaron Burr," 10–18; Donald Barr Chidsey, *The Great Conspiracy*, 72.
21. Steward, *Frontier Swashbuckler*, 82; Pelzer, *Henry Dodge*, 18–19; Bates, *Life and Papers*, 1:116.

prevented the execution of a warrant issued by one of the Judges of the Territory.

You must then I think be convinced that altho' the discretion of the Executive with respect to removals ought to be cautiously exercised, yet that in the present instance, these revocations were the only measures which could be adopted consistently with the interests and the dignity of the Government.[22]

Bates took seriously his obligation to suppress "Burrism, principles of disunion, or other disaffection to the U. States Government" in the territory under his administration. But he did not dismiss Dodge from his position as sheriff. Apparently, Dodge was able to convince the acting governor of his innocence.[23] At least he had not resisted arrest. After the smoke cleared, Smith T and Dodge became bitter enemies.

During the War of 1812, Dodge rose to a high position in the territorial militia. Commanding a force of about 350 mounted men, in 1814, he marched from Ste. Genevieve to the Boonslick area in central Missouri, where Indian tribes were attacking white settlements. Among his soldiers were forty friendly Shawnees, who scouted out the encampment of the Miamis north of the Missouri River near Arrow Rock. After 150 Miamis surrendered to Dodge's superior force, he insisted that they be taken prisoner and that their lives be spared. Some of his recruits balked at this order and cocked their rifles, preparing to shoot the enemy, including the women and children. According to legend, Nathan Boone rode up and stood beside Dodge, who remained steadfast and saved the Indians' lives.[24]

After the war, Dodge vied with Smith T for control of valuable land in the lead mining district. In 1811, Frederick Bates took possession of some property that had been claimed by Smith T at Mine Shibboleth and leased it rent-free to Dodge and two other tenants. A series of lawsuits followed, and a violent confrontation grew more and more likely. Both Smith T and

22. Frederick Bates to John Smith T, St. Louis, May 1, 1807, in Bates, *Life and Papers,* 1:109–10.

23. Frederick Bates to Meriwether Lewis, St. Louis, May 15, 1807, in ibid., 116.

24. Pelzer, *Henry Dodge,* 22–26. Nathan Boone, son of famous pioneer Daniel Boone, had come to the Boonslick area to extract salt from local salt springs. He also served in Missouri's volunteer army. The September 1814 incident involving Dodge and the Miami captives is recorded in Houck's *History of Missouri,* 3:122–23.

Dodge walked around Ste. Genevieve with weapons in their pockets and with their nerves on edge. When they met once by chance, John Scott used his powers of persuasion to prevent a bloody scene. Before the dispute over Mine Shibboleth was settled, Dodge left Ste. Genevieve and headed for Galena, Illinois.[25]

Dodge went on to achieve national prominence. Faced with legal and financial troubles, he joined an exodus of ambitious Missourians to the lead mining areas on the east bank of the Mississippi in northern Illinois, taking his wife, children, and slaves with him. In Illinois, his slaves became free. Before the end of his long life, he moved on to Michigan and Wisconsin. From 1836 to 1841 and from 1845 to 1848, he served as governor of the Wisconsin Territory. In the mid-1840s, he represented that territory in Congress. From 1848 to 1857, he served in the U.S. Senate. In 1850, as the senator from a free state, he voted for the suppression of the slave trade in the District of Columbia and against the repressive Fugitive Slave Bill. When he retired from the Senate, he was seventy-five years old. His wife, Christiana, died in 1865 after sixty-five years of marriage. Dodge passed away two years later at the age of eighty-five.[26]

While Dodge matured from a youthful adventurer to a dignified elder statesman, the people of Ste. Genevieve struggled to maintain a stable community. In 1808, the Court of Quarter Sessions defined the town's boundaries and passed an order of incorporation. James Moore, Jean-Baptiste Vallé, Aaron Elliott, John B. Pratte, and Jean-Baptiste Ste. Gemme served on the first board of trustees. At their first meeting on August 19, 1808, these men elected John B. Pratte as their chair and appointed Nathaniel Pope as their clerk. They passed ordinances regulating the big field and prohibiting the sale of liquor to Indians. In addition, the board required every male resident to keep a bucket and a ladder handy in case of fire. At the next election in 1810, the citizens chose Judge Otto Schrader, Camille Delassus, Charles Gregoire, Francois Janis, and Vital Beauvais to act as trustees. Clearly, the old French elite continued to play a prominent role in community affairs along with German and Anglo-American residents.[27]

25. Steward, *Frontier Swashbuckler,* 117–24.
26. Pelzer, *Henry Dodge,* 29, 188, 193, 196.
27. *Goodspeed's History of Southeast Missouri,* 405–6.

Newspapers recorded the shifting fortunes of the town. Before Ernst founded the *Herald,* at least eleven short-lived newspapers appeared and vanished, and one, the *Ste. Genevieve Fair Play,* began a long run. In 1822, Thomas Foley published the *Correspondent and Record.* Nearly thirty years passed before John K. Smith printed a short run of the *Ste. Genevieve Pioneer* in 1850. During that same year, P. G. Ferguson published the ephemeral *Ste. Genevieve Democrat,* which extolled the virtues of plank roads. In 1857, Rufus Tebbets created the *Ste. Genevieve Independent,* which apparently lasted only a year. From 1855 to 1862 Edward A. Rozier and Oliver Harris published the Democratic *Ste. Genevieve Plaindealer* in the Detchmendy Building at First and Market streets. For a brief period in 1859, H. K. Eaton issued the *Missouri Citizen* from the same building. In 1866–1867, Hallock and Brother published the *Ste. Genevieve Representative.*[28]

Beginning in 1872, Henry Smith issued the *Ste. Genevieve Fair Play* from an office on Market Street, south of the square. During Reconstruction, the *Fair Play* defended the Democratic Party and castigated President Ulysses S. Grant and the Republicans. The paper also supported the temperance crusade, which infuriated Ernst. His paper, the *Herald,* founded in 1882, outlasted its rival and was published weekly through the twentieth and into the twenty-first century.[29]

Ste. Genevieve gradually transformed itself from a backwoods French village that was ruled benevolently by a civil and military commandant to an American county seat that participated in the complex politics of the expanding republic. In-migration from France, Germany, and the eastern United States and out-migration to the mining and agricultural frontiers caused constant shifts in the social and cultural landscape. Political boundaries changed frequently, as Missouri evolved from territorial status to statehood, defining and redefining the system of counties and townships. Gunplay and threats of violence interfered with the electoral process. Public officials sometimes abandoned their duties or flouted the law. Despite all this chaos, between 1804 and 1882, Ste. Genevieve established functioning

28. Copies of these newspapers are on microfilm at the State Historical Society. The *Beobachter* and the *Freie Presse* have apparently not survived.

29. Full runs of the *Fair Play* and the *Herald* are on microfilm at the Ozark Regional Library in Ste. Genevieve.

town and county governments and a weekly newspaper that would continue publishing for well over a century. Not bad for a frontier outpost thousands of miles from the seat of government in Washington, D.C.

During the nineteenth century, the town nurtured five U.S. senators, including the much-admired Senator Lewis Linn. Linn's mother, Ann Hunter Linn, was married to Israel Dodge before she married Linn's father, Asael Linn. Henry Dodge was Linn's half-brother. Born in 1795 and orphaned at the age of twelve, Linn came to Ste. Genevieve to be close to Dodge and his sister Mary, wife of William McArthur. Dodge became a surrogate father to Linn, and their strong bond lasted a lifetime.

In his early teens, Linn studied medicine in his hometown of Louisville, Kentucky, under the tutelage of Dr. William Craig Galt. During the War of 1812 young Linn accompanied Dodge's troops on their mission against the Miamis in central Missouri. He resumed his medical training in Philadelphia after the war, and at the age of twenty, he began practicing medicine in Ste. Genevieve. Three years later, in 1818, he married Elizabeth A. Relfe. Linn combined his medical work with politics, serving in the Missouri Senate in the late 1820s.[30]

During the cholera outbreak of 1832–1833, he risked his own health by attending to victims of the contagion. When a riverboat dumped stricken passengers at Ste. Genevieve in October 1832, he treated them in his own home. At that time, he served on the Land Claims Commission in St. Louis, where he also aided cholera victims. He eventually came down with the disease. Because of his youth, he recovered, although the episode compromised his health. When Senator Alexander Buckner, a Whig, died of the disease, Governor Dunklin asked Linn, a Democrat, to fill his vacant seat.[31]

Linn won reelection in 1836 and 1842 and served in the Senate until his untimely death in 1843. As a senator, he favored the rapid settlement of land claims, economic development, and westward expansion. In the 1830s, he

---

30. Elizabeth A. (Relfe) Linn and N. Sargent, *The Life and Public Service of Dr. Lewis F. Linn*, 16–19.

31. Linn and Sargent, *The Life and Public Service of Dr. Lewis F. Linn*, 69–79; Michael B. Husband, "Senator Lewis F. Linn and the Oregon Question," 3, 18; *Biographical Directory of the American Congress, 1774–1971*, 1294; *Columbia Missouri Intelligencer*, June 29, 1833.

supported President Jackson on Indian removal and made strong statements concerning the need for a military presence on the frontier. With Senator Benton and others, he pressed for approval of the Platte Purchase, which expanded Missouri's boundaries to the northwest. He tried and failed to obtain federal funding for swamp drainage in the state's southeastern lowlands. His great popularity with the voters rested on his staunch support of Missouri's economic interests. He also favored slavery. When northerners petitioned to end slave trading in the District of Columbia, he stood with his party and voted against the measure.[32]

Linn's proslavery stance reflected the views of his local constituents. During his lifetime and until the eve of the Civil War, slave auctions continued to take place on the courthouse steps in Ste. Genevieve. A public notice in the *Ste. Genevieve Independent* announced the upcoming sheriff's sale of all the real and personal property of the deceased Valentine Underwood; the proceeds from this auction were to be divided among his heirs. Included in the public auction were six slaves. The notice described these unfortunate people as "A mulatto man, named Berryman, aged about fifty years, a negro woman named Ann, aged about twenty-six years; a negro boy, child of Ann, aged about one year; a mulatto girl named Ellen, aged twelve years; a negro girl named Louisa Ann, aged five years; also a negro man named Mat, aged about thirty-five years."[33] Admirable as he was in many ways, Linn had defended this abomination.

The political lives of Linn and his half-brother Henry Dodge exemplify the workings of representative government. Nurtured in the same environment, their paths diverged: one moved to free territory, served in the Senate, and promoted an antislavery agenda; and the other became a Missouri senator and staunchly guarded the institution of slavery against the urgent petitions of northern abolitionists. Each represented his constituency, which is exactly what republican ideals would call for them to do. In that sense, their experience reflects the genius of American politics. On the other hand, their diverging points of view were emblematic of the terrible division in American society that would lead to the Civil War.

32. Husband, "Senator Lewis F. Linn," 2; Thomas Hart Benton, Eulogy for Linn, December 12, 1843, *Congressional Globe,* 28th Cong., 1st sess., 1843, 29.
33. *Ste. Genevieve Independent,* December 10, 1857.

Despite their differences, Dodge and Linn loved each other as brothers. When the Senate reconvened after Linn's death in the fall of 1843, Senator Benton delivered an impassioned eulogy. After describing Linn's sudden passing at his home in St. Genevieve at the age of forty-eight, Benton praised his legislative achievements, particularly his support of the Platte Purchase and the Oregon Bill, which was still pending at the time of his death. He spoke eloquently of Linn's compassion, intelligence, courage, and kindness, noting that he had many opponents in Congress but no enemies. More important, said Benton, were Linn's private virtues, particularly his affection for his half-brother. "For twenty-nine years," said Benton, "I have known the depth of that affection, and never saw it burn more brightly than in our last interview, only three weeks before his death. He had just traveled a thousand miles out of his way to see that brother; and his name was still the dearest theme of his conversation."[34]

These bonds were the flesh and blood of an imperfect union based on unrealized principles of liberty and equality. Within two decades of Linn's untimely death and within Dodge's lifetime, the union would break down on the issue of slavery. Human ties, surviving the crisis and enduring through the generations, would be the vital basis for rebuilding the nation on the principles embodied in the Constitution.

Felix Janis, the descendant of an old French family, affirmed the importance of human connections and legal principles in a lengthy speech on "Love of our country; Its Constitution and Governmental Institutions" in Union Hall on April 12, 1883. Union Hall, owned by a German American named Leon Jokerst, was a popular gathering place for beer drinking and socializing.[35] Printed in serial form in the *Ste. Genevieve Herald,* Janis's oration praised the ideals of the Founding Fathers. But it was more than a call for patriotism: it was a thoughtful and erudite analysis of the tense but essential relationship between freedom and authority, rights and responsibility, the people and the government.

Janis reasoned that human beings could not exercise their rights without the protection of the law, and that the law had to protect everyone

34. Benton, Eulogy for Linn, December 12, 1843, *Congressional Globe,* 28th Cong., 1st sess, 1843, 29.

35. Sanders, "Germans in Ste. Genevieve," 10.

equally. No individual, he argued, had authority over another. No class or party could claim the law or the government as its own. "Law is universal," he said, "It extends its protecting aegis over all." In a society that had been divided on the issue of slavery and had recently endured a bloody civil war, he spoke for equal justice for all. "The life of the humblest, the possession of the poorest," he insisted, could claim "in the nation, equally with the great and wealthy this right to justice."[36]

Janis's ringing words must have had a strange resonance when they were spoken by a descendant of an old French family in a German beer hall bearing the name of the Union. With this speech, he clearly appealed to all the diverse people in his community to come together and support a reconstructed nation. The war had brought an end to slavery. Would the nation now embrace the ideal of equality under the law?

36. *Ste. Genevieve Herald,* May 12, 1883.

Chapter Six

Law and Order in Ste. Genevieve

A being capable of free action, of eliciting deliberate acts of the will is a moral being. Such is the nation. It is capable of character, of being loved, respected and venerated. Existing in freedom, governed by law, maintaining order, it moves onward towards the achievement of a conscious aim. It takes cognizance of the actions of men as moral agents. It impresses its character upon them and imbues them with its spirit.

Felix Janis, speaking at Union Hall in
Ste. Genevieve, April 12, 1883

IN HIS SPEECH AT Union Hall in 1883, Felix Janis articulated ideals rather than realities. For most of his community's history before and after the Louisiana Purchase, many of the citizens of Ste. Genevieve did not experience the benefits of "freedom, governed by law." Local authorities often failed to maintain order, and the federal government provided little help. During the Civil War, many local citizens engaged in open rebellion against the authorities in Washington, D.C. When Janis addressed the crowd in Union Hall, he felt the need to tell them that government was not a bad thing but a good thing, "not a necessary evil, but a providential consequence of man's social nature."[1] For people who had grown up on the west bank of the Mississippi River in the nineteenth century, this might have been difficult to believe.

In the expanding republic, peace proved fragile and elusive. Ste. Genevieve was a border town, and Missouri was a border state. The Mississippi River divided the settled East from the alluring West. In the Louisiana

---

1. *Ste. Genevieve Herald,* May 12, 1883.

Purchase lands, Missouri's southern boundary marked the division between slavery and freedom. When the North and the South split apart,
Missouri chose not to secede from the Union, but its young men flocked
by the thousands to the Confederate cause. The new American community struggled to survive in this chaotic world in which the government
seemed powerless to maintain order.

All of the nation's divisions became more obvious on the frontier. Southerners, crossing the Mississippi River, had to reestablish and reaffirm their
racial system. Northerners could no longer keep slavery at arm's length
but had to face it as an everyday reality. Gentlemen of aristocratic pre-
tensions found it necessary to defend their honor in a community full of
newcomers, where not everyone was exactly who he or she appeared to
be. Poor people fought to become wealthy or at least to hold on to their
land. Lawyers came to town, hoping to make money defending land
claims. Greedy people forgot their inhibitions. Restless young men came
looking for easy gratification, and sometimes they found it. Sharpsters,
tricksters, confidence men, and prostitutes offered profits and pleasures or
the illusion of them. Everyone knew how to fight, and everyone had a
knife or a gun.

Before the Louisiana Purchase, it was easy for criminals to cross the river
to escape punishment. For instance, an American named Thomas Allen
raped a twelve-year-old French girl named Marie in Ste. Genevieve in 1800.
When he fled across the river to the American side, Spanish officials could
not pursue him. All they could do was seize the property he left behind.[2]

In the French and Spanish periods, the lower Mississippi and the Gulf
of Mexico harbored pirates such as the notorious Jean Lafitte. After the
War of 1812, New Orleans appealed to the federal government for protection, but none was forthcoming, and piracy increased. Islands in the Mississippi or the wooded swamps in the bottomlands served as hideouts for
rough gangs who attacked boats or lay in wait to rob settlers.[3]

According to historian Philip Jordan, piracy and robbery increased with
the spread of settlement along the river. Organized bands and solitary crim-

---

2. Banner, *Legal Systems in Conflict,* 31.
3. John L. Harr, "Law and Lawlessness in the Lower Mississippi Valley," 55, 58.

inals looted the growing river towns. The arrival of steamboats made matters worse. Many of the paddle wheelers were floating casinos that served liquor and lured passengers into games of chance. Men who behaved themselves at home often left their morals on the dock. Truants and runaways flocked to the Mississippi valley, where they hired on as waiters and cabin boys for the purpose of stealing from passengers. Many of the passengers, even those with money and status, caroused, quarreled, and sought illicit pleasure at houses of ill repute.[4]

Long before the Revolution, prominent American men had adopted the medieval practice of defending their honor by engaging in deadly personal combat. By 1800, many duels in the U.S. were staged events, which allowed the participants to play their parts and then go home unharmed. Some duels, however, such as the shocking Burr-Hamilton contest, ended in bloodshed. On the Missouri frontier, dueling pistols became status symbols, denoting social prestige as well as manliness. The most famous duel in Missouri history occurred on August 12, 1817, when Benton killed Lucas on Bloody Island. In Ste. Genevieve, elite citizens, including Scott, Linn, and Fenwick, and even the local sheriff, participated in the time-honored ritual.[5]

Historian Dick Steward has analyzed the place of the duel in Missouri's developing society. By the early 1800s, the practice dwindled in the northeastern states, where the old-fashioned code of honor gave way to a staunch individualism that scoffed at insults and valued courts of law more than the court of public opinion. In the Old South, dueling became the craze of upper-class men, who connected it with romantic ideals of chivalry, gentility, and courage. For southern aristocrats secure in their social positions, duels affirmed a way of life but did not require the death of an enemy. Duels occurred much more frequently in the old southern states than they did in Missouri. On the Missouri frontier, however, duels were about power, and winning was everything.[6]

The Fenwick brothers—Walter, Ezekial, Thomas, and James—came to the west bank in the 1790s. Three of them lived in the Bois Brule bottom

---

4. Philip D. Jordan, *Frontier Law and Order: Ten Essays*, 24–25, 103–5.
5. Steward, *Duels and the Roots of Violence in Missouri*, 7–8, 58–78.
6. Ibid., 10–11.

south of Ste. Genevieve. Walter, the eldest, became a prominent landowner and physician in town, where Ezekiel reportedly owned a bawdy house. Whether or not this was true, the younger Fenwick had a shady reputation and was constantly in trouble. In 1809 and again in 1811, a man named A. C. Dunn accused Ezekial of counterfeiting and thievery. Attempting to redeem their family's honor, Ezekial's brothers sued Dunn for slander. In response to the lawsuit, Dunn hired an attorney named Thomas T. Crittenden, who won the case by attacking Ezekial's questionable character.[7]

In the aftermath of the trial, Ezekial wrote a note challenging Crittenden to a duel; Ezekial's brother Walter delivered the message. Crittenden refused to fight Ezekial, implying that he was not a gentleman. Walter took his refusal as a personal insult and immediately offered to fight in his brother's place. This time the challenge was accepted. The duel took place on October 1, 1811, on Moreau's Island south of Ste. Genevieve. Sheriff Henry Dodge and attorney John Scott served as seconds. Crittenden emerged unscathed. Walter suffered a fatal wound and died the next day, leaving a widow, Julie, the daughter of Francois Vallé II, and seven children. No charges were filed because dueling was not considered a crime.[8]

In the Mississippi bottomlands, formal contests of honor played out against a backdrop of knifings, shootings, impromptu gunfights, brawls, assaults, and general mayhem. Crittenden and Walter Fenwick observed the rules of honor in 1811. But five years later, De Mun and McArthur chased each other around the square in Ste. Genevieve, ducking for cover, and shooting on the run. McArthur never had to answer for his actions, but the distinction between dueling and cold-blooded murder became a rather fine one. Social position and political connections seemed to have more influence on the justice system than the actual circumstances of the killing.

Murder, pure and simple, was a crime in Ste. Genevieve. Before the establishment of the circuit courts in 1812, Courts of Oyer and Terminer met periodically to try felony cases. In July 1810, a man named Peter Johnston stood trial for murdering John Spear in Big River Township in May

---

7. Ibid., 33–34.
8. *Goodspeed's History of Southeast Missouri*, 312–13; Steward, *Duels and the Roots of Violence in Missouri*, 34.

of that same year. Edward Hempstead was the prosecutor; Henry M. Brackenridge and James A. Graham defended the accused. A panel of judges,
including Otto Schrader, found the defendant guilty of murder in the
first degree and sentenced him to be hanged on August 3. The execution
took place on the top of a hill with a crowd in attendance. As part of the
sentence, the convicted man's body was delivered to Dr. Walter Fenwick
for dissection. A second execution—the last one in Ste. Genevieve—took
place on the same hilltop on March 9, 1812, after Charles Heath was convicted of murdering Hugh Jones in Breton Township.[9]

Justice in Ste. Genevieve was far from blind; status and connections
could save a defendant's hide. The miscreant's reputation for strength,
cunning, and vindictiveness might also dissuade a jury from returning a
conviction. Apparently, this held true in the case of John Smith T, the
same man who conspired and then feuded with Sheriff Henry Dodge.
After their misadventure, Dodge rebuilt his reputation as a solid citizen
and rose to political eminence. Smith T continued his swashbuckling
ways and eventually became a legendary figure known for killing people
and getting away with it.[10]

In 1830, a flare-up in William McArthur's tavern left a man named
Samuel Ball dead. John Smith T was accused of his murder. Ball and
Smith T happened to be drinking in the same room, and apparently the
latter was drinking quite heavily. No one came forward as an eyewitness;
Mary McArthur, who was in another room when the killing occurred, reported that she heard a single shot and rushed in to find Ball's body on
the floor. When she demanded that Smith T turn over his weapons, he
obliged and produced four of them. He was arrested and spent four days
in custody before posting bail. John Scott and a St. Louis lawyer named
Beverly Allen prepared his defense.[11]

Within a few weeks, the Ste. Genevieve Circuit Court tried him and
found him not guilty. On October 9, 1830, the *St. Louis Missouri Intelligencer* reported the story and said Ball had been shot through the heart.
Years later, in 1887, the *St. Louis Globe-Democrat* reflected on the killing

9. *Goodspeed's History of Southeast Missouri*, 311.
10. See Steward, *Frontier Swashbuckler.*
11. Ibid. 185–86.

and suggested that the acquittal was because of fear on the part of the jury. The *Kansas City Journal,* on August 7, 1896, agreed that the trial had been merely a show, as no one in the community had the courage it would have taken to bring down such a dangerous man.[12]

Establishing the rule of law in Ste. Genevieve was an uphill struggle. John Smith T was not unique in his violent behavior or in his defiance of authorities in the trans-Mississippi West. Most American cities, including St. Louis, did not have regular police forces until the latter half of the nineteenth century. Small towns like Ste. Genevieve had to depend upon a county sheriff, who generally had no training or knowledge of police methods.[13] Henry Dodge, Ste Genevieve's second sheriff, seemed more interested in pursuing his own adventures and enterprises than in enforcing the law. Men like Ezekial Fenwick and John Smith T settled disputes in their own way, often by instigating a fight or pulling out a gun. Honest, law-abiding citizens learned to mind their own business and turn their backs on the antics of well-armed and often politically connected men.

Despite these problems, a system of justice took root in Ste. Genevieve. Over the years, the new American order embraced, adapted, and reinterpreted institutions that originated in colonial times. Legal historian Stuart Banner has dispelled the myth that French colonial towns breezed along without functioning legal systems. In St. Louis and Ste. Genevieve, throughout the French and Spanish periods, people acquired and sold property, made wills, settled estates, and sued each other in well-established courts.[14] Even the least powerful people, such as Elizabeth D'Atchurut, exercised their rights to file complaints and to demand reparation for damages when they believed they had been wronged. Problems arose when Anglo-American lawyers, who often had little training, tried to understand French and Spanish legal codes, which were typically unwritten. But these problems were not insurmountable.

After 1803, American officials accepted positions in the Louisiana Territory under a statute that required them to observe existing codes of jus-

---

12. Ibid., 186.
13. Jordan, *Frontier Law and Order,* 106–9.
14. Banner, *Legal Systems in Conflict,* 5.

tice until the codes were replaced by new legislation. Long before new laws were enacted, lawyers and judges had to deal with disputed land claims, demands for the payment of debts, commercial disagreements, and personal grievances that appeared on their dockets. Without a written code to guide them, they sought advice from the French aristocrats, who had grown up with and lived under the old system. Cases involving Spanish land grants often dragged on for decades, finally ending up in the United States Supreme Court. In other legal matters, the territorial and state legislatures acted to bring Missouri into line with standard American practices.[15]

After achieving statehood, Missouri legislators made a slow and systematic effort to bring the state's legal system into line with the legal systems of other states. As time went on, American legislatures and courts relied more on written codes, statutes, and precedents than on custom and oral tradition. A series of statutes regulated wills, probate, and the transfer of estates. In 1849, Missouri followed other states in passing a statute allowing women to own separate property that could not be taken to cover the debts of their husbands. By 1850, Missouri changed its constitution to provide for the election, rather than the appointment of judges, bringing its practices into line with those of other states. Local differences began to fade away, as Americans established a uniform body of law throughout the country.[16]

The national consensus broke down, however, on the issue of slavery. Missouri's admission to the Union followed an ugly debate on the question of whether or not slavery should be allowed to spread into the Louisiana Territory. The Missouri Compromise allowed slavery in the state, but it left many legal questions unsettled. Hundreds of Missouri slaves went to court between 1806 and 1865 to claim their freedom on various legal grounds; some won their cases, but by the 1850s opinion had turned against them. In the *Dred Scott* case, the Missouri Supreme Court reversed its previous decisions and concluded that a slave taken to a free

15. Ibid., 96–99.
16. Ibid., 130–33.

state and then brought back to Missouri remained a slave. The court's decision specifically referred to the abolitionist movement and declared its intention to preserve the institution of slavery. In 1857, the United States upheld this decision, which deprived black people of nearly all their civil rights, including the right to bring suit in federal court.[17]

Ste. Genevieve's local ordinances placed strict limits on African Americans' freedom of action. In 1808, town leaders prohibited slaves from carrying firearms and imposed an 8:00 p.m. curfew during the fall and winter months. Slaves who went out on the streets after dark could be whipped; slaves who assembled unlawfully could receive twenty-five lashes. After 1810, the law said that whites attending such assemblages could be fined. Town patrols hunted runaway slaves, and the local jail sometimes housed fugitives. The laws became increasingly strict in the years leading up to the Civil War.[18]

When the war began, local sympathy leaned heavily toward the southern states that had seceded from the Union. In April 1861, Lincoln's call for troops to quell the Confederate rebellion placed the residents of Ste. Genevieve under severe pressure. Citizens from all parts of the county attended a meeting on May 6, when the circuit court opened its session in the Ste. Genevieve Courthouse. Resolutions drafted before the meeting stipulated that Missouri's interests lay with the protection of slavery, but they did not call for secession. Union loyalists insisted that there could be no neutrality and urged support for the president in putting down the rebellion.[19]

Prominent politicians came to the meeting to argue both sides of the issue. United States congressman John W. Noell, a Virginia-born lawyer from Perry County, championed the Union. He had been elected to the House of Representatives in 1858 as a Stephen A. Douglas Democrat. Missouri senator Conrad C. Ziegler of Ste. Genevieve spoke for the secessionists. Ziegler was also an attorney, who had studied under John Scott and passed the bar in 1833. In partnership with the Pratte family, he

17. Ibid., 132–33.
18. Greg Kester, "They Carried a Heavy Burden: The Use of Slave Labor in the Lead Mines of Southeast Missouri," 42–56; Folders 442, 443, 445, Ste. Genevieve Archives.
19. Bob Schmidt, *Boys of the Best Families in the State: Co. E 2nd Missouri Cavalry,* 333.

had invested heavily in iron mining in the Ozarks. The fact that a Virginian argued for the Union and a German American championed the southern cause demonstrates the complexity of the divisions within the community. The meeting adjourned without settling the question.[20]

Missouri's governor Claiborne Fox Jackson strongly supported the South, but he stopped short of calling for secession. In the spring of 1861, he sent a brigade of the Missouri State Militia to train in St. Louis at Camp Jackson. At the same time, Captain Nathaniel Lyon of the Second U.S. Infantry mobilized local German immigrants as well as regular federal troops to quell any possible rebellion. On May 10, 1861, Lyon's force of seven thousand men marched on the camp and compelled the state militia to surrender. The ensuing victory celebration triggered a riot, in which twenty-eight civilians, including some women and children died.[21]

Although Governor Jackson did not ask the legislature to pass an article of secession, he called for the mobilization of soldiers to protect Missouri from a federal invasion. On May 11, the Military Bill authorized the governor to disband the militia and to form a new organization, the Missouri State Guard, which was to be commanded by former governor Sterling Price. Thousands of men, including the son of Ste. Genevieve's Francois and Mary Vallé, responded to the governor's call and joined the military organization with the intention of keeping Union troops at bay. Throughout the summer of 1861, the state guard crisscrossed the state, engaging with federal troops at Carthage, Wilson's Creek, and Lexington. In the spring of 1862, the state guard retreated into Arkansas, but many of its members joined the Confederate Army.[22]

Francis (Frank) Vallé, who was born in Ste. Genevieve on April 9, 1829, served in the Confederate army throughout the war. He married Columbia E. Holden, the daughter of an attorney, in Perry County on February 2, 1854. In 1860, he was a hotel keeper in Perryville. From September through December 1861, he served as a second lieutenant in the Missouri State

20. Ibid., 333; *Goodspeed's History of Southeast Missouri*, 212, 379, 394, 398–99.

21. Richard E. Peterson et al. *Sterling Price's Lieutenants: A Guide to the Officers and Organization of the Missouri State Guard, 1861–1865*, 4–6.

22. Carolyn M. Bartels, "Preface," *The Forgotten Men: Missouri State Guard*.

Guard under Captain R. B. Holmes before receiving an honorable discharge on Christmas Day.[23] He later served as a first lieutenant in the Seventh Missouri Cavalry and a captain in the Confederate Eighth Missouri Cavalry. On March 11, 1862, he was captured in Wayne County, Missouri, and spent several months in military prisons before being exchanged in September of the same year. After his release, he returned to active duty; he later surrendered at Shreveport, Louisiana, on June 7, 1865.[24]

Another Vallé with the Christian name Francis briefly appeared on the historical stage in the fall of 1861 as a fighter for the Confederate cause. This Captain Vallé, probably a second cousin of the man previously mentioned, joined M. Jeff Thompson's brigade, which carried out a series of raids between St. Louis and the southern tip of Missouri's Bootheel along the banks of the Mississippi River. Most of Thompson's troops were three-month volunteers, who came and went with little fanfare, fading in and out of the general population. In mid-October 1861, Thompson attempted to capture the railroad line at Big River Bridge, forty miles south of St. Louis. According to Thompson's memoirs, during the ensuing skirmish Captain Vallé rushed in on the federal troops and took a bullet through the chest.[25] He survived this wound, but historians have not recorded his subsequent military career. M. Jeff Thompson spent a considerable portion of the war in Union prisons and then faded into obscurity.

Even more obscure was another Vallé, of African American descent, who served on the federal side. Paul Vallé of Ste. Genevieve became a Union solder on August 12, 1863. Details of his life are sketchy, but he was born in Missouri in 1841 or 1842. The 1860 U.S. census lists Melanie Vallé as owning three slaves, including an unnamed nineteen-year-old male, who was probably Paul.[26] By 1863, Lincoln's Emancipation Proclamation and a change in federal policy had opened the doors for black men, including fugitive slaves, to join the Union army.

23. Ibid., 168, 369.

24. Schmidt, *Boys of the Best Families,* 217.

25. M. Jeff Thompson, *The Civil War Reminiscences of General M. Jeff Thompson,* 99–104.

26. U.S. Bureau of the Census, *Eighth Census: 1860, Population Schedule,* NARA microfilm, M653, reel #424.

Paul Vallé enlisted in Company C, Third Arkansas, a segregated unit in the U.S. Army. All of the members of this regiment were black men from Missouri, but the regiment served in Arkansas, mostly in and around Little Rock. Before the war ended, the Third Arkansas was redesignated the Fifty-sixth U.S. Colored Troops. The regiment suffered heavy casualties from combat wounds and disease. Their base of operations was Helena, Arkansas. During the spring and summer of 1864, the regiment saw action at Indian Bay, Muffleton Lodge, and Wallace's Ferry. They made an expedition up the White River in August and September 1864 and then marched south to Friar's Point, Mississippi, in February 1865. After the war ended, they continued to serve as peacekeepers in Arkansas until September 1866.

After the war, Paul Vallé returned to Ste. Genevieve. Apparently, he fell on hard times. Although there is no record of him in the 1870 census, he is listed in the 1880 census as a resident of the county Poor Farm.[27] The *1890 Special Census to Enumerate the Union Civil War Veterans* listed him as living in Ste. Genevieve but gave no other personal information. He did not appear on the 1900 or 1910 census, and there was no record of his death in church or county records.[28]

Returning veterans did not always enjoy a warm welcome. In September 1865, the *Jefferson City Missouri State Times* printed an article by a correspondent describing one former soldier's experience in Ste. Genevieve. The unnamed writer happened to be in town on a day when many people had come in from the countryside to buy or trade goods and possibly to visit the local taverns. After a "general inter-change of opinions," a group of men became unruly and attacked a veteran Union soldier. "For a while," the correspondent wrote, "The act of whipping him seemed to

27. U.S. Bureau of the Census, *Tenth Census of the United States: 1880, Ste. Genevieve County, Missouri,* NARA microfilm, T9, reel #715.

28. Thanks are due to Bill Baehr for primary research on Paul Vallè. Sources of information include the U.S. census population schedules for Ste. Genevieve County, 1860, 1880, 1900, and 1910; U.S. Bureau of the Census, *1890 Special Census to Enumerate the Union Civil War Veterans or Their Widows, Ste. Genevieve, Missouri,* NARA microfilm, M123, reel #28; and Bob Schmidt, *Civil War Veterans of Southeast Missouri for the Counties of St. Francois, Ste. Genevieve, and Washington.*

be a popular one." Someone boasted that he could "lam" any Yankee who showed his face in town. But then the tables turned.

Several other returning veterans came to the rescue of the abused man, and they overpowered the Confederate sympathizers. According to the writer, "The Yankee haters, with bloody noses and bruised heads," ran off in several directions. "Some dashed into the nearest houses to escape the shower of stones, sticks, staves, scrapers, bones and jaw-bones that were flying after them."[29]

Throughout the war, Union and Confederate sympathizers, operating outside any regular military organization, terrorized the state. In southeastern Missouri, the most famous of these guerillas, or bushwhackers, was Sam Hildebrand. He was born in St. Francois County. In 1861, his brother was hanged by vigilantes in Jefferson County (north of Ste. Genevieve), without the benefit of a trial, for stealing a horse. Shortly thereafter, Hildebrand began a bloody crusade to avenge his brother's death.[30] Although Union troops occupied the counties of southeastern Missouri, there were many southern sympathizers who banded together in secret paramilitary resistance groups. Sometime in 1862, Hildebrand emerged as a leader of a band of bushwhackers, who rode through the state wearing federal uniforms, seeking out and killing people they believed were Union spies.

Hildebrand moved quickly up and down the west bank of the Mississippi River from the lead mining towns through the agricultural hamlets of Ste. Genevieve and Cape Girardeau counties, deep into the swamps of the Missouri Bootheel and northeastern Arkansas. After the war, he tried to settle into a peaceful life, but his reputation haunted him. He roamed from county to county and state to state, often with posses on his tail, for several years. In 1872, a stranger in a barroom identified him as a wanted man. Sam went to his wagon to get his rifle, but before he could fire it, a federal marshal knocked him down with a fence picket. After Sam pulled a knife, the lawman shot him dead. He was buried as an unknown person, and for years after his death, people continued to blame him for a variety of crimes.[31]

29. *Jefferson City Missouri State Times,* September 8, 1865.
30. Henry C. Thompson, *Sam Hildebrand Rides Again,* 5–6.
31. Ibid., 102–11.

Outlaws like Hildebrand terrorized—and thrilled—the people of southeastern Missouri long after the war ended. In late May 1873, August Kern offered kindness to a stranger on his farm south of town. The next day he heard that bandits robbed the Ste. Genevieve Savings Association.[32] St. Louis lawmen, who took charge of investigating the crime, attributed it to the Jesse James-Cole Younger gang. But there were plenty of other suspects, including Ed Miller, Dick Little, Frank James, and the deceased Sam Hildebrand.

The *Ste. Genevieve Fair Play* recorded a straightforward account of the bank robbery two days after it occurred. According to the local paper, four men rode into town, hitched their horses in front of a store, and walked nonchalantly toward the bank. Two of the men stayed outside; two others started to go into the bank building. On the front steps, they encountered O. D. Harris, the cashier, and Firmin A. Rozier Jr., the bank owner's son. After saying good morning, Harris followed the robbers into the bank.

Instantly, the robbers drew their pistols and aimed them at Harris's head. One of the robbers said, "Open that safe, damn you, or I will blow your brains out!" Understandably, the cashier opened the safe, and the outlaws took the money. One of them grabbed the terrified man and dragged him outside.

In the meantime, Rozier, who had never gone into the bank, started to shout out the alarm. One of the robbers, standing guard, told him to halt and fired a shot. Rozier fell to the ground and then jumped up and fled. The men who had entered the bank came bursting out, mounted their horses, and took off with their accomplices, firing shots in every direction. Harris hid behind a tree, but Rozier managed to sound the alarm. Local citizens rushed to grab their firearms and horses.

Several men pursued the outlaws. At the edge of town, the bank robbers apparently stopped long enough to let the citizens catch up with them. They fired at their pursuers, who quickly retreated. Others followed, but the robbers got away with the money from the safe and Harris's watch.[33]

32. Kern, interview.
33. *Ste. Genevieve Fair Play,* May 29, 1873.

St. Louis newspapers also picked up the story but added some details. Eventually, the crime found its way into the annals of western outlawry. Frank Triplett attributed the robbery to Jesse James. As he told it, on the morning of May 27, a band of five mounted men, brandishing revolvers, rode into town and stopped in front of the bank. Two of the men dismounted and entered the building, where cashier O. D. Harris was opening for the day's business. Another man, Firmin A. Rozier Jr., the bank president's son, entered the bank at about the same time as the robbers. When the bandits demanded that Harris turn over the bank's cash, Rozier ran wildly into the street, sounding the alarm. People began to gather as the robbers came out of the bank, joined their accomplices, and mounted their horses. The robbers fired a few shots, apparently more to frighten than to kill the people in the crowd.[34]

In another rendition of the story, the bandits relieved the bank of between thirty-five hundred and four thousand dollars in bags of heavy silver coins and headed out of town. A group of citizens pursued them. In the confusion outside the bank, one of the bandits fell from his horse, and the horse bolted with some of the money still in its saddlebags. With the help of an unidentified local man, the outlaws recaptured the horse and recovered a portion of the loot. According to folklore, they told the man to give this part of the money back to the bank. This magnanimous act contributed to the belief that the robber must have been Jesse James, who enjoyed the image of a frontier Robin Hood. In any case, the outlaws rode away, reportedly shouting, "Hurrah for Sam Hildebrand!"[35]

While outlaw bands challenged legal norms, the people of Ste. Genevieve quietly depended on the law and the courts to uphold their human rights. Bandits like Jesse James acquired the mythical reputation of equalizers, who stole from the rich and respected the poor. But this was a fantasy. All the noise the outlaws made and all the attention they received only detracted from the real work of establishing a legal system to serve the needs of the community in a reliable and equitable way.

34. Frank Triplett, *The Life, Times, and Treacherous Death of Jesse James*, 64–66.
35. T. J. Stiles, *Jesse James: Last Rebel of the Civil War*, 228–29.

The Civil War, with all its brutality, brought an end to the ultimate injustice of slavery, but the struggle for equality had just begun. In the reinvented American republic, black people and women continued to be disenfranchised. Mass movements pushing for women's suffrage and black civil rights did not rise to prominence until the twentieth century. In the meantime, individuals had to fend for themselves, demanding their rights by taking their cases to court.

Law and order are two different things: order is about power and control, and law is about fairness. One cannot truly exist without the other. Some level of tranquility must exist before the legal system can function in any dependable way. On the other hand, it is nearly impossible to maintain order when a system denies people the expectation, or at least the hope, of obtaining justice. Powerful people may benefit from order or disorder, justice or injustice. In a just society, the legal system protects not the strong but the weak. The people who have no power are the ones who desperately need the law.

CHAPTER SEVEN

French Women in an American Republic

> The women make faithful and affectionate wives, but will not be con-
> sidered secondary personages in the matrimonial association. The ad-
> vice of the wife is taken on all important, as well as on less weighty
> concerns, and she generally decides.
>
> Henry Brackenridge, *Views of Louisiana*

AS NEW STATES HELD constitutional conventions between 1820 and
1870, delegates had to wrestle with the issue of women's rights. In every
instance, the state conventions decided against equality, generally accepting
the argument that husbands and fathers protected the interests of wives
and daughters, whose physical weakness and emotional delicacy confined
them to a domestic and dependent role.[1] Before the Louisiana Purchase,
French women in Ste. Genevieve enjoyed a degree of independence that
challenged this consensus. After the American takeover, women in Ste. Genevieve continued behaving in ways that contradicted the stereotype of the
timid, deferential female.

In 1811, Henry Brackenridge noted that women in the community expressed their opinions freely, and that their husbands paid close attention
to what they had to say. One year later, the American commandant Amos
Stoddard confirmed this observation, remarking that wives in the former
French colony had more influence over their husbands than wives in most
other communities did. He attributed this, in general, to the customs of

---

1. Rowland Berthoff, "Conventional Mentality: Free Blacks, Women, and Business
Corporations as Unequal Persons, 1820–1870," 753–73.

the mother country and, in particular, to laws that allowed married women to keep and control property of their own.[2]

Historian Susan Boyle examined these assertions by carefully studying public records relating to marriage, death, and property in Ste. Genevieve before 1805. Throughout the eighteenth century, in matters of law, French colonies followed the *coutume de Paris* (customs of Paris). Of particular importance to women were inheritance practices that treated all heirs equally regardless of sex. Under this system, when a woman's parents died, she received a portion of their estate. When French couples married in Ste. Genevieve, they often drew up contracts that specifically separated the property of the bride and her family from the community property to be shared by husband and wife. A widow had the option of keeping her personal property while renouncing her deceased husband's debts. French legal practices gave women a measure of independence and protected them from the careless spending habits of their husbands.[3]

The conditions of life in a frontier community offered women further opportunities for testing their mettle. Men in Ste. Genevieve engaged in a variety of occupations, including farming, hunting, mining, and trading. Well-to-do men spent a great deal of time away from home, supervising operations in the lead mines and saltworks, buying and selling merchandise, and making deals in nearby towns and distant cities such as New Orleans, St. Louis, Detroit, and Quebec. Poorer men had to leave home for months at a time to follow wild game on hunting expeditions, dig and haul lead from the mines, or navigate up and down the river in boats. In the absence of their husbands, women managed farms and gardens, paid and collected bills, hired and fired workers, and purchased items needed for the family. Women participated in public land sales, bid on property, and went to court to demand payment of debts. Widows carried on family businesses, continued to buy and sell property in their own names, and sometimes made trading voyages.[4]

From the earliest period, women in Ste. Genevieve defended their interests in courts of law. When Marie Magdeleine Ridre realized that her

2. Boyle, "Did She Generally Decide?" 775–76.
3. Ibid., 779–81.
4. Ibid., 786–87.

husband had mismanaged the couple's property, she filed for a legal separation and then sued her ex-husband for her share of the assets.[5] The free black woman Elizabeth D'Atchurut sued the estate of the wealthy white man who had fathered her ten children. Another wealthy white man, sitting as judge, validated her claim and awarded her damages. In colonial Ste. Genevieve, the system of justice, as primitive and imperfect as it was, clearly did not exclude the women of the town.

These women stood to lose some of their independence in the new American republic, which increasingly confined women to a private and domestic role in society. Historian Joan Hoff argues that the American Revolution did not improve the lives of women; women did not benefit from the increase in liberty because they lacked the experience necessary to demand a political role in the emerging nation. From her research on white women in the English colonies, Hoff concludes that before 1776 women did not participate in commerce, land acquisition, or local politics and therefore could not readily adapt to a rapidly changing, competitive, increasingly complex world.[6] Her generalizations, however, do not accurately describe the lives of the French colonial women in Ste. Genevieve.

As Brackenridge and Stoddard observed, women in the French community exercised a great deal of authority within their families. This gave them a power base, from which they influenced affairs in the new republic. Hoff admitted that early American women drew strength from their roles as wives and mothers. As the economy shifted into high gear, husbands and fathers increasingly spent their days outside the home, tending to business or laboring in workshops, factories, and mines. Women, confined to a more domestic role, exercised almost absolute authority over the children in their care, at least in the crucial formative years. Women did not vote or hold political office, but they reared the men who did. Mothers held the future of the nation in their hands.[7]

---

5. Ibid., 786.

6. Joan Hoff, "The Negative Impact of the American Revolution on White Women," 76–77.

7. Paula Baker, "White Women's Separate Sphere and Their Political Role, 1780–1860," 110–11.

The ideology of republicanism required an educated citizenry, capable of understanding political issues and of acting in their own best interests and in the best interest of their community, state, and nation. French colonial Ste. Genevieve had been notably blasé about educating its children. After the Louisiana Purchase, American officials urged the creation of an academy to educate the town's young boys. By the late 1830s, a group of nuns arrived in the community to establish a convent school for girls. This institution melded the town's traditional Catholicism with the republican belief in educating female children to prepare them for the important task of motherhood.

Between 1804 and the 1880s, women in Ste. Genevieve embraced their roles as wives and mothers and made their presence known in churches, schools, and places of business. Elizabeth Shannon lifted her daughters out of slavery and established herself as a farmer and property owner. Mary McArthur saw the violent side of frontier life in her husband's tavern. Adeline Ernst managed her family's finances after her husband squandered their resources. "Mama" Odile Vallé spent half of her late husband's fortune funding a church, a cemetery, and local schools. By doing so, she secured her family's legacy.

Common assumptions about female timidity did not stop local women from engaging in business or demanding justice in courts of law. Civil court records abound with the names of female plaintiffs and defendants, attempting to collect small debts or defending their honor. A lack of formal education did not prevent these women from negotiating their way through complex legal tangles. Marie LaPorte, an illiterate French woman, engaged in numerous disputes and frequently won her cases. In at least one instance a free black woman named Lucy Bequette sued Marie LaPorte. Another free woman of color, Pelagie Vital, filed several complaints, always signing with her mark because she could not write her name.

Historian Renae Farris uncovered fascinating information about Marie LaPorte, who was born in Old Ste. Genevieve on July 5, 1766.[8] Her parents

8. Ida M. Schaaf, *Sainte Genevieve Marriages, Baptisms, and Burials from the Church Register, Some Marriages from the Courthouse Records, and a List of Inscriptions from the Protestant Burying Grounds,* 8.

were Simon Hubardeau, a prosperous merchant, and his first wife, Louise Pelagie, who died before her daughter reached the age of seven.[9] Until she was twenty-nine years old, Marie lived in her father's house. Hubardeau appears to have been a colorful and confrontational man. Ekberg noted in *Colonial Ste. Genevieve* that in June 1786 Hubardeau served time in the local jail for making obscene gestures during religious services. Three years later, he engaged in a quarrel with Jean-Baptiste Bequette. Bequette had called him some nasty names, and Hubardeau sued him but apparently lost the case.[10]

Just before her twenty-ninth birthday, Marie Hubardeau married land speculator Francois Guillaume Girouard. During the early years of their marriage, he opened a boardinghouse and billiard hall. In 1803, he was one of four local innkeepers who received official permission to sell alcohol.[11] According to the customs of the time, it is likely that he and Marie conducted their business in a portion of their spacious private residence on the southeast corner of Third and Market streets near the central square in Ste. Genevieve. In September of 1804, Marie's young husband announced publicly that he would make an earnest attempt to pay off all his creditors, indicating that the couple was in financial trouble. Five months later, he died, leaving Marie to run his business and settle his debts.[12]

Three years later, Marie married Louis LaPorte, a native of Bordeaux and an affluent citizen of Ste. Genevieve. She and her new husband lived in the house on Third and Market streets and continued to take in boarders. Louis opposed Sunday liquor sales, an odd stance for an innkeeper. He was involved in some other occupations, including farming, salt making, and operating a store. Information on his business activities is scarce; however, he did purchase lots in the developing town of Cape Girardeau, fifty miles south of Ste. Genevieve, with the final deeds recorded in 1820.

9. Folder 396, Ste. Genevieve Archives.
10. Ekberg, *Colonial Ste. Genevieve*, 328–29.
11. Folder 376, Ste. Genevieve Archives.
12. N. Renae Farris, "French Roots, American Woman: Marie LaPorte of Ste. Genevieve, 1766–1849," 19–24.

By August of that year, he had passed away, but there is no official record of the cause of his death.[13]

At the age of fifty-four, Marie LaPorte became a widow for the second time; she had no biological children. Because she was illiterate, she left no diaries or letters expressing her emotions, but in nineteenth-century America childless women suffered feelings of failure as well as loss. The communal life of Ste. Genevieve helped to assuage these feelings by allowing aunts and godparents to play a role in the rituals of childbirth and baptism. During her second marriage, when it became clear that she would not have babies of her own, Marie and her husband made gifts of land to several godchildren. For instance, in 1817, they gave a house and land to their goddaughter Catherine Buyat on the occasion of her marriage to Gabriel Boyer, and another goddaughter, Marie Langlois, was named in Marie's will.[14]

The LaPortes also showed generosity to the children of friends and neighbors. Louis became the official guardian of the orphaned eight-year-old Marie Vallé after the death of her father in 1814. Official records do not indicate whether the LaPortes raised this little girl to adulthood, but in 1827 and again in 1848, Marie LaPorte gave her substantial tracts of land. Marie LaPorte's will mentioned the offspring of Marie Vallé and her husband, Vital Lalumendiere. Each of the three Lalumendiere boys received a bequest of two hundred dollars and their sister Judith received one hundred dollars. The money was to be used for their education.[15]

As a widow, Marie adopted an infant son, whom she named William Louis LaPorte. There are no official records identifying the birth parents of this child or legally confirming his adoption by Marie. She identified him, however, in her will as her adopted son and left him the bulk of her property, including real estate, slaves, livestock, and cash. She left smaller but substantial amounts to her godchildren and to the Catholic Church, but she made only token bequests to her nieces and nephews.[16] Adopting an infant when she was in her fifties and later snubbing her family in her

13. Ibid., 25–28.
14. Ibid., 38–39.
15. Ibid.
16. Ibid., 41–42.

will were actions that showed strength of character and a degree of contrariness that harked back to the confrontational behavior of her father, Simon Hubardeau.

Following in her father's footsteps, Marie LaPorte became a substantial businesswoman and a fierce combatant in a variety of legal disputes. During the course of her adult life, Marie engaged in farming, innkeeping, slave trading, and moneylending. In 1823, she owned eleven slaves, far more than she would have needed for domestic service. Undoubtedly, they served as agricultural workers. By 1830 she owned fifteen head of cattle, four horses, three oxen, and 526 arpents of land, including sixty arpents in the big field. In 1839, she was the only woman to appear in the county court to register her personal brand for marking free-roaming hogs.[17]

During the three years between her marriages, she continued to operate her first husband's inn. Records indicate that she charged one dollar per day for boarding with an additional charge for laundry service. In addition, she rented out horses for fifty cents per day. Real estate records suggest that she also rented out property. In 1823, the twice-widowed Marie owned at least four houses.[18]

Public records show that Marie was a moneylender and that she could drive a hard bargain. In May 1808, she lent $508 to Joseph Spencer Jr. Spencer promised to repay the loan in three months with interest of forty dollars, but he apparently failed to do so because Marie and her second husband, Louis, later sued him for twelve hundred dollars. The judge ruled in the LaPortes' favor and awarded them 799 arpents of land that Spencer owned on the banks of the St. Francois River. By 1823, these tough business practices made Marie the wealthiest woman in Ste. Genevieve.[19]

Any unfortunate man who owed money to her might very well end up facing her in court. Spencer was not the last man to lose his shirt to this strong-willed woman. In 1820, Pierre Fraichoux purchased a lot with houses on it in Ste. Genevieve from Marie's impecunious half-brother Jean-Baptiste Hubardeau. Shortly before his death, Louis LaPorte loaned $350 to Fraichoux, who signed a mortgage on the property. When Fraichoux refused

17. Ibid., 61–62.
18. Ibid., 65–66
19. Ibid., 66–67.

to pay the money to the newly widowed Marie, she produced her marriage contract stipulating that debts owed to either spouse were community property. Judge Thomas Oliver validated the contract and awarded Fraichoux's property to her.[20]

At least two lawsuits pitted her against other women of Ste. Genevieve. Between 1820 and 1823, she matched wits—and clout—with Catherine Bolduc, the widow of Etienne Bolduc. The trouble began when Catherine loaned money to her son-in-law Rene LeMeilleur. Rene signed a promissory note, which Catherine then signed over to Louis LaPorte presumably in payment for a debt of her own. When Catherine's son-in-law refused to pay his debt, Marie tried to collect the money from Catherine. Joseph Bogy had to intervene to bail Catherine out of jail.

The court case dragged on for three years. John Scott argued Catherine's case, and Marie hired attorney Gustavus A. Bird. During various hearings, Marie consistently testified that she waited one month before attempting to collect the debt. Catherine, on the other hand, kept changing her story, insisting at one point that she had paid what she owed and later, apparently, retracting the statement. Ultimately, the judge ordered Catherine to pay $293 in damages and twenty dollars in court costs. To settle this judgment, she had to auction some of her property at a sheriff's sale in November 1823.[21]

Another woman who faced Marie in court was Lucy Bequette, a free person of color. Details of the case are sketchy, and the outcome is unknown. But what is known is that Lucy was clearly not intimidated by Marie's status or reputation. From surviving documents it appears that Marie boarded an animal on Lucy's property for a period of ten months. In 1831, Lucy took Marie to court to collect a debt of eighty dollars for this service. There were many delays in the case, and a judge dismissed it three years later.[22]

Marie LaPorte survived widowhood, childlessness, and the uncertainties of life on America's western frontier. Many of her male contemporaries could not say as much. Her own half-brother, Jean-Baptiste Hubardeau,

20. Ibid., 70–71.
21. Ibid., 73–74.
22. Ibid., 75.

succumbed to the mania for land speculation that led to a panic and de-
pression in 1819 and 1820. When his various business ventures, including
a sawmill and a distillery, failed, numerous creditors sued him for debt.
Among the creditors was his half-sister Marie, who faced him in prolonged legal proceedings. As his fortunes declined, she was able to save his
fine stone house by purchasing it for sixty-one dollars at public auction.
Eventually, it seems that he lived under her roof. The 1840 census listed a
free white male, sixty to sixty-nine years old, living in her household.[23]

Marie died on September 12, 1849, at the age of eighty-three. Cholera
ran rampant in Ste. Genevieve that year, although no records indicate
that she contracted the disease. If she did, physicians of the time would
have used emetics and laxatives to treat her, which might have hastened
her demise. Above her grave in Memorial Cemetery, her adopted son,
William, erected a tall white marble pillar capped with a draped urn. The
inscription on the monument read,

> *A la memoire de Marie LaPorte*
> *Veuve de Louis LaPorte*
> *Nee le 5 Juillet 1766*
> *Decide de 12 September 1849*
> *Agee de 83 ans*
> *Erige par son fis adoptif*
> *W. L. LaPorte*[24]

Her life challenged traditional assumptions about women and their
place in society. Denied an education, she managed to engage in complicated business transactions and to assert her rights through convoluted
arguments in court. Although women were generally presumed to be weak
and retiring, Marie proved to be a formidable adversary, collecting what
she believed was her due even from members of her own family. At times
she was stubborn and vindictive, but she showed true generosity to the
children of her friends and neighbors. Although she had no children of
her own, she adopted a child and raised him as her loving son.

23. Ibid., 28–30
24. To the memory of Marie LaPorte, Widow of Louis LaPorte, Born July 5, 1766,
Died September 12, 1849, Aged 83 years, Erected by her adopted son, W. L. LaPorte (Inscription on Marie LaPorte's grave stone, Memorial Cemetery, Ste. Genevieve).

Marie LaPorte's success, while unusual, was understandable. Growing up in Old Ste. Genevieve, she could hardly fail to observe her father as he ran his enterprises and fought his personal battles. Working side by side with her two husbands, she learned to manage the farm and the boarding-house. When her protectors passed away, she was already a seasoned busi-nesswoman. Small obstacles such as gender stereotyping and illiteracy did not prevent her from acting in her own best interests. The misfortune of childlessness did not stop her from assuming the hallowed role of mother. A nation that extolled the virtues of self-reliance, fairness, and motherly love could hardly expect her to acquiesce in dependency, injustice, and a solitary old age.

Perhaps Marie was not a typical woman of her time. But she was not the only woman in Ste. Genevieve who defied social norms and demon-strated that a new definition of womanhood was possible, and inevitable, in a democratic republic. On the frontier especially, the vast opportunities that opened up for men could not remain completely closed to bright, energetic women.

Even slavery and racial prejudice could not keep every good woman down. The story of Pelagie Vital provides an example of a lifelong struggle for freedom and personal dignity by a black woman in a slave society. Of French and African extraction, she was born shortly after the Louis-iana Purchase. Along with a small minority of black residents of the area, she was released from bondage long before the Civil War. But the stigma of racial slavery continued to haunt her. Like a small but signi-ficant number of Franco-African women, she raised a racially blended family.

Pelagie was born in Ste. Genevieve on September 20, 1805; she was the illegitimate daughter and the slave of Vital Beauvais. Exactly one month after her birth, the Beauvais family presented the child for baptism in the Catholic Church. When Beauvais died at the age of seventy-seven in 1817, Pelagie became the property of his widow, Felicite Janis.[25] As a young

25. Thanks are due to Anne Herzog for primary research on Pelagie Vital. Sources of information include the Ste. Genevieve Catholic Church, Parish Center, Baptisms and Marriage records, 1760–1860; Ste. Genevieve County, deed book A, p. 182, and deed book B, pp. 443, 285–94.

woman, Pelagie attracted the attention of her white neighbor, Benjamin Amoureux, who became her husband and fathered her children.

On February 13, 1831, Pelagie gave birth to her first son, Joseph Antoine Felix (known as Felix) Amoureux. Sixteen months later, on June 11, 1832, Felicite Janis emancipated both Pelagie and her son. The deed of emancipation stated that it was "the same as if the said Pelagie and Felix had never been slaves."[26]

By the end of 1833, Pelagie occupied a house owned by Francois Dumas Dubuisson. Dubuisson died owing money on the property, and the court ordered the property sold to settle the mortgage. Pelagie may have continued, however, to live there as a tenant. During the next eleven years, she completed her family of four sons and two daughters with the births of Joseph Antoine, Amable Benjamin, Marie Felicitie Heloise, Marie Therese-Claire, and Francis G. All the children were baptized with the name Amoureux, but the 1840 U.S. census listed Pelagie, not Benjamin, as the head of the household.[27]

Public records paint a picture of Pelagie as a light-skinned woman, five foot four inches tall, with a "defective" nose and a feisty disposition.[28] She apparently made some enemies during her lifetime. On more than one occasion, she was attacked by local residents, but she did not submit quietly to their abuse. On February 11, 1840, Jacob Yeally appeared before a justice of the peace to testify against Frances Cromin for allegedly throwing rocks at Pelagie's house. One year later, Pelagie filed suit against a slave named Charles, claiming that he had assaulted her. It appears that she could not read or write because she signed the complaint with her mark.[29]

26. Manumission document in Pelagie Vital and Felix, 1860, Amoureux-Bolduc Papers, Missouri Historical Society.

27. Birth years for Pelagie's children were as follows: Felix, 1831; Joseph Antoine, 1833; Amable Benjamin, 1835; Marie Felicitie Heloise, 1837; Marie Therese-Claire, 1841; and Francis G., ca. 1844 (Ste. Genevieve Catholic Church, parish records; U.S. Bureau of the Census, *Sixth Census: 1840, Population Schedule, Ste. Genevieve County, Missouri,* NARA microfilm, M704, reel #230).

28. This physical description of Pelagie Vital is in the "Registry of Free Negroes and Mulattoes, Ste. Genevieve County, Missouri," Missouri State Archives. She obtained her free black license on July 27, 1836

29. Folder 963, Ste. Genevieve Archives.

The suit against Charles went badly for Pelagie. Apparently some residents of the community had a low opinion of her character. Regarding her claim of assault, the jury found in the defendant's favor and issued a scathing condemnation of Pelagie. The jury said,

> We the jury Called by Simms to try a case of assault—State of Missouri against Charles a slave, the property of Bertel Durocher said suit was instituted by a certain mulatto woman, named Pelagie—know then that we as citizens of the Town of Ste. Genevieve do deeply feel the stain upon the morals of the community by the conduct of said Pelagie and cannot resist this mode of expressing our heartfelt sorrow that such a woman should be allowed to come into a court of law and ask for the aid and protection of the laws which she is daily in the habit of [trampling] under foot to the injury of this place and a bad example to the community. We now close our verdict by unanimous voice that her charge is groundless, without testimony and sufficient evidence to sustain a suit against said Charles.[30]

It is impossible to know exactly what the all-white jury had against her. That she was a woman of color bearing a white man's children surely upset some of her white neighbors. But black people also seemed to bear enmity toward her. In 1845, she swore out another complaint, on oath before justice of the peace Joseph D. Grafton, stating that Henry Badeau, a free man of color, tried to harm her. Badeau allegedly grabbed her while she was walking down the street, shook her, and threatened to strike her. After she took shelter on the gallery of Ichabod Sargent's house, Badeau cursed her. Again, she signed the papers with her mark.[31]

A change occurred in her household during the 1850s. The 1850 U.S. census once again listed Pelagie as the head of a household. Six others resided in the home. All were listed as mulatto. Among the residents were nineteen-year-old Felix Amoureux and his wife, Mary; Joseph Amoureux, age seventeen; Amable Amoureux, age fifteen; and Marie Amoureux, age twelve. In 1859, Benjamin Amoureux sold a property on St. Mary's Road and moved in with this mixed-race family. In 1860, the census officially

30. Ibid.
31. Folder 1130, ibid.

listed Pelagie as the wife of Benjamin C. Amoureux, a white male, resid-
ing with her in the same household.[32]

Perhaps this new living arrangement incited persecution by white neighbors. Descendants of Pelagie have long believed that Felicite Janis tried to
reclaim her former slave. In May of 1860, Pelagie and her eldest son, Felix,
who was about thirty years old, had to go to court to prove that they were
not slaves. Felix Vallé and Bartholomew Durocher, the witnesses to their
emancipation documents, testified that they were indeed free.[33]

Despite these difficulties, the family remained in Ste. Genevieve throughout the Civil War and Reconstruction. In 1868, Pelagie's son Felix purchased a vertical log house on the road that led from Ste. Genevieve to
St. Mary—the same property his father had sold in 1859. When Pelagie
died on November 11, 1890, at the age of eighty-five, her death notice in
the *Ste. Genevieve Herald* read, "Died: at her home in Ste. Genevieve on
Tuesday, November 11, 1890 Mrs. Pelagie Amoureux, relict of Benjamin
C. Amoureux, aged 85 years, two months, six days. The deceased leaves
five children of whom two, Felix and Joseph Amoureux, are well-known
citizens of Ste. Genevieve."[34] The house in which she died has been preserved by the state of Missouri, an important legacy for a woman who
was born a slave.

In 2002, Phillippe Amoureux, a direct descendant of Benjamin and
Pelagie, and his wife, Fran Barker, traveled from Seattle, Washington, to
Ste. Genevieve to visit the sites connected with his family history. According to Fran, they flew to St. Louis and then drove down Interstate 55 to
the Ste. Genevieve exit. Barker recalled that after leaving the highway,
they "immediately saw rolling green hills and a mist, fingers of mist, and
a huge harvest moon hanging ahead of us. It was like going back through
the centuries, with the moon and the mist, and when we got to the town,
it got dark."

With no map and no previous knowledge of the town, they searched
for the Inn St. Gemme Beauvais, a bed and breakfast. After turning a few

32. U.S. Bureau of the Census, *Seventh Census: 1850, Population Schedule,* NARA microfilm, M432; *Eighth Census: 1860, Population Schedule,* NARA microfilm, M653.
33. Amoureux-Bolduc Papers, Missouri Historical Society.
34. *Ste. Genevieve Herald,* November 15, 1890.

corners, they stopped in front of a sign that read "Beauvais House." Barker "went to the front door, knocked on it, and found out it was the Beauvais house that his great-great-grandmother had been a slave in." The inn was a block away. Two days later, the owner of the Beauvais house invited them to dinner.

The couple also visited the Amoureux House, which Benjamin and Felix had owned, on St. Mary's Road. The house reminded Phil Amoureux of the stories he had heard about Pelagie. His father, Louis Phillippe Amoureux, who passed away in 1993, had often told him "about the big Frenchman that went next door and fell in love with her and basically took her away and married her over in Kaskaskia." According to the family tradition, "He [Benjamin] used to walk right down the street with Pelagie on his arm." The couple defied convention, and the family treasured their legacy of defiance.

Of his family, Phil Amoureux said, "I'm proud of the fact that we survived so long, and that Benjamin and Pelagie's personalities—their toughness, their belligerence—have survived. If you're nice all the time, you get stepped on. My great-great-great-grandmother and Benjamin weren't about to get stepped on by anybody. I'm very proud of the toughness that they had."[35]

Strong women such as Pelagie Vital and Marie LaPorte challenged the prevailing gender ideology, not by articulating a feminist agenda, but by defending themselves, their families, and their sense of personal dignity. When Pierre Fraichoux refused to pay a debt to Marie LaPorte because she was a widow—and a woman—she produced the marriage contract that validated her claim to her deceased husband's assets. When a man attacked Pelagie Vital on a public street, she took him to court. The jury heaped more abuse upon her, but she did not accept defeat. Several years later, she went back to court and filed a similar complaint against Henry Badeau.

Both women found validation in the traditional institution of motherhood. In her fifties, Marie LaPorte, the richest woman in Ste. Genevieve, adopted a baby. At the age of fifty-five, Pelagie finally shared a home with

35. Phillippe Amoureux and Fran Barker, interview with the author, January 13, 2005.

the white father of her children. Despite racism and abuse, she and her family continued to live in Ste. Genevieve through the Civil War and Reconstruction. It was not until her death that the community recognized her sons as substantial citizens.

These women did not rebel against or even openly question the legal arrangements of the new republic. Within the existing system, they simply acted in their own best interests and in the interests of their families and the community. Other women in Ste. Genevieve did the same thing. Wealthy women like Odile Vallé "mothered" the townspeople with generous gifts. Poor women like Elizabeth Shannon set an example of self-reliance for generations to come. A group of nuns opened a school to educate young girls. Women whose struggles have been forgotten put food in the mouths and ideas in the heads of future citizens of the republic—a republic that denied these women the rights of citizenship. Because of their actions, from day to day, year to year, and generation to generation, the system began gradually to change.

CHAPTER EIGHT

Slavery and Freedom

The wretchedness of slavery, and the blessedness of freedom were perpetually before me.

Frederick Douglass, *Narrative of the Life of*
Frederick Douglass, An American Slave

ELIZABETH D'ATCHURUT sued the estate of a powerful white man for support of her children. Elizabeth Shannon gained her own freedom, purchased freedom for her daughters, and became the legal owner of real property. Paul Vallé joined the Union army and fought for his own liberation. Pelagie Amoureux braved insults, defended herself in court, and raised a racially blended family in a society that divided white from black. All of these black people challenged prevailing norms that demanded whiteness as a prerequisite for citizenship, and none of these individuals accepted the bleak assumption that the law and the courts would always be against them. Even in a slave society, the legal system offered narrow openings for society's weakest members to argue for justice and to claim their rights. Before and after the American takeover, slavery existed in Ste. Genevieve, but so did the basic building blocks of freedom.

At the time of the Louisiana Purchase, slavery was well established in the French colonies west of the Mississippi River. African slaves were the labor force in the French sugar islands, and French colonists used the same labor source in the Mississippi River valley as early as 1712. The first African slaves on the eastern bank of the Mississippi River migrated with the French colonists from the Caribbean Islands. Ekberg concluded that the Jesuits were the first and largest slaveholders in the Illinois Country.

In 1732, African slaves accounted for one-third of the population of the Illinois Country, and the slave population continued to grow. Many of the French families who settled Ste. Genevieve came from the Illinois Country and brought slaves with them. Throughout the colonial period, slaves accounted for forty percent of the local population. The labor required of the slave population included fieldwork, domestic service, lead mining, and manning the oars on riverboats.[1]

The French Code Noir (Black Code) of 1724 and its Spanish revision of 1777 loosely regulated slavery in the Upper Louisiana Territory on the west bank of the Mississippi. The code subjugated people of color but provided some legal protection for slaves. Originally, the French code recognized slaves as property that could be bought and sold, but it also acknowledged that slaves were human beings with certain rights of their own. Masters were required to provide religious instruction, adequate food, and clothing for their slaves; the code prohibited torture and forbade the separation of husbands, wives, and children less than fourteen years of age. Of course, masters differed in their levels of cruelty and compassion, and officials looked the other way even when they knew about violations. The Code Noir was nearly impossible to enforce. Local conventions, customs, and directives possessed more authority in *le petit village* of Ste. Genevieve.[2]

Under the Spanish regime, slaves could not marry without their owner's consent, and marriage or cohabitation with whites—even though it did happen—remained illegal. But Spanish authorities generally did not punish couples for cohabitation or intermarriage. The new regime also allowed masters to free their slaves by signing documents of manumission. Under Spanish rule, slaves could and sometimes did purchase their freedom. There were no fixed rules for these transactions. Masters had to agree to a price and conditions of the sale. The exact legal status of the freed slaves, however, remained unclear.[3]

---

1. Ekberg, *Colonial Ste. Genevieve,* 196–212.

2. Ibid., 208–9; Greene, Kremer, and Holland, *Missouri's Black Heritage,* 9–10.

3. Carl J. Ekberg, *French Roots in the Illinois Country: The Mississippi Frontier in Colonial Times,* 147–48; Thomas N. Ingersoll, "Free Blacks in a Slave Society: New Orleans, 1718–1812," 177–78, 180.

After 1803, the legal status of slaves and free black persons rested precariously on a system undergoing an uncomfortable transition between French and Spanish customs and the new American order.[4] The laws of many states severely restricted a slave's ability to purchase his or her freedom. An expansion of the federal Fugitive Slave Act of 1793 defined as "fugitives" all those who had obtained their freedom illegally. States and territories had the right to regulate the influx of free black people across their borders.[5] Missouri's territorial code, derived from Virginia statutes, defined slaves as personal property. The code did not distinguish, however, between lifelong slavery and limited servitude for a specified term of years; therefore it was still possible for a slave to obtain freedom by legal means.[6]

As Missouri statehood approached, lawmakers vacillated over proposals to bar free black people from living in the state. In 1820, when applying for admission to the Union, the delegates to Missouri's constitutional convention considered a provision prohibiting free black individuals from entering the state for any reason whatsoever. This measure was not adopted. Free black people continued to live in Missouri, but their lives became increasingly difficult in the years leading up to the Civil War. In the 1830s and 1840s, the Missouri legislature placed heavy burdens on free African Americans.[7]

By 1835, free black residents were required to post a monetary bond and secure a license in the county courts to document and maintain their free status and residence in the state. Pelagie Vital and twelve other Ste. Genevieve residents obtained their licenses in 1836, but few people obtained licenses in the late 1830s or in the 1840s. The law, revised in 1843, was designed to prevent free black migration into the state. By 1847, the language of the statute had been modified to state that "no free negro or mulatto shall, under any pretext, emigrate to this State, from any other State

---

4. Banner, *Legal Systems in Conflict*, 96.

5. Ingersoll, "Free Blacks in a Slave Society," 196–99.

6. Harrison Trexler, *Slavery in Missouri, 1804–1865*, 58–60.

7. Charshee McIntyre, *Criminalizing a Race: Free Blacks during Slavery*, 83; Bellamy, "Free Blacks in Antebellum Missouri," 198–99, 204–5; Greene, Kremer, and Holland, *Missouri's Black Heritage*, 62–74.

or territory."[8] Black people who came to the state risked pursuit and capture as runaway slaves.

Ste. Genevieve residents vigorously pursued runaways. Felix Vallé posted a reward of three hundred dollars for three of his slaves who escaped in the summer of 1845. In an advertisement in the *St. Louis Missouri Republican,* he described the fugitives as "a bright mulatto boy named Batiste, about 21 years old, 5 feet 6 or 7 inches high, thick set, lively, and speaks fast. Also a dark mulatto named Batiste, heavy set, about 20 years old, has a dull and downcast look. Also, a black boy named Henry, about 30 years old, about 5 feet 10 inches high, very slender, speaks very slow." Vallé promised a reward to "any one who will apprehend said negroes and confine them in jail, so that I can get them, or deliver them to me, at Ste. Genevieve."[9]

Authorities sometimes confined runaway slaves in the Ste. Genevieve jail. A notice in the *Missouri Republican* on January 4, 1850, informed the public that a sixteen-year-old boy, who called himself "General," had been apprehended. This boy, "about 5 feet high; a mulatto, had on an old cloth cap, cassimere pants, blue roundabout coat, white pleated bosom shirt." He apparently told officials that his owners, two men named Conner and McAfee, lived in Memphis and St. Louis. The public notice announced that if these owners did not claim their property, the young man would be sold to the highest bidder at the courthouse door in Ste. Genevieve on March 20.[10]

The pressure on free blacks to prove their legal status intensified after 1850, when the United States Congress passed a stringent Fugitive Slave Law.[11] In Ste. Genevieve during the 1850s at least twenty-seven local free black residents appeared in county court to pay their bond and obtain licenses from the county. For example, in August 1851, the court issued a summons ordering Mary Boynton (or Byington), the twenty-one-year-old wife of Felix Amoureux, to comply with the law. To receive her license,

8. *Laws of the State of Missouri,* Fourteenth General Assembly, First Session, 1847.
9. *St. Louis Missouri Republican,* September 2, 1845.
10. Ibid., January 4, 1850.
11. Perry McCandless, *A History of Missouri: Volume II, 1820–1860,* 250–52.

she had to post a bond of one hundred dollars. Her white father-in-law, Benjamin Amoureux, signed the bond document.[12]

Despite hostile attitudes and restrictive laws, the free black population of Ste. Genevieve grew from ten free persons of color in 1787 to sixty-five in 1850.[13] In-migration was a factor in this growth, and it seems likely that the licensing laws did not completely stop the migration of free black persons into the community. Several of the town's free black residents hailed from other states and countries. Michel Badeau was born in Port au Prince, Haiti; Clarisse Janis was born in Virginia, as were Lucy Bequette, Gerder Harris, and Ned Logan. The 1850 U.S. census for Ste. Genevieve listed seven free black individuals as having come to the area from other states: three were from Illinois, two were from Kentucky, one was from Indiana, and one was from New York. The census also indicated that one of Ste. Genevieve's free black residents had emigrated from Canada.[14]

Local slave owners could, and occasionally did, grant freedom to their slaves, with or without any monetary compensation. In some cases, masters simply wanted to escape the responsibility for caring for elderly slaves. For example, the owners of Arkange Vallé gave the old woman her freedom. Manumission documents stipulated that she was to be cared for by the Recole family, a black family, if she became infirm.[15]

More often, however, slaves purchased their own freedom. Between 1806 and 1856 several enslaved individuals emancipated themselves in Ste. Genevieve. Jacob Auguste purchased his freedom in 1817 from his owner—Auguste Aubuchon—for the sum of seven hundred dollars.[16] The price

12. Licenses, bonds, and summons documents on file in the County Clerk's office, Ste. Genevieve County Courthouse. Thanks are due to Jadie Eisenhower for primary research on Mary Boynton.

13. Greene, Kremer, and Holland, *Missouri's Black Heritage,* 20; Schroeder, *Opening the Ozarks,* 205–6; Bellamy, "Free Blacks in Antebellum Missouri," 200; *Spanish Census of Ste. Genevieve, Missouri,* 1787, Census Collection, 1732–1980; U.S. Bureau of the Census, *Seventh Census: 1850, Population Schedule,* NARA microfilm, M432.

14. U.S. Bureau of the Census, *Seventh Census: 1850, Population Schedule,* NARA microfilm, M432; *Eighth Census: 1860, Population Schedule,* NARA microfilm, M653.

15. Folders 911 and 931, Ste. Genevieve Archives.

16. Ste. Genevieve County, deed book B, pp. 477–78.

of emancipation varied widely in Ste. Genevieve—six hundred dollars for Antoine Recole in 1816; one hundred dollars for Ignacio Moreau in 1849; and twelve hundred dollars for Mary Vallé in 1852. In several cases, slaves who purchased their own freedom also bought freedom for their children. Elizabeth Shannon, for example, purchased her daughters, Eliza and Mary, in 1845 for $600 and $240, respectively. Peter Brown purchased freedom for his son first and then his own freedom one year later.[17] In 1855, Brown paid fifteen hundred dollars for the freedom of his son, Peter Pratte. Brown's own freedom cost two thousand dollars.[18] When calculating the price required for emancipation, slave owners took into account past and future financial investments, estimated remaining years of service, faithfulness, and their own sentimental responses of benevolence and humanity.

To survive independently, free black people had to earn a living. Many but not all worked as farmers or laborers. Some became artisans and craftsmen. For example, Michel Badeau brought his two sons, Israel and Henri Eli, into his carpentry business. By 1850 the census enumerated three carpenters, one wheelwright, seven farmers, and six laborers in the free black community, along with numerous others whose occupations went unlisted.[19] Occupations of free black women also varied. Pierre Delassus listed two free black women on his 1797 census, reporting their names as Lisette (probably Elizabeth D'Atchurut), age forty-five, and Rose, age sixty. Lisette and Rose made their living by farming and raising livestock.[20] Women also worked as domestic servants. Mary Boynton Amoureux, the

17. Manumission and Free Black Licenses, 1836–1857, County Clerk's office, Ste. Genevieve County Courthouse.

18. Antoine Recole's manumission was recorded in Ste. Genevieve County, deed book B, p. 410; manumission papers for Ignacio Moreau, Mary Vallè, Peter Pratte, and Peter Brown are with the Manumission and Free Black Licenses, 1836–1857, in the County Clerk's office, Ste. Genevieve County Courthouse.

19. Deed of emancipation, June, 1832, in Amoureux-Bolduc Papers; U.S. Bureau of the Census, *Seventh Census: 1850, Population Schedule,* NARA microfilm, M432; *Eighth Census: 1860, Population Schedule,* NARA microfilm, M653.

20. Greene, Kremer, and Holland, *Missouri's Black Heritage,* 16; *List and Census of the Population of the Post of New Bourbon of the Illinois and Its Dependencies,* 1797, folio 347, legajo 2365, Papeles de Cuba, New Orleans Collection, Missouri Historical Society.

wife of Felix Amoureux, was listed as a housekeeper in federal census records for forty years beginning in 1850.[21]

Property ownership was common in the free black community. According to the 1850 census, seven of the fifteen free black households living within the city of Ste. Genevieve owned real estate valued between one hundred and six hundred dollars. Two additional families were listed as property owners in the Jackson and Saline townships of Ste. Genevieve County.[22] Jacob Auguste, a free person of color, acquired his first lot in 1826 for forty dollars and his second in 1834 for four hundred dollars.[23] In 1850, Michel Badeau owned property worth two hundred dollars, and he also purchased land in the big field for agricultural use—suggesting the possibility that he was supplementing his income from carpentry work with growing commercial crops. In 1850, Jacob Auguste, John Micheau, and Antoine Cavelier were listed as free black men, who owned property. Cassimere, a free person of color, purchased property for thirty dollars in 1854.[24]

Sometimes white masters provided property holdings to emancipated slaves. Dr. William James liberated his "good, faithful, and honest" slaves— Louis, Eliza, Thomas, Sophy, Moses and Diggish—in his will and bequeathed them four hundred dollars each. He suggested that they use the money to move to Canada or Liberia. But if they chose to stay in Missouri, according to the doctor's will, they would also be given land, homes, farming implements, and livestock so that they could earn a living. He bequeathed parcels of land and fifty dollars each to his slaves Eliza and Samuel, who were to be emancipated after they reached the age of thirty.[25]

21. U.S. Bureau of the Census, *Seventh Census: 1850, Population Schedule,* NARA microfilm, M432; *Eighth Census: 1860, Population Schedule,* NARA microfilm, M653; *Ninth Census: 1870, Population Schedule, Ste. Genevieve County, Missouri,* NARA microfilm, M593, reel #807; *Tenth Census: 1880,* NARA microfilm, T9, reel #715.

22. U.S. Bureau of the Census, *Seventh Census: 1850, Population Schedule,* NARA microfilm, M432.

23. Ste. Genevieve County, deed book D, p. 145.

24. Ste. Genevieve County, deed book F, p. 254.

25. Will record book C, 1836–1869, Probate Records, Circuit Court Clerk's office, Ste. Genevieve County Courthouse.

Gender was not a barrier to property ownership in Ste. Genevieve. Free black women like Lucy Bequette and Margaret Recole owned real estate in the Ste. Genevieve region: Elizabeth Shannon purchased land from Conrad Ziegler in 1845, and Clarisse Janis purchased property from Antoine Recole in 1850.[26] Property ownership must have had great significance for these women, because it helped to ensure their economic survival, even in the absence of a husband or a master.

Free black individuals in Ste. Genevieve sued, testified, and settled disputes in the local courts. Michel Badeau, who inherited $127 from his father, Francois, had to settle a dispute over a borrowed saddle before he could collect the money.[27] Michel returned to court in 1839 regarding a debt of nine dollars owed to Antoine Janis and again in 1845 over a debt of one dollar that was owed to Louis Buat.[28] Three of the former slaves of Dr. James took a property issue to the court in 1861. Louis, Thomas, and Eliza James filed complaints when the court issued annexation orders against their land, and even in those troubled times, they won their case.[29]

Free black persons left wills and estates. Probate files, created upon a person's death, tell much about the day-to-day existence of the free black community. For example, outstanding claims against Jacob Auguste's estate remained at the time of his passing. These included an invoice for sugar, coffee, whiskey, and a chicken. Another document noted a debt for services rendered by Lucy, a free black woman, who tended to Jacob's wife between March and July of 1863.[30] Like their white counterparts, free black people died with or without wills, leaving unfinished business.

To remain in the community, free black people needed a support network. Traditionally, in Ste. Genevieve, where most residents were Catholic, the church was an important source of strength. Although it condoned and even practiced slavery, the church also recognized black people as members of the parish. According to historian Emily Clark, Catholicism helped

---

26. Ste. Genevieve County, deed book F, p. 254.
27. *Badeau,* March 1813, Orphan's Court Records, Ste. Genevieve County Courthouse.
28. Ste. Genevieve Catholic Church, Parish Center, Burial records, 1766–1860.
29. Ste. Genevieve County, deed book P, pp. 176–77.
30. *Jacko,* 1864, Probate Records, Circuit Court Clerk's office, Ste. Genevieve County Courthouse, box 13, file 349.

people of different races maintain connections in the French colonies.[31] By administering the sacraments to people of color, both free and slave, priests recognized their humanity and encouraged their sense of belonging to the community.

During the final decade of the eighteenth century, a special dispensation from Rome allowed priests to perform marriages for couples who were not baptized in the Catholic Church. This dispensation, designed to decrease the number of illicit relationships, allowed priests to solemnize the vows of mixed-race couples. By doing so, the church was recognizing the facts of life on the colonial frontier. Enslaved, free black, and Indian women made up a significant portion of the female population. French colonial leaders pleaded for more women to emigrate from France, and after 1720 white French women came to Upper Louisiana in greater numbers. Census data for Ste. Genevieve confirms, however, that the male population was significantly higher than the female population throughout the eighteenth century. White women made up 25 percent of the population in 1752 and 43 percent of the population by 1800.[32]

After the Louisiana Purchase and well into the nineteenth century, priests in Ste. Genevieve baptized, married, and buried slaves and free black persons and their offspring. In performing these rites, the priests ensured that the names of these slaves and free black persons would be entered into church records. By looking at these records, we know that the children of Elizabeth Shannon were baptized in Ste. Genevieve parish even though she was a slave at the time of their birth.[33] Free black residents Felix Amoureux and Mary Boynton were married in the Ste. Genevieve parish, as were John and Mary Ribault. The Badeau and Amoureux children were all baptized in the Ste. Genevieve parish. Jacob Auguste, a free person of color eighty to eighty-six years of age, was buried in the Catholic cemetery of Ste. Genevieve in 1864.[34] Clarisse

31. Emily Clark, "By All the Conduct of Their Lives: A Laywomen's Confraternity in New Orleans, 1730–1744," 792–93.

32. Boyle, "Did She Generally Decide," 775–89.

33. Ste. Genevieve Catholic Church, Parish Center, Baptisms and Marriage records, 1760–1860.

34. Ste. Genevieve Catholic Church, Parish Center, Burial records, 1766–1860.

Janis, Antoine Recole, Francois St. Cyr, Arkange Vallé, and various members of the Amoureux and Badeau families also received Catholic burials.

With the support of the church, black and mixed-race families endured the turmoil of Missouri statehood, the collapse of the Union, and the Civil War. The descendants of Catherine Coton de Mahi, for instance, lived, worked, and raised children in Ste. Genevieve from the late eighteenth through the late nineteenth century. In the 1787 Spanish census, Catherine is listed as Caterina Alemande. Her race was not recorded, but her descendants were documented repeatedly as "mulatto," indicating that they were of mixed race, black and white. Catherine was enumerated as a *comercianta* (merchant). The 1787 census contains many errors, but it provides some evidence of Catherine's residence in Ste. Genevieve and of her five children: Charles, Antoine, Louis, and twin daughters, Hyacinth and Mari.[35] It also reports that she had no boarders. The Spanish word *alemande* might be translated to the word "German." Her surname later appeared in documents as Coton de Mahi, or "Cotton of the Corn." These varying names are an interesting mystery since Indian, black, and German women were all represented in the region in the eighteenth century.[36]

Church records reveal that on December 9, 1790, Catherine Coton de Mahi died. According to her estate records, Catherine left behind a black and white cow with a broken horn, pigs "to be fattened," a salting tub, a shovel in poor condition, one wooden dish, two pewter spoons, and a *couchette* (crib). Catherine also left behind four living children.[37] Her fifth child, Louis, had apparently died. What Catherine did not leave behind was clear evidence of the paternity of her children, and Catherine and her descendants did not leave diaries or other personal writings. It is difficult to know absolutes about this case study, but the documents point to an early multiracial family.[38]

35. Folder 237, Ste. Genevieve Archives.

36. Vaughn B. Baker, "Cherchez les Femmes: Some Glimpses of Women in Early Eighteenth-Century Louisiana," 21–37.

37. Folders 150 and 237, Ste. Genevieve Archives.

38. U.S. Bureau of the Census, *Seventh Census: 1850, Population Schedule,* NARA microfilm, M432; *Eighth Census: 1860, Population Schedule,* NARA microfilm, M653. In her church marriages and marriage contracts database, Susan C. Boyle notes after Mari's name that she was "Possibly part Indian."

Following Catherine's death, her daughter Mari Coton de Mahi entered the household of a Frenchman named Etienne Parent, who agreed to provide for her nourishment and support. His wife, Elizabeth Bolduc, was the daughter of a wealthy businessman, and their household was an affluent one. Mari did not leave this household until she married Louis Cavelier. It may be a coincidence, but Parent served in the Ste. Genevieve Militia with a man of the same name. It is very likely that this was the same man who became Mari's husband.[39]

In 1780, Louis Cavelier served in the first Ste. Genevieve Militia. He was listed as a chasseur on the militia roster. Louis Cavelier's race is unknown, but it was common for free black men, as well as white men, to serve in the militias for the French and later Spanish regime. In fact, free black militiamen were a significant force in defending colonial strongholds throughout the eighteenth century.[40] During the American Revolution, the Ste. Genevieve Militia represented the community on behalf of the Spanish regime in defending St. Louis in May 1780 against British attack. Ekberg conjectured that many of the men on the militia roster were chosen without regard to race because they were good marksman and experienced Indian fighters.[41] In the summer of 1780, Louis Cavelier, who had established a trading relationship with the Pottawatomie tribe, assisted the Spanish government in keeping the Pottawatomie people neutral during a Spanish and British dispute at a British post named St. Joseph.[42]

The Catholic parish in Ste. Genevieve recorded Mari's marriage to Louis Cavelier on April 6, 1799 and listed several prominent Ste. Genevieve citizens as witnesses—Etienne Parent, Louis Leclerc, Francois Aubuchon, Antoine Aubuchon, and the colorful Irish priest, Father James Maxwell, the vicar general of Upper Louisiana.[43] The presence of these individuals

39. Folders 150 and 237, Ste. Genevieve Archives; Ekberg, *François Vallé and His World,* 298. The name *Cavelier* is recorded in documents as Chevallier, Chevellier, and Cavalier.
40. Ira Berlin, *Slaves without Masters: The Free Negro in the Antebellum South,* 112.
41. Ekberg, *François Vallé and His World,* 63–66.
42. Lawrence Kinnaird, "The Spanish Expedition against Fort St. Joseph in 1781, a New Interpretation," 173–91.
43. Ste. Genevieve Catholic Church, Parish Center, Baptisms and Marriage records, 1760–1860, marriage register, April 6, 1799.

at the wedding shows that the couple had strong support from the community and the church. It is not clear from the records whether the couple were of the same race, but their offspring would be identified in records as being of mixed race.

After their marriage, Mari and Louis Cavelier lived on a parcel of land on the North Gabouri Creek, where they raised six children and where their descendants would reside for more than a century. Their oldest daughter, Caroline, who was born in 1800, married Michel Badeau, the carpenter. She died on the eve of the Civil War in 1860 and was buried in Memorial Cemetery in Ste. Genevieve. Mari, who lived to be nearly one hundred, spent her final years on the family homestead in the household of her youngest son, Antoine.[44]

Antoine Cavelier was born January 20, 1809. According to the parish records, he married Julienne Ricard sometime around 1845. Both husband and wife were listed as "mulatto" on census records and on bond documents. The only exception was the 1870 census, which listed Antoine, Julienne, and his mother as "white." In 1845, Antoine and Julienne, continuing the family tradition, had twins, whom they named Israel and Philomena. Between 1845 and 1853 they had seven children.[45]

While they raised their family, Antoine and Julienne Cavelier experienced threats to their free black status. Antoine Cavelier's family had lived as free residents in Ste. Genevieve for nearly seventy years, but in the 1850s the changing social and racial climate made his position insecure. He and Julienne posted bond in October 1857 — fifty dollars each — with the county sheriff. The summons, forcing Antoine to appear in court, declared that "Antoine . . . a person of color . . . a mulatto, not being a citizen

44. Carla Jordan, Richard Taylor, Jason Moen, and Jason Williamson conducted extensive research in county and church records and the U.S. census population schedules for Ste. Genevieve County, 1850, 1860, 1870, and 1880. Mari and Louis Cavelier's land was located on U.S. Survey 344; the land previously granted to Louis Cavelier was auctioned in 1899, and John White (Louis's son-in-law) bought it for fifty dollars. Caroline's tombstone is still extant and legible in the Memorial Cemetery in Ste. Genevieve.

45. U.S. Bureau of the Census, *Seventh Census: 1850, Population Schedule,* NARA microfilm, M432; *Eighth Census: 1860, Population Schedule,* NARA microfilm, M653; *Ninth Census: 1870, Population Schedule,* NARA microfilm, M593, reel #807; Probate Records, Circuit Court Clerk's office, Ste. Genevieve County Courthouse; Manumission and Free Black Licenses, 1836–1857, County Clerk's office, Ste. Genevieve County Courthouse.

of any one of the United States, but claiming to be free, is abiding within the County of Ste. Genevieve, in the State of Missouri, without having obtained a license, or acquired any other right to reside or remain within this State."[46] The classification "free but not a citizen" marked the low point of the Cavelier family's disenfranchisement.

On the bond documents the family changed its name to "Louison." The name "Louis' Son" expressed Antoine's attachment to his father and his pride in the family's heritage of freedom. The family name was listed as "Cavelier" on the 1850 and the 1860 census. On the 1870 census, their Christian names were Anglicized, and the family was listed as "white" under the race category. In 1880, the census taker listed the family as "Louison," but someone crossed it out and wrote "Cavelier," providing the clue that made it possible to trace the family's history.

Name changes represented a common and significant metamorphosis in the emancipation process. The Cavelier family changed its name—not because of its emancipation—but to sustain its freedom. Freed slaves often did this to confirm their altered status or to guard their newly won privacy. Historian Leon F. Litwack explained that free black people often changed their names in case white people changed their minds and tried to reenslave them.[47]

The Caveliers (Louisons), the Amoureuxes, and other free black families survived the Civil War, which ended slavery without establishing racial justice. Many black men, both slave and free, fought for the Union and the liberation of their people.[48] John White of Ste. Genevieve served as a private in the Union Colored First Missouri Artillery. After completing his service, White married Antoine and Julienne Cavelier's daughter Mary at the family home on the North Gabouri.[49]

---

46. Manumission and Free Black Licenses, 1836–1857, County Clerk's office; and Probate Records, Circuit Court Clerk's office, both housed in the Ste. Genevieve County Courthouse.

47. Leon F. Litwack, *Been in the Storm so Long: The Aftermath of Slavery,* 249.

48. John David Smith, ed. *Black Soldiers in Blue: African American Troops in the Civil War Era,* 29.

49. U.S. Bureau of the Census, *1890 Special Census, Ste. Genevieve, Missouri,* NARA microfilm, M123, reel #28; Marriage License books, Recorder's office, Ste. Genevieve County Courthouse.

After the war, members of the Cavelier family continued to live in Ste. Genevieve. The 1880 census listed the family as "mulatto" and indicated that they had a "black boarder" named John White living with them. Surely this odd listing reflects the racism of the census taker, who misunderstood or misrepresented the true status of this black man. John and his wife, Mary, raised five children on the homestead of her ancestors.[50] Their offspring—like the generations before them—played in the clear waters and climbed the rocky banks of the North Gabouri. These descendants of Catherine Coton de Mahi were baptized in the Roman Catholic Church. They became respected citizens, were literate, and remained an active part of the Ste. Genevieve community well into the twentieth century.

The *comercianta*, Catherine Coton de Mahi, matriarch of an American family, now finds a place on a long list of women who contributed to the settlement of the Upper Louisiana frontier. Catherine was the mother of antebellum free black children. Her descendants sustained their freedom through their connections with the prominent citizenry, through the support of the Catholic Church, through their efforts as militiamen and soldiers, and through land ownership. Catherine's children preserved their family unity through multiple generations and her daughter Mari lived on the home place well into her ninetieth year. When you walk the vacant homestead on the banks of the North Gabouri Creek today, the only reminders of the family who resided there for more than a century are two vertical log fence posts, some handmade barbed wire, a field of grass, and several mounds of earth. The landscape belies the rich story of a free black family that resided as early settlers in Ste. Genevieve.

Before, during, and after the Civil War, African Americans took many paths to emancipation: some purchased their freedom or received it from their masters, others simply ran away and created lives for themselves and their children in towns like Ste. Genevieve. Like other residents of the community, they cared for their elders, worked the land, practiced their trades, received the sacraments of the church, took their cases to the local

---

50. U.S. Bureau of the Census, *Tenth Census: 1880*, NARA microfilm, T9, reel #715; Ste. Genevieve Catholic Church, Parish Center, Baptisms and Marriage records, 1760–1860.

courts, and remained united as families, despite the dehumanizing policies of local, state, and national governments. Many black men fought for their own liberation by joining the Union army. For most African Americans, however, there were no glorious battles, only day-to-day struggles for economic survival, justice, and human dignity.

The life stories of Elizabeth D'Atchurut, Elizabeth Shannon, Paul Vallé, Pelagie Amoureux, and Missouri's other black residents demonstrate the truth of at least one of Tocqueville's observations: of all the factors necessary to create a democracy—circumstances, laws, and the customs of the people—the third one far outweighs the first two. For people of African descent, circumstances created an intolerable burden and laws supported a system of oppression. But the people endured and transcended these hardships, advancing by slow and labored steps toward the ideals of equality and freedom.

There is no foolproof formula for democracy. Those who are looking for it will not find it in the soil, the resources, the demographics, or the economic profile of the country. Despite the great importance of the law, they will not find it in the law books. They will find it where they find the people: in courtrooms and on juries; in the workplace and in the home; and in schools, churches, sick rooms, death beds, taverns, ballrooms, and the streets.

PART THREE

CUSTOMS OF THE PEOPLE

CHAPTER NINE

Work and Family in Ste. Genevieve

And, as Poor Richard likewise observes, He that hath a trade hath an estate, and he that hath a calling, hath an office of profit and honor; but then the trade must be worked at, and the calling well followed, or neither the estate nor the office will enable us to pay our taxes. If we are industrious, we shall never starve; for, as Poor Richard says, At the working man's house hunger looks in but does not enter.

Benjamin Franklin, "The Way to Wealth," 1757,
in *Benjamin Franklin: Writings*

ON HIS TOUR of America, Tocqueville noted that nearly every man, regardless of his wealth, worked at some occupation. This, he believed, resulted naturally from the spread of democracy and the lack of a landed aristocracy. Citizens of the new republic respected industry, not leisure, and according to Tocqueville, this took all the glory away from idleness. In America, he encountered wealthy young men, who had no financial need to work, but who nevertheless pursued a profession. Even those who preferred a leisurely life felt pressured by public opinion to find some employment.[1]

Observers of life in early Ste. Genevieve contrasted the indolence of the old French residents with the driving ambition of the American settlers. German immigration added a contingent of industrious craftsmen and tradesmen to the supposedly lazy Creole community. But these ethnic stereotypes add little to our understanding of the culture of Ste. Genevieve. Francois Vallé I came close to fitting the mold of the self-made man, and

1. Tocqueville, *Democracy in America,* 2:237.

American newcomers sometimes allied themselves with the old French aristocrats. John Scott, for example, made his living defending these aristocrats in court. French-born women, such as Marie LaPorte, could drive as hard a bargain as the shrewdest American businessman. Michel Badeau and his racially mixed family made a name for themselves as carpenters and joined in the economic prosperity of the Americanizing town.

Landed families could build and retain their wealth in America, but they could not depend on their good names and connections alone. Pierre and Domitille Delassus came to the United States with grand visions but failed to thrive in the backwoods environment of New Bourbon. The Vallé family adapted to the new world order and triumphed. The contrasting stories of the Delassus and Vallé families illustrate Tocqueville's insight that the American-born sons of these families had to join the ranks of doctors, lawyers, merchants, bankers, prospectors, and others who scrambled for wealth and position.

Despite this fact of life in the republic, class divisions remained obvious in Ste. Genevieve, and class often corresponded to ethnicity. Historian Barbara Sanders observed that throughout the nineteenth century descendants of the town's early French settlers formed an elite group of wealthy farmers and entrepreneurs.[2] Eloy S. LeCompte, for example, established a flour mill that remained the largest such operation in Ste. Genevieve from 1856 through the remainder of the nineteenth century.[3] French surnames attached themselves to a host of enterprises, including the Vallé lead mines, the Menard and Valle mercantile business, the Bolduc trading establishments, the Bogy copper mines, and the Rozier stores and banks.

Some Anglo-Americans found their way into this elite group, often through marriage. As previously mentioned, three of Ichabod Sargent's daughters married into prominent French families. At a later period, another ambitious young American named O. D. Harris made an advantageous union that connected him to the prominent Janis and Rozier families. Harris's career would ultimately end in ruin and disgrace, but his compli-

2. Sanders, "Germans of Ste. Genevieve," 9–10.
3. *Goodspeed's History of Southeast Missouri,* 410.

cated story demonstrates that in nineteenth-century Ste. Genevieve, business connections and family connections were often one and the same.

The Janis-Rozier-Harris saga began with the Louisiana Purchase. Recognizing new opportunities with the influx of Anglo-Americans, Francois Janis opened an inn in a spacious vertical log building on the road between Ste. Genevieve and New Bourbon (St. Mary's Road). The Green Tree Tavern had large stone fireplaces, spacious rooms under a roof supported by heavy Norman trusses, and a long gallery overlooking the Gabouri Creek.[4] In 1806, the English traveler Thomas Ashe spent some time in Ste. Genevieve and remembered staying at Janis's inn. On the road into town, Ashe heard the church bells ringing. Hurrying toward the sound, just before sunset, he "put up at an inn which had strong indications of comfort. I was by no means disappointed; the landlord, a lively Frenchman, looked after my horses and his wife made me a cup of coffee with as much perfection as ever I drank at the *Palais* Royale or at the food of Point Neuf."[5] This Frenchman was Francois Janis.

The Rozier family established itself in Ste. Genevieve during this early territorial period. As mentioned in chapter 3, Ferdinand Rozier came to America with John James Aududon, settling first in Philadelphia, then in Kentucky, and finally in Ste. Genevieve. Audubon left the community, but Rozier stayed, engaged in business, married, and raised a family. In 1820, the year Missouri became a state, his son Firmin was born.[6]

Firmin Rozier, known in his later years as "the General," left his mark on Ste. Genevieve. He completed his education St. Mary's College in Perry County, Missouri. As a young man, he found a job as a clerk on the steamboat *Vandalia,* which traveled up and down river between St. Louis and New Orleans. In 1841, he abandoned his life on the river and opened a business in St. Louis. A financial crisis forced him to seek another occupation, and he decided on the law. He went to Bardstown, Kentucky,

---

4. At the end of the twentieth century, Hilliard Goldman purchased this property, and architect Jack Luer supervised a very accurate restoration of the building to its eighteenth century appearance.

5. Thomas Ashe, *Travels in America Performed in 1806,* 288.

6. Rozier, *History of the Early Settlement of the Mississippi Valley,* 5, 286–90.

and Transylvania Law School in Lexington, Kentucky, to complete his education. In the 1840s, he joined the South Missouri Guards and set out to accompany John C. Fremont on an expedition to California. The company of 115 men, handpicked by Thomas Hart Benton, made it as far west as Fort Leavenworth, Kansas, before winter weather prevented them from crossing the Great Plains. After being mustered out of that company, Firmin joined the militia of Southeast Missouri. During four years of service, he attained the rank of major general.[7]

In the 1850s, after an unsuccessful campaign for the United States Congress, Rozier returned to Ste. Genevieve, where he entered the banking business and served as mayor. By 1858 he became president of the Ste. Genevieve branch of Merchant's National Bank of St. Louis. Within a few years, he phased out this bank and established the Ste. Genevieve Savings Association. In 1872, Rozier was elected to serve in the Missouri Senate.[8] His son, also named Firmin, took over some of his duties at the bank. It was this younger Firmin Rozier who gave the alarm during the robbery in 1873. At the time of the incident, O. D. Harris was the bank's cashier.

O. D. Harris, an Anglo-American, had personal as well as business connections with the Rozier and Janis families. The son of Oliver and Mary Dudley Harris, he was born on June 23, 1840, in St. Louis, Missouri. When he was fifteen years old, he moved with his parents to Ste. Genevieve. From 1856 to 1862, he worked as a bookkeeper at the Ste. Genevieve branch of Merchant's National Bank of St. Louis. In 1863, he married Louise Isabella Janis, a cousin of Firmin Rozier's wife, Mary. Witnesses to the ceremony at the home of Felix Janis were the senior Firmin A. Rozier and O. D.'s father, Oliver Harris.[9] O. D. and Louise had four children.

In the 1860s, Harris tried to capitalize on the discovery of copper deposits south of Ste. Genevieve. A German farmer named Simon Grass found pieces of a green-colored mineral near his farm and showed it around in various taverns in Ste. Genevieve. Several years later, Harris sent a piece

7. Ibid., 5–6.
8. Ibid.
9. Thanks are due to Leslie Dingman for primary research on O. D. Harris; Deeds and Marriage Records, Recorder's office, Ste. Genevieve County Courthouse, book A, 163.

of the ore to a geologist in St. Louis. Scientific analysis revealed that the specimen contained 17.75 percent metallic copper. In 1868, Harris directed explorations on Grass's property, but nothing developed from them immediately. Four years later, Harris and the Roziers obtained a twenty-five year lease on the property, offering Grass a 10 percent royalty. During the first few years of the operation, the Chicago contractor they hired to run the business failed to turn a profit. After 1876, Harris ran the enterprise under the name of the Cornwell Copper Mines.[10]

Harris had a competitor in the mining business, which remained risky for everyone. Leon Jokerst, a German American businessman, discovered another deposit of copper ore about four miles north of the Cornwell operation. In partnership with John L. Bogy and Leon Bogy, Jokerst opened the Swansea Copper Mines and extracted a large amount of ore that contained 20 to 27 percent metallic copper. Both the Cornwell and the Swansea mining operations depended on the labor of independent contractors, working under the supervision of a mine boss. The miners received one cent per pound of ore, regardless of the percentage of metal it contained. This system provided no incentive for dressing the ore to separate valueless rock from valuable metallic copper.[11] In addition, problems with machinery and equipment plagued the operations, and neither of these mines lived up to the expectations of their owners.[12]

In 1874, while he struggled with the mining business, Harris opened a bank in partnership with his wife's cousin Jules Janis. Janis died in 1883, and within a year, under Harris's management, the bank failed. Angry depositors demanded that Harris turn over stock in the mines to compensate them for the losses he had caused them. As the true picture of Harris's financial misconduct emerged, others called for a criminal investigation into his business practices.[13]

Compounding his errors, Harris apparently misappropriated county funds for his own use. In 1884, he succeeded his deceased cousin Jules Janis

---

10. Stuart Weller and Stuart St. Clair, *Geology of Ste. Genevieve County, Missouri,* 331.
11. Ibid.
12. Yealy, *Sainte Genevieve,* 140; *Ste. Genevieve Fair Play,* April 5, 1877.
13. *Ste. Genevieve Fair Play,* March 28, 1885.

as treasurer of Ste. Genevieve County.[14] After the bank failure, the *Ste. Genevieve Herald* published accusations of official misconduct, which proved to have a basis in fact. In the spring of 1885, attempting to clear Harris's name, county official C. W. Hamm alleged that although Harris had at one time owed the county more than seventeen thousand dollars, he had repaid all but eight hundred dollars of that amount.[15] This assertion, however, proved to be false.

According to the official records from later that year, the county court found a deficit of $2266 in county revenues chargeable to Harris as treasurer. The court ordered him to replace the missing money by October 1, 1885. If he failed to do so, he faced criminal charges. The court referred the matter to Prosecuting Attorney Henry S. Shaw.[16] After the state of Missouri charged him with embezzling county funds, Harris resigned as treasurer. Sixteen years later, he died of a heart attack and was buried in Ste. Genevieve Catholic Cemetery.[17]

While the Harris' fortunes tumbled, the Roziers entered into a business partnership with the Jokerst family. In the 1840s, Joseph and Charles Jokerst emigrated from Baden to Ste. Genevieve. Joseph, a stonemason, helped to construct many important buildings in the community. Charles died a few years after coming to America, and his two sons, Francis L. and Charles C., went to work in their early teens. Francis eventually joined Henry L. Rozier to create the Rozier and Jokerst merchandising firm. Charles C. went to work as a tailor and fitter in their store.[18]

Most residents of Ste. Genevieve did not find their way into the elite group headed by the Vallé, Janis, Rozier, Bogy, and other French families. As late as 1880, well-connected Frenchmen still dominated local businesses, politics, and professions. They held powerful positions in local stores and banks. Five of the seven lawyers and two of the four physicians in town had French surnames. There was one Anglo-American lawyer. The other

14. November 14, 1884, and February 10, 1885, County Court Record, 1884–1886, County Clerk's office, Ste. Genevieve County Courthouse.

15. *Ste. Genevieve Fair Play,* April 10, 1885.

16. Saturday, August 15, 1885, County Court Record, 1884–1886, County Clerk's office, Ste. Genevieve County Courthouse.

17. *Ste. Genevieve Herald,* November 2, 1901.

18. Sanders, "Germans of Ste. Genevieve," 8–10.

lawyers and physicians were all members of the Hertich family, who had emigrated from Switzerland. Half of all the city and county officials listed in the 1880 census were French, and this included one woman, the postmistress, Augustine Menard. Her twenty-three-year-old son Saucier assisted her in this position.[19]

By 1880, German-born residents had established themselves in middle-class society as business owners, craftsmen, tradesmen, and clerks. Six out of seven local saloon keepers, all three brewers, all six butchers, both bakers, four out of six millers, and all three stonemasons in Ste. Genevieve had German surnames. Of those working as clerks in offices and stores, six were German, five were French, and one was Anglo-American. Five of eight coopers and four of eight blacksmiths also had German surnames; the others were French and Anglo-American. Other Germans held the skilled occupations of saddler, tinner, wagon maker, tailor, engineer, cigar maker, and gardener. One was a school teacher, and one owned a soda factory.[20]

Despite a few conspicuous men like O. D. Harris, Anglo-Americans remained underrepresented in the upper reaches of local society and even in the middle class. Only three out of nine merchants and one out of seven lawyers had English surnames. Both printers, the town's only dentist, and the only photographer, however, were Anglo-American. Of the local carpenters, seven were Anglo-American, six German, and five French. Other residents with Anglo-American surnames worked as teamsters, shoemakers, and tailors.[21]

African Americans had virtually no access to skilled jobs or professions. Of all those listed in the 1880 census, other than farm workers and housewives, eight were "day laborers," five were servants, two were "washerwomen," and one was a teamster. The end of slavery had not brought about a dramatic change in the way Ste. Genevieve's African American residents made their living from day to day.[22]

Women's occupational choices also were limited. Most were "keeping house" for their husbands or male relatives. Of those with other occupa-

19. U.S. Bureau of the Census, *Tenth Census: 1880,* NARA microfilm, T9, reel #715.
20. Ibid.
21. Ibid.
22. Ibid.

tions, the largest number (twenty) were servants. By contrast, only five males were listed in the 1880 census as servants. Ten women worked as dressmakers or seamstresses. Of these, six were Anglo-American, three were German, and one was French. Nine women were listed as nuns; these women were, presumably, also schoolteachers. Three, including two African Americans, were laundresses. Two were saloon keepers. One was a baker, and one was a midwife.[23]

Of all the occupations in Ste. Genevieve in 1880, the most uncertain and least secure was laborer. In all, thirty-eight men (but no women) fell into this vague category. Interestingly enough, fifteen of these men had French surnames. Nine were Anglo-Americans; six were Germans, and, as previously mentioned, eight were African American. For these individuals, jobs—any jobs—could be insecure and hard to find.[24]

Manufacturing did not play a significant role in the local economy in the nineteenth century. In January of 1875, the editor of the *Ste. Genevieve Fair Play* urged local businessmen to follow the lead of investors in other Missouri communities and establish a woolen mill or some other kind of factory. Bemoaning the lack of entrepreneurial spirit in "the people of this benighted place," he pointed out that a factory would "furnish employment to your young men, many of whom are now spending their time in idleness simply because they can find nothing to turn their hands to that would be useful and profitable."[25] According to the 1880 census, however, only 122 men and five children worked in manufacturing jobs in all of Ste. Genevieve County, which had a total population of more than ten thousand. No women were reported as having manufacturing jobs.[26]

Throughout the nineteenth century, Ste. Genevieve's entrepreneurs invested in mines and quarries to the north, south, and west of town. Prominent families, including the Vallés, the Roziers, and the Bisches profited from lead mines in Jefferson, Madison, and St. Francis counties northwest of Ste. Genevieve. When all danger from the Osage had been eliminated, the mines operated year-round. After the Civil War, the Vallés and others

23. Ibid.
24. Ibid.
25. *Ste. Genevieve Fair Play,* January 7, 1875.
26. U.S. Bureau of the Census, *Compendium of the Tenth Census, 1880,* pt. 2, 989.

shifted from slave to free labor. Black and white miners and their families worked and lived in company towns, such as the town of Valle Mines, and bought supplies at company stores. By the end of the nineteenth century, large corporations dug deeper mines with sophisticated machinery, eventually putting the old shallow mining operations out of business.[27]

The testimony of ex-slave John McGuire, recorded in the 1930s, provides insight into the lives of black workers in the lead mines. McGuire was born at Valle Mines. His mother, Sophie, was the slave of Henry Bisch, and his father, Philip, was owned by a man named John McGuire. Philip McGuire worked in the lead mines, while he and his wife brought up eleven children. After the Civil War, the family moved into a log cabin, and Philip continued to work in the mines. As John recalls, his family had a difficult time when they set up housekeeping as free people. His father's wages depended on how much lead and zinc he could dig. Some days he made two dollars; some days he made nothing. Philip McGuire's sons eventually left Valle Mines to find work elsewhere. John went to St. Louis, where he "worked in a boiler room, in the steel works and drove a team," hauling cinders, lumber, and dirt.[28]

In addition to lead and zinc, the rugged land west of the Mississippi River contained huge deposits of limestone and sandstone. "Quicklime," composed mainly of calcium carbonate, found in the bluffs north of Ste. Genevieve, proved useful in making mortar and cement, but this local industry did not take off until the late nineteenth century. By the 1870s, however, several large sandstone quarries operated about four miles south of town. Buff-colored blocks chiseled from huge gashes in the bluffs provided construction materials for the Eads Bridge and other prominent structures in St. Louis.[29]

During their brief heyday, the sandstone quarries reportedly employed hundreds of men. According to the state geologist, the Richardson quarry had four hundred to five hundred workers, and the Bogy quarry had

27. Materials on file at Missouri Mines State Historic Site, Park Hills, Missouri.

28. *Born in Slavery: Slave Narratives from the Federal Writers' Project, 1936–1938*, 238, Manuscripts and Prints and Photographs Division, Library of Congress.

29. E. R. Buckley and H. A. Buehler, *The Quarrying Industry of Missouri*, 2:194–97; Weller and St. Clair, *Geology of Ste. Genevieve County*, 330.

three hundred to four hundred names on its payroll. Most of these workers, apparently, did not live in Ste. Genevieve but in small hamlets and mining camps in the surrounding countryside. In the spring of 1876, the sandstone quarry workers went on strike, demanding higher pay. According to the *Fair Play,* the company was paying $1.75 per day, and the workers were demanding $2.50. The superintendent offered a temporary raise of twenty-five cents per day until he could consult with the company's officers. The newspaper did not report the outcome of the strike. The sandstone quarries ceased operations before the end of the century, after the Mississippi River meandered away from the bluff line, depriving the operators of cheap transportation.[30]

Farming remained the mainstay of the local economy, and old French families retained large landholdings. Despite the confusion about French and Spanish land claims and the legal delays in confirming land ownership, the founding families managed to keep their farms. A plat map of Ste. Genevieve in 1877 reveals that French families retained the largest tracts in town, in the outlying agricultural areas, and in the big field. Francois Vallé owned a tract of more than six hundred acres at the southwestern edge of town, two long lots of sixty arpents each in *le grand champ,* and other smaller parcels in town. His nearest neighbor, Francois Janis, owned a tract of about one hundred arpents, which bordered by Vallé's tract on the south and Louis Cotteux's tract on the north. The long lots in the big field belonged almost exclusively to families with French surnames, including Pratte, Misplait, Bogy, Aubuchon, Beauvais, Janis, Guibord, Caron, Dufour, Trudeau, Moreau, Thomure, and St. Gemme.[31]

Family solidarity was the key to acquiring and retaining agricultural land. The misfortunes of the Delassus family opened the way for Anglo-American and German American families to acquire large farms. Martin Sweek and Ichabod Sargent each owned a portion of the old Delassus property for a short period. The Kern family managed to hold onto this

30. Buckley and Buehler, *Quarrying Industry,* 2:196–97; Weller and St. Clair, *Geology of Ste. Genevieve County,* 330; *Ste. Genevieve Fair Play,* April 13, 1876.

31. Connected Plat of the Town of Ste. Genevieve, Situate in T. 38 N. R. 9 E., 5th P.M., drawn by Emile P. Vogt, July 1877, on file in the Recorder's office, Ste. Genevieve County Courthouse.

farm for more than a century by pooling its labor and maintaining its kinship ties through several generations.

Family connections sometimes transcended racial divisions. When Jean Ribault, a French widower, died at the age of eighty in 1849, his mixed-race family inherited a house on the road between Ste. Genevieve and New Bourbon (now St. Mary's Road) and a strip of land in the New Bourbon common field. Court records confirm that Ribault fathered a son by Clarisse, a former slave of the Janis family. Clarisse's son, John Ribault, appeared in court and received a free black license on October 11, 1851. According to the license, he was mulatto, twenty-four years old, five feet eight, and 154 pounds. Sixteen years later, he married Mary Jane Bahr.[32]

For many years, Clarisse Janis and John Ribault, his wife, Mary Jane, and their children occupied a vertical log house on St. Mary's Road and farmed a small tract in the common field. Clarisse passed away in 1886, John Ribault died in 1899, and Mary Jane passed away in 1926. The couple and all their children were buried in Valle Spring Cemetery with their names inscribed on the same marker: John Ribault, 1826–1899; Mary Jane, 1841–1926; Laura, 1873–1944; Anna, 1884–1949; Levi, 1878–1954; Louis, 1880–1968, and Alonzo, 1890–1969. The house remained standing in the twenty-first century.[33]

Another kind of dwelling sheltered those who had no property of their own and who could not support themselves. At an annual cost of more than five thousand dollars, the county maintained a poor house on a tract of land outside the city limits on the road to the ferry landing.[34] County officials appointed a woman named Catherine Brown to oversee this establishment, which had seven residents according to the 1880 census. One of them, Dick Woods, a white man, was sixty-nine years old; he was identified as a "servant" in the facility. Two others, Rufus Johnson and Ansehlm

32. Lucile Basler, *Pioneers of Old Ste. Genevieve,* 73; Manumissions and Free Black Licenses 1836–1857, County Clerk's office, Ste. Genevieve County Courthouse; Deeds and Marriage Records, Recorder's office, Ste. Genevieve County Courthouse, book A, 212.

33. Crystal Rose, a student in the summer field school, did primary research on the Ribault family. On July 1, 1999, Rose interviewed Marge Wilhauk, who shared the results of her own research on the family. See also Melburn Thurman's essay on this house in *Building a House in Eighteenth Century Ste. Genevieve.*

34. *Ste. Genevieve Herald,* June 3, 1882. The Poor House was also called the Poor Farm.

Byer, were elderly white men, seventy-five and seventy-four years of age.
A forty-year-old white woman, Sally Roth, lived there with her six-year-
old daughter, Josephine. The other resident was thirty-eight-year-old Paul
Vallé, the former slave, who had fought for the Union in the Civil War.[35]

Many counties throughout the new republic operated poor houses,
which were based on the old English model of the almshouse or the work-
house made famous (or notorious) in the fiction of Charles Dickens.
According to historian Ethel McClure, the early American colonists
transported the principles of the English Poor Law to the new continent.
Under this law, the parish or the county took responsibility for the relief
of misery by appointing an overseer of the poor. This official tried to put
able-bodied people to work and to provide direct relief, or aid, to those
unable to earn a living. Relief might take the form of "indoor" shelter in
an almshouse or "outdoor" relief to families in the community.[36]

Following this model, county officials in Ste. Genevieve provided direct
relief to destitute individuals and families. These unfortunate people,
many of whom were elderly or disabled, were stigmatized as "paupers."
County records for 1884 and 1885 included a list of charges for the aid of
"Paupers, not in Poor House":

> May 12, 1884, $5.00, for medicine for the Laplante family
> May 12, 1884, $10.00, for nursing for Lena L[illegible]
> May 12, 1884, $6.45, aid for the Laplante family
> May 14, 1884, $20.00, nursing for Wash Scott
> May 16, 1884, $9.00, nursing for Martha Hays
> August 11, 1884, $4.50, aid for the Laplante family
> August 12, 1884, $4.00, coffin for a "colored" man
> August 16, 1884, $9.00, nursing for Martha Hays
> November 10, 1884, $1.50, coffin for a pauper
> November 12, 1884, $4.00, coffin for a pauper
> November 12, 1884, $20.00, medicine for a pauper
> February 10, 1885, $2.00, aid given to a pauper
> February 10, 1885, $4.00, coffin for a pauper
> February 10, 1885, $20.00, aid for Cecile Govro

35. U.S. Bureau of the Census, *Tenth Census: 1880,* NARA microfilm, T9, reel #715.
36. Ethel McClure, *More than a Roof: The Development of Minnesota Poor Farms and Homes for the Aged,* 1–2.

February 10, 1885, $9.00, coffin and digging grave

March 9, 1885, $12.00, aid for Mr. and Mrs. Heil

April 11, 1885, $50.00, advanced to a man who was "insane"[37]

"Hunger looked in" the windows of many houses in Ste. Genevieve, and working men and women struggled to keep it from entering their doors. For example, in 1880, Sarah A. Morris, a fifty-eight-year-old widow, operated a dressmaking business in her home. Her two younger sisters, Elizabeth Labruyere, forty-nine, and Emily Kinnison, forty-four, lived in her household and assisted her in the business. Together, these middle-age sisters cared for Sarah's eight-year-old granddaughter, Daisy Morris.[38]

Many local families needed multiple breadwinners. Christian Baum, forty-four, a German-born shoemaker, headed a large household. His wife, Louisa, thirty-two, brought in some income as a dressmaker. His nineteen-year-old son Henry worked with his father in the shoe shop. Two of Henry's brothers, Anton, fifteen, and Charles, fourteen, hired out as farmhands. The household also included Christian's five younger children: Louise, twelve; Frank, ten; Annie, eight; May, five; Genevieve, three months; and his step-daughters, Louise and Lizzie Schneider, ages thirteen and eleven.[39]

Even in well-to-do families, sons added income to their parents' households. In 1880, Charles Hertich, a fifty-nine-year-old physician of Swiss descent, suffered from paralysis. His wife, Mary, fifty-six, kept house. Three sons still lived with them at home. The census listed no occupation for Villars, age twenty-eight; however, Bert, twenty-five, worked as a drug clerk and Augustus, twenty-two, was a lawyer. The Hertichs' two daughters, Clara and Blanche, ages nineteen and sixteen, also lived at home. In addition, the family had two servants, Mary Jane Orter, a thirty-year-old black woman, and her three-year-old son, George Orter.[40]

The Hertich family demonstrated the essential accuracy of Tocqueville's observation about Americans' work ethic. Sons of prominent fathers

37. May 16, 1885, County Court Record, 1884–1886, County Clerk's office, Ste. Genevieve County Courthouse.

38. U.S. Bureau of the Census, *Tenth Census: 1880*, NARA microfilm, T9, reel #715.

39. Ibid.

40. Ibid.

joined in the family business or engaged in professions of their own. Bert and Augustus Hertich worked to support their ailing father and his household. Their older brother Charles, thirty-two, lived next door with his wife, Sarah, twenty-five, and their one-year-old son, Vivian. The younger Charles Hertich followed in his father's footsteps and practiced medicine.[41]

Tocqueville did not give a complete picture of work and workers in the new republic. For instance, he did not broach the subject of women and work. Although their occupational choices were limited, women in Ste. Genevieve participated in the productive labor of the community as servants, housewives, dressmakers, and saloon keepers. Some women, such as dressmaker Sarah Morris, headed households; others added to the income of their families. Nine women had renounced traditional family life to live together in a convent and teach school.

Tocqueville exaggerated, of course, when he said that everybody worked. In the 1870s, the local newspaper took note of the fact that the town lacked manufacturing enterprises and that, as a result, many young men had no productive employment. Local records demonstrate that some families and individuals could not support themselves without governmental assistance. There were no federal or state programs to provide such aid. By the 1880s, the county formally recognized its duty to care for the indigent through direct relief or institutionalization.

For most people in the new republic, the keys to prosperity and survival were the strength and solidarity of their families. The wealthy Vallé family demonstrated this through several generations, clinging to large landholdings, developing wide-ranging enterprises, and attaching their family name to many landmarks. John Kern acquired land from the disassembled estate of an old French aristocrat, and his family held onto that land for more than a century. Jean Ribault provided land through his estate to his African American wife and their children. O. D. Harris launched his ill-starred career by marrying into the Rozier family. After Harris sank into personal disgrace, the Rozier family remained solid, formed new alliances, and continued to prosper.

41. Ibid.

People without illustrious names or advantageous connections also relied on their families. Christian Baum, a shoemaker, depended on the paid work of his wife and elder sons to provide for his large household of children and stepchildren. Sarah Morris and her sisters combined their labor to support themselves and Sarah's granddaughter. Even the sisters in the convent, having renounced traditional married life, lived and worked together as a family.

CHAPTER TEN

Home, Church, and School

Truth alone can make and keep us free; while adherence to falsehood is the enslavement of the mind. Let us cultivate our own minds and hearts that we may be worthy members of the Republic.

Felix Janis, speaking at Union Hall in Ste.
Genevieve, April 12, 1883

SOLID CITIZENS OF A democratic republic do not drop like ripe fruit from the liberty tree. They arrive as ignorant babies and receive their first crucial lessons about freedom in the home. But homes do not exist in a vacuum: the values taught in kitchens and in bedrooms reflect the ideals of the larger society, which are communicated through religious and educational institutions. Schools are an essential bulwark of participatory democracy, but schools, like homes, are enmeshed in an intricate network of social relationships that shape, and are shaped by, people's deeply held beliefs.

For most children growing up in Ste. Genevieve, home life conformed to a traditional patriarchal pattern. French law allowed women to inherit and claim their own property, but men still occupied the position of head of the household. English law supported inheritance through the male line, assuring that Anglo-American males would maintain their position as property owners, breadwinners, and authority figures. German American men also guided their families with a strong hand, although women participated actively in economic life as helpmates for their husbands. African American and racially blended families tended to follow the same pattern.

Despite this general truth, life on the frontier produced a significant number of families that did not fit the accepted mold. Short male life spans created numerous widows, who either quickly remarried or became heads of their own households. Marie LaPorte lost two husbands and had no biological children. She took charge of her own economic affairs and created her own family by adopting a son and acting as a benefactor for several godchildren. The Catholic Church supported this kind of family arrangement by recognizing the connection of adults other than the biological parents to the physical and spiritual protection of the child.

Ste. Genevieve differed from many American communities in that the population was overwhelmingly Roman Catholic. The parish church played a particularly active role in educating the young. Because of this, the secular public school system made slow and halting progress in the community during the nineteenth century. Throughout the history of Ste. Genevieve, church-based education played a dominant role in shaping citizens of the republic.

Formal educational institutions were sorely lacking in French colonial Ste. Genevieve. According to Ekberg, the vast majority of residents of the old town could neither read nor write. Even the town's most prominent residents, including Francois Vallé I, owned few or no books. In New Ste. Genevieve, as early as 1787 schoolmasters offered classes sporadically. Henry Brackenridge studied under one of these men in the 1790s, but this teacher's name remains unknown. Pierre Delassus tried to persuade the Spanish government to provide a stipend for a school teacher named Fremon de Lauriere, a French émigré who held classes in the town from 1795 to 1799, but the funds never materialized. Education in colonial Ste. Genevieve remained privately funded and unsystematic. Nevertheless, Ekberg concludes that literacy increased markedly by the time of the Louisiana Purchase.[1]

By teaching the catechism and preparing young people for confirmation, Catholic priests often acted as the only school teachers in the French colonial settlements. But their numbers dwindled after the French and Indian War. In 1763, the Ste. Genevieve community relied on the services of Father Sebastian Louis Meurin, an aging Jesuit, who was one of only two priests remaining in all of Upper Louisiana. Two years later, the death

1. Ekberg, *Colonial Ste. Genevieve*, 172–82.

of Father Luke Collet left Meurin as the only priest serving the west and east bank parishes, including Kaskaskia, Cahokia, and Prairie du Rocher. In 1768, a younger priest, Father Pierre Gibault, arrived in the region, but he also divided his time among parishes in Illinois and on the west bank, coming to Ste. Genevieve only to preside over baptisms and marriages and to visit the sick. By the fall of 1773, he had left the region.[2]

Ste. Genevieve's first actual parish priest, Monsignor Francis Hilaire de Genoveaux, had a brief and unhappy career in the community. When he arrived in 1773, he decided that he needed a servant and asked his parishioners to pay the cost of purchasing a slave. The heads of numerous local families complained about the situation, informing the Spanish authorities that Father Hilaire asked too much of them, considering that he seemed very lax in his duties. The Spanish governor covered the cost of a slave, and Father Hilaire remained in the community for another four years before he mysteriously disappeared in 1778.[3]

During the troubles of the 1780s, when the villagers moved their town to higher ground, Ste. Genevieve existed without a regular pastor. Father Paul de Saint Pierre, a Carmelite friar, ministered to the people during the year of the big waters in 1785, but he returned to his previous post at Cahokia the following year. In 1789, he returned to Ste. Genevieve, where he had already won the affection of the people. Father Paul was a German, whose name at birth was Paul von Heiligenstein. He had come to America during the Revolution as a chaplain to French soldiers. Authorities in the French church asked him to go to the western frontier.[4]

Local historian Francis Yealy credits Father Paul with establishing regular services, observing all the feasts and holidays, providing excellent religious instruction, and bringing stability and order to the religious life of the new town. In 1793, Father Paul persuaded local citizens to build a new church. The parishioners decided to disassemble the old log church in the abandoned village and rebuild it in the central plaza of New Ste. Genevieve.[5]

---

2. Mary Lucida Savage, *The Congregation of Saint Joseph of Carondelet,* 27–28; Yealy, *Sainte Genevieve,* 43–49.

3. Yealy, *Sainte Genevieve,* 54–55.

4. Ibid., 63–67.

5. Ibid.

At the time of the Louisiana Purchase, an Irish priest, Father James Maxwell, served as pastor of Ste. Genevieve and vicar general of Upper Louisiana. Maxwell's story is a strange one. Although he came from Dublin, he studied theology at the University of Salamanca in Spain. In 1794, the Spanish government sent him on a mission to America. The bishop of Louisiana appointed him to replace Father Paul, who was transferred to Iberville Parish. Maxwell arrived at his new parish in April 1796 and remained until his death in 1814. When the Spanish authorities appointed him to the post, they hoped he would convert the American newcomers to Catholicism.[6]

In 1808, Maxwell established the Ste. Genevieve Academy, a Catholic school for boys, with the support of prominent local citizens. The academy's board of trustees included Otto Schrader, Jean-Baptiste Vallé, John Scott, William Shannon, and Henry Dodge; Maxwell served as the board's president. William Shannon took charge of erecting an impressive stone building on a hilltop northwest of the town limits. Shannon owned the building, but he leased it to the trustees, who operated the school under a charter from the governor of the Louisiana Territory. In 1810, the academy opened with Daniel Barry as instructor; in 1812 Mann Butler replaced him. Teachers came and went, and the school suffered financial difficulties, closing and reopening several times in its history.[7]

In 1808, an American traveler named Christian Schultz recorded his impressions of religious life in Ste. Genevieve. At that time, he noted, the French inhabitants held a low opinion of the Americans' devotion to religion. Schultz observed, however, that several Frenchman overcame their prejudices and freely associated with the impious Americans. He remarked that in general the male population attended mass less frequently than their female relatives did. Schultz himself "frequently attended at their low mass, when I was the only male person present except the priest and bell-ringer."[8]

6. John Rothensteiner, *History of the Archdiocese of St. Louis,* 1:198–99.

7. *Goodspeed's History of Southeast Missouri,* 408; Rothensteiner, *History of the Archdiocese,* 1:205.

8. Christian Schultz, *Travels on an Inland Voyage through the States of New-York, Pennsylvania, Virginia, Ohio, Kentucky, and Tennessee, and through the Territories of Indiana, Louisiana, Mississippi, and New-Orleans, performed in the years 1807 and 1808,* 2:67–68.

Despite some laxity, Schultz described a community with a strong and somewhat naïve faith in their church and their priest. While he was in Ste. Genevieve, local residents told him about an incident that had occurred a few years before his arrival. The flooded Mississippi threatened to overflow the big field and destroy the crops. Local inhabitants convinced the priest (presumably Father Maxwell) to form a procession and drive back the waters. As the waters crested, the chapel bell rang. Men, women, and children of all ages answered the call, solemnly chanting Pater Nosters and Ave Marias. As they marched toward the edge of the Gabouri Creek, where the priest forbade the water to rise any higher, the flood subsided.[9]

Sundays, according to Schultz, provided a day of rest and amusement rather than worship for many local residents. The high mass on Sunday morning lasted only half an hour. For the rest of the day, people went about their business or enjoyed themselves in the billiard parlors, which were always open on Sunday. In times of need, however, the residents came together and demonstrated their faith. Schultz observed numerous processions, led by Father Maxwell in pontifical robes, on behalf of the ill and the dying. When the bells rang, every local Catholic, white or black, male or female, ran to join in these pageants to pray for those in need.[10]

Although Father Maxwell was active in the community, he was not always attentive to his duties. During his tenure, he devoted a great deal of energy to his dream of creating a haven for Irish Catholics on a wild tract of land in the Ozarks. On October 15, 1799, he petitioned Lieutenant Governor Charles Delassus for a huge grant of sixteen square leagues (more than 150 square miles) of land on the Black River. Early in November, Delassus approved the grant for a settlement of immigrants who would be faithful to the Spanish crown. Maxwell promised to build a church on the tract, which was surrounded by miles of rugged hills and separated from Ste. Genevieve by eighty-six miles of ridges, valleys, and swift-flowing rivers.[11]

Maxwell never gave up on his plan, even when Irish immigrants failed to arrive. After the Louisiana Purchase, he petitioned the board of land com-

9. Ibid., 2:63–64.
10. Ibid., 2:62–65.
11. Schroeder, *Opening the Ozarks,* 351–56.

missioners to confirm his claim. The commissioners rejected it twice, on June 28, 1806 and May 29, 1812, on the grounds that the tract exceeded the size authorized by Spanish policy and that the terms of the grant, specifying the relocation of Catholics from Ireland, had not been met. After Maxwell's sudden death, his nephews and heirs tried again to validate the claim, but they suffered another rejection in 1833. In the meantime, American settlers took up residence on the Maxwell grant.[12]

Maxwell's obsession with the Ozarks may have angered some of his parishioners. Visitors to Ste. Genevieve in the early nineteenth century noted the priest's absence. Brackenridge accused him of paying more attention to his hunting dogs and guns than to his priestly offices. It seems likely that Maxwell visited his land grant often and probably took along his dog and his gun. In 1810, Father Stephen Badin, the region's first American-born priest, wrote to the archbishop to petition for the removal of the Irish priest from his parish. Father Maxwell defended himself vigorously, pointing out that Father Badin had an interest in obtaining the post in Ste. Genevieve. Amid the controversy, Maxwell continued in the post until he died on May 28, 1814, at the age of seventy-two after falling from his horse.[13]

Maxwell's troubled career and sudden death left a void in the community. There was no parish priest in Ste. Genevieve for more than a year. In the summer of 1814, Bishop Benedict Joseph Flaget visited parishes in the Mississippi River valley. On August 21, he made his first appearance in Ste. Genevieve, where a large crowd turned out to honor him. According to the official history of the Archdiocese of St. Louis, he astonished the dance-loving citizenry by preaching against balls, and he administered the rights of confirmation to 361 individuals.[14]

After a trip on horseback to other parishes on the west bank, Bishop Flaget returned to Ste. Genevieve. On this second visit near the end of October, he preached to a congregation of nearly five hundred black people from Ste. Genevieve and the surrounding towns. John Rothensteiner, a church historian, has written that Flaget became indignant when he learned

12. Ibid., 356–58.
13. Rothensteiner, *History of the Archdiocese,* 1:206–9.
14. Ibid., 1:196–97.

that legal marriage was uncommon among slaves. He threatened slave owners with excommunication if they did not change this situation.[15]

After Flaget's visits, Henri Pratte, Missouri's first homegrown priest, assumed the post left vacant by Maxwell. Born in Ste. Genevieve in 1788, Pratte was the son of Jean-Baptiste Sylvestre du Pratte and his wife, Therese Billeron. Henri's sister Odile would later marry Felix Vallé. As a boy, Henri Pratte attended the local grammar school headed by Francis Moro. In 1803, his parents sent him to the Sulpician Seminary in Montreal, where he was ordained as a priest in 1815. As a newly ordained priest, Pratte offered to come back to his hometown.[16]

In 1817, Louis William Valentin Du Bourg, the bishop of Louisiana, made grand appearances in St. Louis and Ste. Genevieve. Pratte went to St. Louis to assist in the solemnities. In the meantime, Father Felix DeAndreis, acting as local pastor, welcomed the bishop and his entourage to Ste. Genevieve on New Year's Eve. According to church history, Father DeAndreis and forty other local men on horseback went to the landing with a carriage to escort the dignitaries back to town. The visitors went first to the rectory, where they donned vestments, and then led a procession, accompanied by bells, to the church. On New Year's Day 1818, the bishop celebrated a pontifical high mass. This was the first time that such a mass was held in Ste. Genevieve.[17]

Pratte's tenure as priest, while filled with promise, was tragically brief. According to Rothensteiner, Ste. Genevieve "owes to Father Pratte the renewal of its piety and the blessing of Christian education to the children; to teach the Catechism was his delight."[18] Under his supervision, workmen enlarged the old log church, plastered the walls, and installed a new roof and a new floor. With his guidance, the academy reopened in 1818, under the direction of the Christian Brothers. Brother Antonin, Brother Aubin, and Brother Fulgence taught classes for three years in the stone building that had been erected in 1808. But these men left the community after Pratte's untimely death in 1822.

15. Ibid.
16. Yealy, *Sainte Genevieve*, 100–101.
17. Rothensteiner, *History of the Archdiocese*, 1:265.
18. Ibid., 1:362.

In the summer of 1822, Joseph Rosati, the future bishop of St. Louis, invited Pratte to assist in celebrating the feast of St. Vincent. Pratte sent a letter of refusal, saying that too many people in Ste. Genevieve and Kaskaskia were ill and in need of his services. This may have been the last letter he ever wrote.[19] Early in August, he came down with yellow fever. After suffering for three weeks, he died on September 1, 1822. Rosati conducted the funeral services, which drew a large crowd from Ste. Genevieve and the surrounding countryside. Pratte was buried under the sanctuary of the church.[20]

His successor, Francis Xavier Dahmen, arrived in Ste. Genevieve before the end of the month. A native of Germany, Dahmen was fluent in three languages—German, French, and English. When he was a young man, his homeland west of the Rhine River came under French dominion. He served in Napoleon's army as a cavalry soldier and took part in several battles. After he was discharged, he studied for the priesthood in Rome. Bishop Du Bourg encouraged him to come to America. He made his final vows in 1818 at the Congregation of the Mission at Perryville, a Vincentian seminary. After his ordination in St. Louis, he served as pastor of Vincennes and temporary pastor at Florissant before coming to Ste. Genevieve.[21]

Dahmen's erect military bearing, fluency in languages, gruff good humor, and kindliness made him a popular and effective spiritual leader. According to Rothensteiner, the priest "was not a grave man of learning, but alert in mind and direct in rugged speech, yet a very loveable character withal."[22] When German Catholics settled in Ste. Genevieve in the 1830s, they found a welcoming father figure who spoke their language and understood their customs. Church announcements made it clear that he offered sermons in three languages: French, German, and "sometimes English."

He supported efforts to build a stronger community. As Rothensteiner wrote, "When the citizens of Ste. Genevieve wished to form a Literary Society, Father Dahmen was with them heart and soul."[23] Beginning in

19. Ibid., 1:366.
20. Ibid., 1:361–62, 366; Yealy, *Sainte Genevieve*, 104, 128.
21. Yealy, *Sainte Genevieve*, 109–10; Rothensteiner, *History of the Archdiocese*, 1:367–68.
22. Ibid., 2:556–57.
23. Ibid., 1:368–69.

Old stone church, shown here in the 1870s, was constructed in the 1830s in Ste. Gene-vieve's center square. Photograph courtesy of the Missouri Historical Society, St. Louis.

Ste. Genevieve in 1832. The stone church is under construction. The old log church has been moved to an adjacent lot. To the right of the church is the brick courthouse with its cupola. This historically accurate diorama shows old French vertical log houses interspersed with brick and stone buildings of the American period. Diorama created by Lewis Pruneau; researched by Jim Baker. Photograph courtesy of Bill Naeger.

1831 he supervised the construction of a new stone church on the site of the original log building, which seems to have been moved to an adjacent lot. Bishop Rosati consecrated the new church on November 12, 1837, with Father Dahmen and twenty other priests, mostly Vincentians, in attendance. At the time of the dedication, witnesses remembered that the old log church was still standing.[24]

Dahmen played an important role in establishing a stable educational system in Ste. Genevieve. In the spring of 1837 he brought Mother Agnes Hart and five Sisters of Loretto to town to open a convent school on land purchased from Catherine Bolduc. Among the sisters was Odile Delassus Pratte Vallé, the daughter of Camille and granddaughter of Pierre Delassus. After inheriting a portion of her father's estate, Odile married Sylvester Pratte, a fur trader, who died of mountain fever. Her second husband, Louis Vallé, died young after being bitten by a mad dog. That same year, Odile also lost her infant son. In 1835, she became a novice in the convent of the Sisters of Loretto in Perryville. Two years later, she used her personal wealth to purchase two lots. The lots contained one brick and one frame building, and these buildings were used for the convent school. In 1837, the school had twelve boarders and forty-five day students.[25]

French, German, and Anglo-American residents of Ste. Genevieve struggled to maintain their educational institutions after Father Dahmen left the parish in 1840 to teach at the seminary in Perryville.[26] In 1847, eighty residents of Ste. Genevieve pledged money for labor and materials to repair the old stone academy on the hill. One year later, Firmin Rozier acquired the property and reorganized the academy with forty students. After securing a new charter, Rozier constructed a two-story addition on the building and reopened the school in 1854. According to the 1861 prospectus, Rozier was the academy's principal and the school had four instructors. Within one year, the upheaval of the Civil War forced the school to close.

---

24. Yealy, *Sainte Genevieve,* 111.

25. Ibid., 128–30: Rothensteiner, *History of the Archdiocese,* 1:370; Women's Club of Ste. Genevieve, "Historical Highlights of Ste. Genevieve, 1735–1972."

26. According to Rothensteiner, Dahmen's successors, Hyppolite Gandolfo, Father St. Cyr, and Philip Lawrence Hendrickx, were not very distinguished or effective (*History of the Archdiocese,* 1:370 and 2:70).

During this period, its financial difficulties worsened. The tuition was too high for most residents. After 1861, the academy was dissolved, but Rozier kept the property.[27]

By the late 1850s, the Sisters of Loretto withdrew from the convent school. Father J. M. St. Cyr, the parish priest, appealed to Reverend Mother St. John Facemaz of the Sisters of St. Joseph of Carondelet, Missouri, to send teachers to replace them. On August 28, 1858, Sisters Gonzaga Grand, Bridget Burke, Theodora McCormack, Clemence Motschman, Dorothea Rufine, and Dosithea Grand left Carondelet and reached Ste. Genevieve on the same day.

Their chronicler, Sister Mary Lucida Savage, describes what they saw when they arrived: "From the landing at the foot of the village's main street, they looked upon an attractive rural scene. Grouped about the old stone church as a center were the low white houses with gabled roofs, broad verandas, and outside chimneys built from the ground. The gardens were bright with late summer flowers, and elm and pecan trees shaded the gravel roads." The large frame convent occupied a plot of several acres. Near this property stood the house of Felix and Odile Vallé, who were financial benefactors of the Catholic school.[28]

The superior, Sister Gonzaga, dignified and reserved, apparently had a talent for organization. According to Savage, she "quickly endeared herself to the kindly villagers." She returned to the Mother House in Carondelet in 1860 but served another two years at the school in Ste. Genevieve in 1877–1878. Between 1858 and 1885, the Academy of St. Francis de Sales had eight different mother superiors, including Mother Gonzaga Grand, Mother Cecilia Rating, Mother Gabriel Corbett, Mother Blanche Fogarty, Mother Lidwina Jarre, Mother Leonie Martin, Mother Mary Assumption Vincent, and Mother Irene Facemaz.[29] Under their administration, the school drew local students from Ste. Genevieve and boarders from surrounding communities.

27. Yealy, *Sainte Genevieve,* 128.

28. Savage, *Congregation of St. Joseph,* 115–16.

29. Ibid., 116; List on file in the archives of the Sisters of St. Joseph of Carondelet, St. Louis Province Motherhouse, Cardondelet, Missouri.

The convent school's 1860 prospectus described an impressive curriculum that included instruction in the "English, French, and German languages (taught by the ladies of each nation), Reading, Writing, Arithmetic, Book-keeping, Grammar, Sacred and Profane History," and a variety of other subjects. For boarding students, the cost was substantial: one hundred dollars for board and tuition per year (September through June). Tuition for day students was eighteen dollars per year for lower level students and twenty-four dollars for the higher levels. "Half boarders," who took meals at the school, paid one dollar per week. There were additional charges for painting, piano, guitar, and accordion lessons and for laundry and bedding. Thursday was visiting day for parents and other relatives. Students wore pink and white uniforms in summer, red and black in winter, with white or green bonnets. Catholic and non-Catholic girls could attend classes, but everyone had to attend religious exercises.[30]

The convent school was still functioning in 1865, when the new parish priest, Francis Xavier Weiss, found the church building and the priest's residence in disrepair. Weiss went to work immediately, reaching out to the German Catholics in town and the surrounding countryside. In 1867, he supervised the construction of a substantial stone house. Weiss occupied the upper story, and the lower story accommodated a school for boys. By 1880, with generous donations from the Vallés and others, Weiss was able to build an imposing brick church with a soaring spire.[31]

While Father Weiss revived the local church, the Sisters of St. Joseph expanded parochial education for local children. During the Civil War, the school had lost many of its boarders, but the sisters continued to offer classes for day students. In 1867 the order built a new brick school building,[32] and in 1871 it erected a new convent. Three years later, the church issued a writ to the order to administer, in perpetuity, two parochial schools: one for girls and one for boys under the age of twelve in the city and county of Ste. Genevieve. This document indicated that Felix Vallé provided an endowment of seventy-five hundred dollars for

30. The prospectus appeared in the *Ste. Genevieve Fair Play,* August 31, 1860.
31. Rothensteiner, *History of the Archdiocese,* 2:70–72.
32. Dorothy Meirink, "From Carondelet down the Road a Piece to Ste. Genevieve," 24.

the repair of the girls' school and furnishing everything necessary for the boys' school.[33]

A newspaper account of the girls' commencement exercises at the convent school in June 1877 offers a glimpse of local attitudes toward education, religion, gender, and race. The writer described the occasion as "a very agreeable entertainment," consisting of "addresses, recitations, instrumental and vocal music and a drama, founded upon the efforts of the Catholic Church to Christianize the Chinese." Clearly, the school provided religious, not secular, education. Even the "Observer" who wrote the article had misgivings about "the propriety of religious dramas," not because they undermined education, but because they seemed "to inspire a flippant, careless familiarity with sacred subjects."[34] Despite his reservations, the "Observer" gave a detailed account of the drama and its presenters.

The plot centered on a Chinese orphan rescued by her mother from an "opium-eating" father. The mother then handed the girl over to a group of nuns. In telling the story, the reporter betrayed a deep-seated prejudice against Chinese society, which was apparently also expressed in the play, when he wrote of the need to "preserve from the wholesale slaughter, then prevalent in that country, the poor little almond-eyed waifs, who were so unfortunate as to have been born gal babies instead of incipient statesmen and fire-cracker manufacturers." The rudiments of a feminist message became embedded in a pervasive contempt for people of color.

In terms of performances, the writer spoke glowingly of Miss Blanch Ziegler, who played the reverend mother of the Hong Kong Orphan Asylum, and Miss Clara Hertich, who played Sister Margaret and "looked the sister of charity to perfection." But in his view the stand-out in the cast was Gussie Menard, portraying an "impulsive, benevolent Irish woman," who stowed away on a ship, landed in Hong Kong, and evidently helped restore the orphan to her natural mother. In one brief drama, the students

33. A copy of this handwritten document, or writ, is on file in the archives of the Sisters of St. Joseph of Carondelet.

34. *Ste. Genevieve Fair Play,* June 28, 1877.

at the academy seemed to affirm the values of piety, pluck, and mother-hood, while figuratively shouldering the "white man's burden."[35]

The students also demonstrated their accomplishments in vocal and instrumental music, poetry, and rhetoric. Sallie Carlisle delivered, in verse, an address to the graduates, prompting the reporter to comment that she was "one of the lights of our beauties," who possessed "talent that only needs appreciation and a judicious guidance to develop into something more than a worker of ottomans or chenilles." Again, the writer managed to undercut a feminist affirmation with a patronizing attitude. Father Weiss presented gold medals to outstanding scholars, giving masculine approval to the education of young ladies. The reporter praised the work of the Sisters of St. Joseph, but clearly their efforts occurred within a framework of a patriarchal church.[36]

While the Catholic schools persevered, secular education made a halt-ing start in the community. Joseph Hertich opened a school called the Asylum in rural Ste. Genevieve County in the 1820s. Hertich was born in Switzerland in 1775 and attended school in Europe. There he learned the pedagogical methods of Pestalozzi and became a teacher. He immigrated to the United States in 1796 and opened a mercantile business in Ste. Genevieve around 1810. In 1816, he married Mercalite Villars, daughter of Louis and Marie Vallé Villars, and fathered seven children. He owned a piece of land near the Little Saline about ten miles southwest of town, where he opened his school for boys.[37]

Following the doctrines of Pestalozzi, Hertich emphasized applied rather than abstract knowledge. His classes attempted to prepare young men to function in the real world and emphasized moral and religious develop-ment. In 1830, Missouri's governor appointed Hertich as one of three commissioners to design a system of primary school instruction for the state, but the state never put his ideas into practice. Hertich retired from

---

35. Ibid.
36. Ibid.
37. Yealy, *Sainte Genevieve*, 128; *Goodspeed's History of Southeast Missouri*, 408; and marriage records located at the Ste. Genevieve Catholic Church, Parish Center. Thanks are due to Brandon Kuehn and David Kreidler for primary research on Joseph Hertich.

teaching around 1830, and he died in 1852. One of his students, Lewis V. Bogy, represented Missouri in the United States Senate from 1874 to 1877. Two other students, George W. Jones and Augustus Dodge, eventually became U.S. senators from Iowa. Hertich's daughter Clara Ann married Augustus Dodge.[38]

Other efforts to provide education in Ste. Genevieve faltered in the years before the Civil War. From 1824 to 1842, schoolmasters offered classes in John Price's brick house at Third and Market streets. Beginning in 1846, citizens made a concerted effort to establish a system of schools. Eloy S. LeCompte, Felix Vallé, Francis C. Rozier, Eugene Guibourd, and Ichabod Sargent served on the first board of directors of the common schools. Despite their good intentions, no school was built for more than ten years. In the 1850s, Matthew Doyle and A. H. Parker conducted classes on the site of the old fort on the South Gabouri.[39]

Finally, in 1860, the citizens of Ste. Genevieve built a public school on Washington Street. The first teachers were John Bodkin, Elvira Adams, and Amanda Chadwell. In 1872, the school board acquired property that had belonged to John Scott next door to the original convent school of the Sisters of Loretto. On this property they erected a two-story school building with a basement at a cost of six thousand dollars. The principal was Joseph Ernst, and the first teachers were Felix Janis and his wife. Until 1911, the public schools offered only primary education. Students had to go to private academies for high school classes. The schools were segregated. During Reconstruction, the old school building on Washington Street became Lincoln School, a segregated facility, for African American children.[40]

The public schools had trouble attracting students. On September 24, 1874, after the school year had begun, Felix Janis and John Bodkin, published this plea,

> To the Parents and Guardians of Ste. Genevieve. Public schools of this
> city are now in operation, but the number in attendance, though greater

38. Yealy, *Sainte Genevieve*, 129; Floyd C. Shoemaker, *Missouri and Missourians: Land of Contrasts and People of Achievement*, 1:322, 333 and 2:625.

39. *Goodspeed's History of Southeast Missouri*, 409; Yealy, *Sainte Genevieve*, 129.

40. *Goodspeed's History of Southeast Missouri*, 409; Yealy, *Sainte Genevieve*, 129.

than usual, is not what it should be. Did parents and guardians consider the importance to all concerned of having all the pupils take an even start, we presume they would be more punctual in sending them on the first day. We respectfully request those who intend to patronize the Public schools of this city the present year, to send as soon as possible, especially young or backward children, as every new pupil after the first day or two will start a whole class.[41]

In 1880, according to an official report submitted by Ernst, less than thirty percent of eligible young people attended the public schools. From a population of 517 white children between the ages of six and twenty, only 137 (23 percent) were enrolled in public school. More than half of the black children (39 out of 71) were enrolled in the "colored" school. On average, though, the students enrolled in the public schools actually attended less than half the time (93 out of 200 school days).[42] These were dismal statistics, somewhat mitigated by the fact that many of the white children attended the parochial school.

Institutions, such as public schools, do not spring full-blown from abstract ideals or words or the exercise of force or even the will of the majority. Viable institutions develop gradually from preexisting human relationships, shared traditions, and deeply felt beliefs. Descendants of Ste. Genevieve's old French families supported education under the American regime. Felix Janis, the eloquent champion of republican values, became a teacher and vigorously recruited students to the public schools. But the oldest and most prominent of the original French families, the Vallés, threw their support behind Catholic education. The parochial schools were able to thrive partly because of the Vallés' patronage and partly because of their intimate connection with the parish church, which had a long history in the community and physically embodied the people's common faith.

41. *Ste. Genevieve Fair Play,* September 24, 1874.
42. Public Schools of the State of Missouri, *Thirty-first Report of the Public Schools of the State of Missouri,* 144–45.

CHAPTER ELEVEN

Life, Death, and Remembrance

To our most beloved boy
February 28, 1833
Having visited us in our house
October 11, 1844
He returned.

Translation of the Latin inscription on the grave marker of young
John Ichabod Sargent in Memorial Cemetery, Ste. Genevieve

IN 1844, ICHABOD and Anstes Sargent lost their only son; he was
only eleven years old. Details of this boy's brief life and tragic death are
unknown, but the inscription on his tombstone testifies to his family's
sense of love and loss. Four years later, Ichabod died at the age of fifty-six,
leaving Anstes and their four daughters a substantial estate. Anstes, who
was at least a decade younger than her husband, lived until 1876. The
placement of the parents' graves in Memorial Cemetery, flanking that of
their young son, confirms his importance in their affections.[1]

Early death was commonplace in America before the twentieth century.
According to the aptly named historian Margaret Coffin, young people
died of many causes, including childhood diseases such as mumps and

---

1. U.S. Bureau of the Census, *Sixth Census: 1840, Population Schedule,* NARA microfilm,
M704, reel #230, lists Ichabod Sargent as the head of a household. The household also included one white female age thirty to forty, one white male between the ages of five and
ten, four white females between the ages of five and twenty, and four slaves. Names of
family members are recorded in parish records of the Ste. Genevieve Catholic Church.
Ichabod Sargent's will is recorded in Ste. Genevieve County, deed book H, p. 118; Anstes
Sargent's will is recorded in deed book D, p. 142. Grave markers for Ichabod, Anstes, and
their son remain legible in Memorial Cemetery, Ste. Genevieve.

Grave marker of Mary Louise C. Contancin (Marie L. C. Contancin) with inscriptions in French and English in Memorial Cemetery, Ste. Genevieve. Photograph by B. H. Rucker.

measles for which there were no treatments. Malarial fevers and tuberculosis ran rampant in the new republic, and there were periodic epidemics of yellow fever and typhoid fever. Coffin argued that the principal reason for high death rates was ignorance. Although there were several medical schools, including Transylvania in Lexington, Kentucky, physicians lacked a basic understanding of the use of anesthesia and antiseptics, and they continued to employ traditional and questionable procedures, such as bleeding.[2]

With limited medical knowledge, American physicians had to contend with a variety of contagious diseases, including cholera. Before the nineteenth century, cholera epidemics occurred mainly in Asia, but advancements in trade and transportation spread the contagion around the world. Victims of the disease suffered sudden acute diarrhea, spasmodic vomiting, cramps, chills, and dehydration. Death could come within hours or days. Until the 1880s, physicians did not understand that the cause of the disease was a bacterium that attacked the human intestine. The bacteria bred in the water supplies of large, crowded cities with poor sanitation. In St. Louis, for instance, where there were no sewers, people drank water directly from the river. The disease often flared up among groups of travelers, crowded on steamboats. Steamboat crews sometimes ejected and abandoned sick passengers on levees and landings.[3]

In 1832 and 1833, Lewis Linn and Ichabod Sargent treated cholera-stricken people in Ste. Genevieve. The remedies they used included bleeding (taking as much as fifteen ounces of blood from the sufferer), sweating (bathing patients' feet in warm water or placing warm stones in their beds), and opiates such as laudanum. In a letter to the editor of the *Columbia Missouri Intelligencer,* in late June 1833, Linn stated that he and Sargent had used these remedies "last year, and since, during the existence of the disease at Ste. Genevieve, with almost universal success."[4] Although these

2. Malarial fevers were also referred to as autumnal and intermittent fevers, and bleeding is sometimes referred to as bloodletting (Margaret M. Coffin, *Death in Early America,* 16–33).

3. Patrick E. McLear, "The St. Louis Cholera Epidemic of 1849," 178. For an interesting description of the cholera epidemics in New York, see Charles E. Rosenberg, *The Cholera Years: The United States in 1832, 1849, and 1866.*

4. Lewis Linn, "Cholera Remedies by a Missouri Physician."

treatments represented standard medical practices at the time, they were unlikely to cure cholera patients, who lost fluids at such a rapid rate that they often died of dehydration. After his letter appeared in the newspaper, the death rate climbed. On October 5, the paper reported that "the cholera still continues to prevail in the town of Ste. Genevieve. Last week we understood there were nine deaths."[5]

Linn bravely tried to do his duty, but he did not understand the situation in which he found himself. In his June letter, he theorized that cholera was brought on by fear, anger, misuse of alcohol, and exposure to drafts. Given the state of medical knowledge, he could not have understood the relationship of microorganisms to the spread of the disease. In fact, he argued that "this disease is surely not contagious; the common belief that it is so, has been the cause of acts disgraceful to us as men; more horrid to see than the sight of the disease in its most terrific form:—be firm and do your duty to each other."[6] A few months after this exhortation appeared in the newspaper, Linn himself came down with cholera, but he was able to recover.[7]

During the horrible summer of 1849, cholera killed at least forty-five hundred people in St. Louis, where the death rate was higher than it was in any other American city. Because of contaminated water and poor sanitation, the disease ran rampant there from January through August, killing 6 percent of the city's total population of seventy thousand. During the first month, thirty-three people died, and the death toll kept mounting. In June alone, there were 1,259 deaths. Many residents and local officials fled the city. In August, there were only fifty-four deaths. After that the contagion quickly passed.[8]

In Ste. Genevieve, at least twenty-two adults and five children died of cholera during the 1849 epidemic. Jean-Baptiste Vallé, eighty-nine, succumbed to old age in that year, but his family did not escape the disease. Sixty-nine-year-old Francois Vallé, two-year-old Sargent Vallé, and five of the Vallé slaves died from the contagion during the summer. The Missouri

5. *Columbia Missouri Intelligencer,* October 5, 1833.

6. Linn, "Cholera Remedies."

7. *Columbia Missouri Intelligencer,* October 5, 1833.

8. McLear, "St. Louis Cholera Epidemic," 174–79; Linda A. Fisher, "A Summer of Terror: Cholera in St. Louis, 1849," 189, 207.

mortality schedules for 1849–1850 also recorded that Marie LaPorte expired from old age, but that two of her slaves died of cholera. Misdiagnosis and mistakes in record-keeping probably resulted in underestimation of mortality from this disease. In the twelve months before the 1850 census, at least sixteen children and six adults in Ste. Genevieve died from unknown (or unrecorded) causes. Of the seventy-eight local residents who passed away in that time period, twenty-seven were children under eighteen years of age, thirty-six were adults between the ages of eighteen and sixty, and fifteen were more than sixty years old.[9]

In Memorial Cemetery, the only surviving grave marker that mentions cholera is that of Martin Sweek. At the time of his death on April 25, 1849, Sweek was fifty years old. His wife, Caroline, died on May 2, 1849, at the age of forty-six. The single stone that marks both of their graves lists their names, places of birth (Virginia for Martin and England for Caroline), and ages. The last three lines of the inscription read,

> The above named persons
> Died of cholera leaving
> A family of 12 children.[10]

In one week's time, the Sweek children lost both their parents.

For the young people of Ste. Genevieve, life held many terrors. An epidemic of whooping cough killed sixteen people in 1859 and 1860, all of whom were under the age of eighteen. The mortality schedules for Ste. Genevieve in the twelve months before the 1860 census listed many other causes for the deaths of infants and children. In official records, physicians listed such ailments as teething, croup, fever, hives, diarrhea, bloody flux, colds, lung disease, heart disease, scrofula, and worms. Six young people died of unknown or undiagnosed illnesses, bringing the total death toll among children to forty-five.[11]

Conditions did not improve significantly for children in the two decades after the Civil War. It appears that physicians learned how to diagnose a larger number of ailments because the mortality schedules for 1870 and

---

9. U.S. Bureau of the Census, *Missouri Mortality Schedules, Ste. Genevieve, Missouri,* 1850.
10. Grave marker in Memorial Cemetery, Ste. Genevieve.
11. U.S. Bureau of the Census, *Missouri Mortality Schedules, Ste. Genevieve, Missouri,* 1860.

Sweek family monument in Memorial Cemetery, Ste. Genevieve. Photograph by B. H. Rucker.

Close-up of the inscription on the Sweek family monument. Photograph by B. H. Rucker.

1880 attribute no deaths to unknown causes. In some cases, however, the diagnoses were vague. Thirteen children in 1869 and 1870 died of various fevers, and five succumbed to "spasms." Malaria claimed four victims, and typhoid fever took three children's lives in that year. Diphtheria and pneumonia each claimed two victims. Other children died of colds, croup, consumption, and dysentery, bringing the toll to thirty-seven. A decade later, in 1879–1880, sixty-five children died of the following causes (in descending order of frequency): pneumonia, dysentery, cholera infantum, croup, cold, stillbirth, measles, malaria, fever, diarrhea, whooping cough, typhoid fever, tumors, sunstroke, cramps, epilepsy, convulsions, hives, and bleeding at the navel.[12]

For young women, pregnancy posed a danger. In January 1850, twenty-five-year-old Margaret Holmes died in labor. Mortality schedules for the year preceding the 1860 recorded that Rosine Miller, nineteen, and Elvira Larson, twenty-five, also died in childbirth. No such deaths appeared in the mortality schedules for 1869–1970, but ten years later Therese Schweiss, twenty-six, died while giving birth. In that same year, thirty-year-old Fern Ferguson succumbed to "child bed fever," probably due to a secondary infection.[13]

Residents who survived through young adulthood often had bad habits that hastened their demise. Daniel Drake, an Ohio physician, studied the lifestyles and diseases of the inhabitants of "the Interior Valley of North America," including the settlements along the Mississippi River, and described them in a treatise published in 1850. His book provides telling

12. Ibid., 1870 and 1880.
13. Ibid., 1850, 1860, 1870, and 1880.

glimpses of the daily lives and environment of the American pioneers and the old French settlers of the region. These factors, in addition to epidemics and inadequate medical care, make it a wonder that any of them lasted long enough to die of old age.

According to Drake, the American pioneers and early French settlers ate too much meat, fat, and carbohydrates. Rich soil, game-filled forests, and rivers teeming with fish provided an abundance of food, and the people partook of it freely. He noted that both adults and children ate meat three times a day, consuming beef, pork, veal, and cured meats, such as bacon and sausage, in large quantities. Poultry, waterfowl, eggs, and fish graced the tables of rich and poor alike. Many people drank milk or buttermilk and ate buttered bread with their meat. "Fermented (yeast) wheat bread is far from universal," Drake reported, "and hot unleavened biscuit, with fat, is a favorite article on the breakfast and supper table, especially in the southern half of the Valley."[14] In addition to meat and fat, people consumed large quantities of fruits and vegetables, which provided them with adequate nutrition. But the people ate too fast and chewed too little, which led to overeating, and they consumed too much fat.[15]

Former slaves, who told their stories to interviewers for the Federal Writers' Project in the 1930s, recalled eating similar foods. "Uncle" Fil Hancock of Rolla, Missouri, remembered that when he was a child in the 1850s, "We got to eat what the white folks did," including salt meat, biscuits, cabbage, potatoes, and other vegetables.[16] Mrs. Tishey Taylor of Poplar Bluff said that the slaves did not eat what they wanted, but what the masters gave them—beans, potatoes, corn bread, milk, and "sometimes round hog killin' time he pass out the jowl meat."[17] Mrs. Hattie Matthews of Farmington told her mother's stories about eating "scraps from the white folks' table."[18]

Although many people worked hard at physically demanding tasks, they did not understand the need for regular exercise. Drake, who did

14. Daniel Drake, *Malaria in the Interior Valley of North America*, 654–55.
15. Ibid., 654.
16. *Born in Slavery*, 147–49.
17. Ibid., 342.
18. Ibid., 249.

understand this, expressed dismay at the habits he observed. Children, he wrote, "both at home and in the school or college, are allowed to grow up in bodily listlessness; and consequently, they suffer under numerous infirmities of health and frame, from which, by proper physical discipline, they would be protected."[19] Adults in sedentary occupations, such as shopkeepers, often engaged in no regular outdoor exercise. Women, who did not work outside the home, experienced "many infirmities, which are the consequence of bodily indolence and inactivity; some of which, in the end, prove fatal."[20]

Smoking was a common and dangerous habit. French people, including women, often used powdery dry tobacco, or "snuff," which they sniffed into their noses or rubbed onto their teeth and gums. Germans, according to Drake, were "great smokers," who preferred pipes over cigars. Among Anglo-Americans, chewing remained more popular than smoking. Many boys began chewing or smoking tobacco before puberty, sometimes at the early age of seven or eight. Generally, the habit continued throughout their lives. Although Drake did not know about the connection between smoking and lung cancer, he did believe that smoking had bad effects on the nervous and digestive systems, sometimes depressing the appetite and keeping "the individual in a state of comparative emaciation."[21]

Alcohol consumption at all times of the day was customary. Anglo-American settlers brought with them the habit of drinking "morning bitters" and mint juleps, which were made of whiskey and served to all members of the family, including children. According to Drake, this practice had declined by 1850, but barroom drinking by adult males had increased. "The times for this kind of drinking," Drake lamented, "are the morning, the forenoon, the afternoon, and the night."[22] Beverages included whiskey and other distilled spirits, wine, malt liquor, and hard cider. Although Drake admitted that a man might drink any or all of these beverages in moderation and live to a ripe old age, he had also seen numerous people

19. Drake, *Malaria in the Interior Valley of North America*, 697.
20. Ibid., 697.
21. Ibid., 674–75.
22. Ibid., 668–69.

with alcohol-related diseases, including inflammation of the liver, dropsy (edema), convulsions, delirium tremens, and "suicidal monomania."[23]

The water the people drank and bathed in came from springs or from the river. There were no purification plants, and, as Drake observed, water sometimes contained organic matter and minerals that might be harmful to people's health. Drake noted that Americans in the middle of the continent hardly ever bathed. He found this to be regrettable. He advised those who could not immerse themselves in water to sponge or sprinkle their bodies every morning or, in the winter months, to stand at an open window and take "an air bath, which should not be prolonged after a slight shuddering has commenced."[24]

Whether or not they took this interesting advice, the people of the Mississippi River valley suffered frequently from fevers, chills, and respiratory congestion. In the French colonial period, residents of Ste. Geneviève often contracted malaria, a mosquito-borne disease that causes all these symptoms and that may result in anemia and enlargement of the spleen. By the time the Americans arrived in large numbers, the French inhabitants had developed some resistance to the disease. In the first decade of the nineteenth century, Amos Stoddard remarked that Anglo-Americans, especially northerners, fell victim to malaria far more often than their French neighbors did.[25]

Nineteenth-century physicians, including Drake, struggled to discover the cause and cure of malaria. He did not connect the disease with mosquitoes but attributed it to heat, moisture, and atmospheric gases or to "living organic forms, too small to be seen with the naked eye."[26] Like other physicians of his time, he advocated a variety of treatments, including bloodletting. He also recommended administering emetics to bring about "full evacuation of the stomach" and cathartics to empty the bowels.[27] More salubrious medications included sulphate of quinine, which did

23. Ibid., 672.
24. Ibid., 666, 679.
25. Schroeder, *Opening the Ozarks*, 55–60.
26. Ibid., 716–22.
27. Ibid., 743–44.

seem to arrest the disease. But Drake also advocated opium to relieve chills and convulsions.[28] Most of these treatments would not have been helpful, and some were probably dangerous.

By far the leading cause of death for adults in Ste. Genevieve in the twelve months before the 1860 census was consumption, which might have indicated tuberculosis. It could also have meant any lung disease that caused the patient to waste away. Eleven people between the ages of eighteen and sixty died in this manner; two others officially succumbed to lung disease. Four people died of pleurisy, which may actually have meant pneumonia, and one died of a cold. At least a few of these deaths probably resulted from smoking. Two people died of liver disease, which may have been related to alcohol use, and two died of dropsy (kidney disease). Other residents under the age of sixty passed away because of a variety of fevers (some probably malarial), apoplexy, and sunstroke. Four deaths among people over sixty were attributed to old age. Three other elderly people died of palsy and two of unknown causes; one poor soul died of hiccoughs, bringing the total number of adult deaths to forty-three.[29]

Ten years later, physicians attributed ten deaths of people under sixty to pneumonia and six deaths to consumption. Typhoid fever claimed three lives. One man's death resulted from an epileptic seizure. Others died of various fevers, flux, heart disease, neuralgia, and palsy. Doctors, who seemed to be getting better at identifying illnesses, attributed only one fatality to old age. One man committed suicide by cutting his throat, and one man was killed by a slingshot. The total number of adult deaths in the twelve month period before the 1870 census was thirty-nine.[30]

Pneumonia and consumption remained the leading causes of death a decade later, claiming at least fifteen and nine lives respectively in the year before the 1880 census. Physicians identified at least nine victims of heart disease and two victims of cirrhosis of the liver. Malaria and typhoid fever killed five people, and measles killed one adult in addition to the children previously mentioned. Unfortunately, the mortality schedule for

28. Ibid., 747–48.
29. U.S. Bureau of the Census, *Missouri Mortality Schedules, Ste. Genevieve, Missouri,* 1859–1860.
30. Ibid., 1869–1870.

this period contains many illegible entries. It is apparent, though, that pneumonia and lung diseases were the leading causes of death. In addition to deaths from natural causes, the schedule listed two accidental deaths and one fatal gunshot wound, bringing the total number of adult deaths to seventy-five.[31]

From these numbers, it is possible to imagine real life in this Mississippi River town, where fever and contagion appeared out of nowhere, leaving a trail of bodies behind them. Physicians struggled against forces they could not comprehend, using remedies that did not work. Children were as likely to die as adults, and young women risked their lives bringing infants into the world. People ate and drank abundantly, smoked incessantly, and paid an unwitting price for their minor vices. Danger lurked everywhere, and death could come at any moment.

Many poor souls lost their lives in the river. Some of these deaths were accidental, and others resulted from acts of violence. A shifting population of wild and desperate men roamed the banks of the Mississippi, finding work or getting into mischief aboard the steamboats that moved up- and downstream between New Orleans and St. Louis. Some of these men ended up as anonymous corpses on the west bank at Ste. Genevieve.

Drowning, accidental or deliberate, occurred regularly. In the mid-nineteenth century a local man named Peter Moro supplemented his income by pulling bodies from the river and the Saline Creek. For instance, in July 1846, the state of Missouri requested Moro and five other "good and honorable men" to assist the coroner in collecting and examining a body found in the river. Fees of twelve dollars were paid for this service and the person's burial. Another record dated April 11, 1850, documents essentially the same transaction. Other files in the Ste. Genevieve archives make it clear that Moro and his son John performed this service on a regular basis.[32]

Steamboat accidents, minor and major, littered the river with wreckage. The most frequent mishaps were groundings or collisions with submerged objects, such as snags, rocks, or sunken vessels. Windstorms could

31. Ibid., 1879–1880.
32. Thanks are due to Brandon Kuehn for primary research on Peter Moro (Folders 1085 and 1087, Ste. Genevieve Archives).

turn boats into piles of kindling. Wooden hulls were vulnerable to punctures. Upper decks made of pine and covered with oil-based paint were tinder boxes, ready to catch fire from boilers, stoves, and lamps. Boiler explosions caused the greatest number of fatalities, but collisions with bridges and other steamboats also wreaked havoc.[33]

According to steamboat historian James V. Swift, at least seventeen boats sank near Ste. Genevieve.[34] On November 25, 1823, the *Franklin Missouri Intelligencer* reported that the steamboat *Cincinnati* had sunk while in the Mississippi between Ste. Genevieve and Kaskaskia. During its passage from St. Louis to New Orleans, the *Cincinnati* attempted to cross from the west to the east bank to take on a cargo of flour. According to the newspaper, the boat "struck a snag, and went down in 7 or 8 feet of water.—She was but partly freighted with lead and other imperishable articles, which it is believed, will be principally recovered, the water being very low."[35] The steamboat *Robert Morris* also hit a snag and sank near Turkey Island, four miles north of Ste. Genevieve, on Christmas Day in 1846.[36]

Official records and press accounts of steamboat disasters were sparse and uninformative. For example, on December 23, 1828, the *St. Louis Missouri Republican* printed these two short sentences: "The Steam Boat Pilot, on her passage to New Orleans, sprung a leak, and sunk at Ste. Genevieve. She was laden with lead."[37] The St. Louis paper made no mention of any casualties, and unfortunately there was no Ste. Genevieve newspaper at the time.

According to local historian Firmin Rozier, on August 22, 1852, a flue collapsed in the steamboat *Doctor Franklin No. 2* at Turkey Island. Rozier reported that billowing water scalded and killed twenty to thirty of the passengers and crew. The blast catapulted the vessel's two engineers into the river. Other people jumped overboard and drowned. A few passengers

---

33. Michael Gillespie, *Come Hell or High Water: A Lively History of Steamboating on the Mississippi and Ohio Rivers*, 209–210.

34. James V. Swift, "Several Boats Were Lost at Ste. Genevieve," 14.

35. *Franklin Missouri Intelligencer*, November 25, 1823.

36. Folder 1095, Ste. Genevieve Archives.

37. *St. Louis Missouri Republican*, December 23, 1828.

escaped without injury. Burned and blistered corpses and screaming survivors were mingled in the cabin, as rescuers towed the disabled boat to the Ste. Genevieve wharf. Local citizens rendered assistance to those who were injured and buried the dead in a mass grave in Memorial Cemetery.[38] To date, however, that mass grave has not been located, and corroboration of Rozier's account of the event has proved elusive.[39]

The body of one unknown white man apparently floated from the site of the explosion at Turkey Island downriver to the Little Rock Ferry Landing. Ste. Genevieve County coroner M. J. Amoureux held an inquest on August 23. The coroner's jury concluded that the drowned man, who was approximately thirty-five years old and appeared to have been a deck passenger, "must have died in consequence of the explosion of the steamer Dr. Franklin No. 2."[40] This official record confirms that an explosion occurred, but it does not document the extent of the tragedy.

In 1880, the *Ste. Genevieve Fair Play* published an account of the "greatest calamity that has ever befallen our community." This was not a steamboat wreck but a boiler explosion at the Cone Mills, a flour milling facility. An hour before noon on July 17, the newspaper reported, "every building in town was shaken from top to foundation, and a roaring, as of wind, was heard." The engine room had blown up; the main building had three holes in its side. The smokestack flew into the air and landed two hundred feet away from the site. One of the flues hit a stable, and another one landed in a beer garden. After the steam abated, a crowd rushed in and found the engineer, I. L. Koenemann, lying dead on the floor "with the whole upper portion of his head blown off." Two other men were injured, but Koenemann only one fatality.[41]

Until the 1880s, the people of Ste. Genevieve buried their dead near the Catholic Church on a gently sloping tract granted to the community by the Spanish government sometime before the Louisiana Purchase. The

38. Rozier, *History of the Early Settlement of the Mississippi Valley*, 132.

39. Frederick Way Jr. reported that the *Dr. Franklin No. 2* "Burned at St. Louis on July 7, 1853" (*Way's Packet Directory, 1848–1983: Passenger Steamboats of the Mississippi River System since the Advent of Photography in Mid-Continent America*, 131). It is possible that there was a previous unrecorded accident.

40. Record of the coroner's inquest, August 23, 1852, folder 1173, Ste. Genevieve Archives.

41. *Ste. Genevieve Fair Play*, July 17, 1880.

exact date of this grant remains in question; the earliest death date still legible on a grave stone is 1807. Priests recorded the names of the deceased, but they did not keep track of burial sites in the cemetery. Prominent families, such as the Vallés, claimed family plots and enclosed them with walls or fences. But the land was held in common; mourners selected plots at will in sunny spaces or in the shade of trees. Friends and family erected monuments, many of which have crumbled away, and residents frequently disturbed old graves when digging new ones. Local authorities closed the old cemetery, allowing no new burials after 1881. Odile Vallé, who donated land for a new burial ground, received special permission to be buried in the old one in 1894.[42]

Monuments in Memorial Cemetery marked the resting places of ordinary citizens as well as those of prominent families. For example, in June of 1844, Dennis McGill, an Irish American laborer, died alone in the woods. Two of his fellow workers, Christopher Maydwell and Joseph Cox, served as jurors at an inquest. The court determined that there was no foul play, but that the young man died of apoplexy. In the old cemetery, sixteen of his friends erected a tall, imposing monument, bearing symbols of the stonemason's craft, with the following inscription, "Sacred to the memory of Dennis McGill, a native of Killybegs, Ireland, died June 22, 1844, aged thirty-three years. This monument was erected by the shopmates of the deceased. A. L. Grave and Co., contributors." Cox and Maydwell's names appear on the monument along with fifteen others.[43]

The end of a man's life, even in a frontier town, awakened a sense of awe and dread. One of Ste. Genevieve's old French inhabitants, Alexis Thomure, died a shocking death in the winter of 1885. On February 28,

42. Under the auspices of the Foundation for Restoration of Ste. Genevieve, with a Save America's Treasures (S.A.T.) grant from the National Park Service, B. H. Rucker is coordinating a massive effort to document and preserve the old cemetery. Carl Ekberg calls it the Old Town Cemetery, but it is more commonly known as Memorial Cemetery. The exact date of the Spanish land grant that created the cemetery remains in question. Local historian Lucille Basler gives the date of 1787, but no documents have been found to confirm this.

43. "Inquests on unidentified bodies found drowned in the Mississippi River and on the bodies of Dennis McGill; Morose, a free man of color, and Thomas Fugason," folder 1039, Ste. Genevieve Archives; monument in Memorial Cemetery, Ste. Genevieve.

the *Ste. Genevieve Herald* reported that two German American men, Frank Sexauer and Frank Stoeckle, out riding through the countryside, noticed that Thomure's small cabin seemed abandoned. According to the newspaper, the elderly man's house looked "deserted, no smoke issuing from the chimney, no signs of life about the premises, which the morning being very cold, appeared to them as singular."

Thomure, a widower, had been unwell for some time but had continued living alone in his place off the plank road. Although he had many relatives in town, he had never gone to them for nursing care. On that February morning, Sexauer, "more in a spirit of levity than from any suspicion of any thing being wrong, proposed to his companion to go and wake Lexis up."

After going to the cabin and raising the window, the two men saw a horrible sight. The newspaper described what they saw in ghastly detail:

> on the bed lay the aged and solitary occupant alone and dead, at his feet lay his faithful dog, pinched and starved but faithful to the end; upon his breast was perched a cat, which with the instinct of self preservation uppermost and regardless of gratitude for past protection, was prolonging its existence by devouring the face and exposed parts of its late master.

Sexauer and Stoeckle rushed into town to tell the coroner, who held an inquest that same evening. An investigation revealed that Thomure had frozen to death and that he had been dead for several days before the two men found him. The dog, though starving, remained on guard and would not budge until a member of the coroner's jury struck him with a club. According to the newspaper, "The cat had however eaten all the fleshy parts of [Thomure's] face and neck as far as he could reach for the shirt collar and clothes."[44]

The old Frenchman's death and the discovery of his body by two German American men revealed a great deal about Ste. Genevieve society. Family was important to local residents, but the old man, who had many relatives in town, chose to live a hermit's life after his wife passed away. The absence of smoke coming from the chimney of his cabin signaled

44. *Ste. Genevieve Herald,* February 28, 1885.

danger and inspired a neighborly response. Two prominent townsmen went looking for him on a cold winter morning, perhaps out of concern, perhaps merely as a prank or joke, to get the old man out of bed. What they found was shocking enough to merit a long article in the newspaper. The message was clear. This sort of thing should not happen in our town.

The fact that death was commonplace did not make it easier to bear. Life was precious. Memorial Cemetery's ornate monuments with their sentimental inscriptions expressed a desire to remember loved ones who had passed. The Sargents clearly mourned the loss of their young son, although they still had four daughters to raise, a household to maintain, and work to do. Sargent was a doctor. He had seen the grim face of death when he treated cholera patients in 1833. Like his colleague, Lewis Linn, he had to remain firm and do his duty. But there was more to life than duty and hardship.

The inscription on the young boy's grave expressed not only grief but also wistfulness and hope. The "beloved boy" had "visited" his parents' house and then "returned," presumably to the place from which he came, a place that was not temporal but eternal. His brief visit had been a gift that had enriched his parents' lives; the joy he brought to them did not vanish after he passed away. Even a short life had value and meaning that deserved to be remembered.

In this frontier community, grief was real, but so was the pursuit of happiness. And so was the quest for human freedom.

CHAPTER TWELVE

Holidays and Celebrations

The Old Year will be buried and the birth of the New Year duly celebrated by the recurrence of the annual Guignolee at the New Year's Eve
Ball at Union Hall on Wednesday Evening, December the 31st, 1884.

Ste. Genevieve Herald, December 20, 1884

NUMEROUS OBSERVERS HAVE contrasted the free and easy, fun-
loving ways of the French with the piety, sobriety, and industriousness of
Americans in the new republic. Amos Stoddard, Thomas Ashe, and Christian Schultz all noted that the French inhabitants of the territory did not
believe in a rigid observance of the Sabbath. While they might attend
mass on Sunday morning, they felt perfectly free to enjoy themselves by
visiting neighbors, dancing, drinking, and gambling on any day of the
week. This behavior, the commentators implied, contrasted with the more
puritanical ways of the Anglo-American settlers. Historian Harvey Wish
developed this theme in a well-known article on the assimilation of the
French in the Mississippi valley, but his essay told only part of the story.
Assimilation was not a one-directional process but a complicated web of
relationships through which French-speaking, English-speaking, and
German-speaking people created a blended community within the American republic. This cultural blending became particularly apparent in the
enjoyment of recreational activities, holidays, and public celebrations.[1]

In early Ste. Genevieve, religion and worldly enjoyments coexisted hap-
pily. As Ashe, a British visitor, entered the town in the summer of 1806,

---

1. Harvey Wish, "The French of Old Missouri (1804–1821): A Study in Assimilation,"
181, 184–87; Sanders, "Germans of Ste. Genevieve," 19–22.

he heard the sweet sounds of vespers from the Catholic Church. After services in the evening, he and others noted that the women of the town continued their housework, while the men played instruments, sang songs, and told stories on the galleries or in the courtyards. When the heat of the day dissipated, local residents gathered together to dance. Both the French and the Anglo-American residents enjoyed dancing. The French favored European dances like the waltz, while the Americans introduced more sprightly tunes like "Old Dan Tucker" and the "Sailor's Hornpipe."[2]

Schultz observed during his 1808 visit that gambling was as popular as dancing among both the French and the Anglo-Americans. "Whenever there is a ball given by even the most rigid and superstitious of these Catholics, there is always one room set apart for gambling. *Vingt-un* is the word; and never did I see people with so much spirit and perseverance to win each other's money, as in this little village." Sometimes, he reported, players would sit for thirty hours at the card table with no food, only coffee and wine, and sometimes they would win or lose more than a thousand dollars. "Nor is it the French alone who pursue this destructive habit: the Americans likewise (with a very few laudable exceptions)," according to Schultz, "have followed the same scandalous practice."[3]

Missouri statehood brought restrictions on the enjoyment of these innocent, or naughty, pastimes. From the beginning, Missourians placed legal restrictions on people's activities on Sunday, the Christian Sabbath. The convention that drafted the state's constitution adjourned from Saturday until Monday, and the legislature adopted various bills compelling the observance of Sunday as a day of rest. The revised statutes of 1835, for example, made it a misdemeanor, punishable by a fine of up to five dollars, to labor or cause another person to labor on Sunday, exempting those whose religious faith named another day as the Sabbath. The early statutes specifically prohibited horse racing, cockfighting, card playing, or gambling on Sunday. Fines for those offenses might be as much as fifty dollars. Another state law required stores or dram shops (businesses that

2. Wish, "French of Old Missouri," 186–88.
3. Schultz, *Travels on an Inland Voyage,* 2:61.

sold liquor) to close their doors on the Christian Sabbath and forbade any sales of merchandise, except for medicines or other dire necessities.[4]

The Missouri Supreme Court upheld these Sunday closing laws, ruling that they did not violate the First Amendment right to the free exercise of religion. On the contrary, the court ruled that these laws secured "a full enjoyment of the rights of conscience" for those who believed Sunday was a holy day. The law did not compel anyone to go to church, but it afforded workers and others the freedom to do so if they wished. How could Christians enjoy their hallowed day, the court asked, "amidst all the turmoil and bustle of worldly pursuits, amidst scenes by which the day was desecrated, which they conscientiously believed to be holy?" The court recognized that the religion of those who framed the state constitution was Christianity, but it gave scant attention to those of other faiths and no attention at all to those who felt perfectly comfortable observing the Lord's day amidst the hustle and bustle of everyday life.[5]

Many local residents resisted Ste. Genevieve's city ordinances, which prohibited merchants, grocers, and dram shop keepers from opening their stores or warehouses or selling "any goods or liquors between the hours of nine o'clock A.M. and four o'clock P.M., on the first day of the week, called Sunday." Offenders had to pay a fine of five dollars for each offense.[6] Joseph Ernst wrote numerous editorials denouncing this law as ridiculous and unfair. He believed that it discriminated against German Americans who owned many of the grocery stores and other local establishments that sold alcoholic beverages. Sunday closing laws prevented merchants from making an honest living while prohibiting other hardworking people from enjoying the company of their friends in the beer hall on that day. More fundamentally, in Ernst's view, these laws restricted personal freedom. For many German immigrants, freedom was the lure that brought them to America.[7]

---

4. *Revised Statutes of the State of Missouri, 1845,* art. 8, chap. 47, sec. 31, 32, 33, 34, p. 405.
5. *State of Missouri v. Ambs,* Supreme Court of Missouri, St. Louis, 20 Mo. 214, 1854 Mo. LEXIS 174, October 1854.
6. Ste. Genevieve town ordinances, August 7, 1867, on file at Ste. Genevieve City Hall.
7. Sanders makes this point very clearly in "Germans of Ste. Genevieve."

On a Sunday afternoon in July 1883, the members of the Progressive Cornet Band, a German musical ensemble, flouted the law by taking an excursion up the river on a flatboat owned by Gottlieb Rehm. By going up the river, they left the state of Missouri. According to Ernst, "They had provided themselves with sundry kegs of lager and boxes of bottled beer and succeeded even in arranging a dance—some kind of a hornpipe we believe—which was performed by the jolly butcher and Miss Soupe Bone." As there were no women in the ensemble, "Miss" Soupe Bone must have been a sight to behold. With their liquid cargo and their musical instruments, "The party landed at some point above the lime kiln where they made themselves comfortable and passed the time pleasantly and profitably in evoking the echoes of the neighboring hills [with their loud songs], drinking beer and admiring the Terpsichorean feats of the above mentioned" twosome. Ernst reported the incident gleefully as a defiance of "the Puritanical Sunday law of old Ste. Genevieve."[8]

German Americans and Anglo-Americans helped save the traditional French New Year's custom of *La Guillonee* from suppression by moralistic local authorities. The word *Guillonee* defies translation. According to Wilson Primm, a descendant of one of the early French families of St. Louis, the ancient Gauls presented each other with branches of *gui* (mistletoe) at the beginning of *la Nouvelle Annee* (the New Year). A Gui la Nouvelle Annee might have been transformed into La Guillonee. But the highly stylized activities comprising La Guillonee seem to have begun in the North American colonies, without a clear antecedent in France.[9]

In Ste. Genevieve and other French towns in Missouri, just after dark on New Year's Eve, young men dressed in masquerade costumes and gathered in an agreed upon place. Each man would carry a bucket, basket, or sack for receiving gifts of food or beverages. The inebriated revelers would parade from house to house singing "La Guillonee," a song that had twenty verses. In the first verse, the singers greeted the master and mistress of the house; in subsequent verses, they asked for food or other gifts. But the

8. *Ste. Genevieve Herald,* July 28, 1883.
9. Wilson Primm, "New Year's Day in the Olden Time of St. Louis."

real gift they requested was *la fille ainee* (the eldest daughter), promising to warm her feet and to take her into the woods and show her a good time.[10]

During the verse in which the group proposed to entertain the young lady, a soloist would break in with romantic verses about doves and nightingales. At this point the master and mistress of the house were expected to provide a donation of sugar, coffee, lard, rum, eggs, meat, or poultry for an upcoming celebration. After receiving the gifts, the revelers would dance and sing wildly before proceeding on their rounds. On January 6, the feast of the Epiphany, the young girls of the town would take the provisions gathered during La Guillonee and transform them into an elegant meal for an event called the King's Ball.[11]

In the mid-nineteenth century, New Year's Eve revelers faced threats from a local ordinance that prohibited "disturbing the public peace within the town by any unusual noise either by singing, loud hallooing, or using profane language." Violators could be fined up to ten dollars and/or confined in the county jail for ten days.[12] Clearly, this ordinance exposed participants in La Guillonee to charges of disturbing the peace. Nevertheless, the tradition continued year after year, with large crowds taking part in the merriment.

In 1873, the *Ste. Genevieve Fair Play* described the event vividly. According to the newspaper, about thirty young men wearing costumes and masks went through town and ended up at Munsch's Hall, where they chose partners and led the first dance of a New Year's ball. Two of the costumes represented "an old whiskey toper and a jovial, good-natured old gentleman—however, they both had the big-head. Their antics were peculiar, being so constructed that the head could be raised or lowered by the

10. *La Guillonee: A French New Year's Custom and Song, a collection of Essays.*
11. Primm, "New Year's Day."
12. Ste. Genevieve town ordinances, August 7, 1867, on file at Ste. Genevieve City Hall. On January 4, 1936, the *Ste. Genevieve Fair Play* published an article stating that in 1855 the city passed an ordinance banning the La Guillonee. The article described a trial of revelers and a spirited defense by John Scott. But the truth of this story cannot be verified. City ordinances before 1867, with a few exceptions, have not been preserved. A search of court records for 1855 did not unearth an account of this trial.

operator—presenting at one time a short thick set dwarf, while at the next instant they presented the spectacle of a long slim dangling awkward giant."[13]

During the midnight supper, which featured a French bouillon (chicken stock pot), another set of masked revelers arrived, singing "the French song peculiar to the occasion." By this time, there were about two hundred and fifty people in the hall, and the party continued almost until dawn. The newspaper carefully noted, however, that the people "conducted themselves well and no disturbance occurred to mar the pleasure of the night."[14]

The tradition continued. In the winter of 1884–1885, Leon Jokerst, the German American manager of the Union Hall, invited everyone who could pay a fifty cent admission to attend the annual celebration of La Guillonee. The *Fair Play* announced that "the several Guignolee [*sic*] bands will meet at the Hall in full costume at about 12 o'clock m. and chant the old time Song of the Guignolee." After that, there would be a costume ball. For an additional twenty-five cents, revelers could enjoy a traditional French bouillon. "Everybody is invited," the newspaper said, and "perfect order will be maintained."[15]

Every year the people of Ste. Genevieve came together to observe secular and religious occasions with a series of balls. For example, in October 1882, French, Anglo-American, and German American civic leaders funded a banquet and dance at the Union Hall "to celebrate the great success of the Ste. Genevieve Copper Industry." Among those sponsoring the event were Harold Vallé, Henry S. Shaw, Joseph A. Ernst, and Firmin A. Rozier. Because of his "unswerving energy and untiring perseverance in developing the copper mines," Leon Jokerst was the guest of honor. This event united French joie de vivre, Anglo-American industry, and German conviviality in one elaborate event.[16]

The cycle of Christian holidays inspired an endless round of celebrations, including the King's Ball, which marked the Epiphany, and Mardi Gras balls, which ushered in the period of Lent, followed by Easter, and,

13. *Ste. Genevieve Fair Play,* January 9, 1873.
14. Ibid.
15. Ibid., December 20, 1884.
16. *Ste. Genevieve Herald,* September 23, 1882.

of course, culminating in Christmas feasts. In 1874, the editor of the *Fair Play* described "A Christmas Ramble" that included a prodigious amount of eating and drinking. On a cold day, with a few snowflakes falling, the editor put on his best clothes and "walked majestically down town" where

> All the little ones and big ones—knowing how generous and wealthy we are shouted "Christmas gift" in our ears on all sides. No doubt they are still exulting over the many magnificent gifts they received from our benevolent hand.
>
> As we are a noted personage—for our capacity for eating—of course we were invited to all the lunches and such. We first stopped at the Union Hall Saloon, where we found everybody and his grandmother, getting outside of Hot Toms, Lager Beer and other Christmas Trix—you bet they were doing them justice too. In a short time Leo arranged his square tables in line and mounted them with a fine lunch, consisting of roast turkeys, roast beef, roast pork, chickens, gobblers, pickles, sour kraut, Bologna sausage, and many other articles, all dressed and cooked in the most approved style.

After this lunch, he visited other public houses, where he found people competing with each other in loud singing or sleeping off their liquor in quiet corners. In the evening, he had a "hearty supper," and he woke up the next morning with a "slight head ache, probably caused from not eating enough the day previous."[17]

The Catholic and the Lutheran churches outdid each other in proclaiming the joy of Christmas. For Catholics, according to the *Fair Play*, Christmas day began long before dawn, with a four o'clock high mass. In the early morning darkness, "The church was resplendent with light and floral decorations." The day continued with low mass at seven o'clock in the morning, high mass and sermon at ten o'clock, and vespers at three in the afternoon. At the Lutheran Church, there was a Christmas Eve service with hymns and a morning service featuring a sermon on the life of Jesus. "Two large Christmas trees, filled with presents for the children of the school, and other floral decorations and a brilliant illumination made the church resplendent with light and beauty."[18]

17. *Ste. Genevieve Fair Play*, January 1, 1874.
18. Ibid., January 2, 1886.

The German custom of decorating an evergreen tree with candles and baubles became widely popular. St. Nicholas evolved into Santa Claus, the man who brought gifts to delight the children. In the 1880s, according to Joseph Ernst, Christmas in Ste. Genevieve was "a day which makes children glad and through them the older people as well; a day which is suggestive of forgiveness and charity, and the exercise of the better emotions generally." Throughout the town on that day, he said, "we sniff the breeze and it is fraught with turkey. Yum! Yum!"[19] One assumes that turkey was not the only thing consumed; the revelers most likely also enjoyed plenty of beer, wine, and hard liquor.

By the mid-nineteenth century, the easy alliance of religion and secular life, work and recreation, good food and strong drink rubbed up against the stern momentum of the nation's temperance movement. During the early years of the republic, Anglo-Americans rivaled and quite possibly exceeded their French counterparts in the consumption of alcohol. Historian W. J. Rorabaugh has convincingly documented a "great alcoholic binge," in the United States at the beginning of the nineteenth century. By 1830, however, America's drinking spree had reached its peak. It suddenly leveled off and then began a sharp decline as a result of a fervent, widespread, and well-organized campaign to promote abstinence and demonize liquor.[20]

The temperance crusade appealed to many Americans' evangelical Christianity, desire for wealth, and belief in the perfectibility of human society. Between 1795 and 1837, charismatic Protestant ministers identified alcohol as a dark temptation that could lead the country to economic ruin and moral damnation. Evangelists held revivals and circulated tracts throughout the republic. Wives and mothers who had suffered, or seen other women suffer, from the abuse and neglect of alcoholic men flocked to the temperance banner. Industrialists, seeking a sober work force, and ambitious men, wanting to climb the social ladder, embraced abstinence as the way to increase productivity and achieve success. Optimists and idealists of many varieties came to believe that control of liquor consump-

19. *Ste. Genevieve Herald*, December 22, 1883.
20. W. J. Rorabaugh, *The Alcoholic Republic: An American Tradition*, 25, 187–88.

tion would uplift private and public morality, increase prosperity for every-one, and lead to a better world.[21]

Initially, the reformers relied on moral persuasion to promote abstinence, but eventually they sought legal restrictions on the sale and use of alcohol. By the 1830s, temperance advocates were pushing local authorities to stop issuing licenses for the sale of liquor, and by the 1850s they had succeeded in "drying up" some counties in New England.[22] In the 1840s, Missouri state law required county clerks to collect license fees from merchants selling food or liquor. According to the revised statutes of 1845, "No person [should], directly or indirectly sell intoxicating liquors, without taking out a license as a grocer or dram-shop keeper." A person could operate a grocery store and could sell liquor, but he or she needed to purchase a separate license for each purpose. This could be expensive. County clerks determined the exact fees, and the state allowed them to charge up to fifty dollars every six months (or one hundred dollars for a grocer who also sold liquor). According to local records, Ste. Genevieve merchants paid less than eleven dollars in fees to operate a general store but fifteen dollars (the minimum required by the state) to maintain a "dram shop," which sold distilled spirits. Saloons with billiard rooms paid a whopping one hundred dollars for a license.[23]

These pre-Civil War licensing laws clearly discriminated against merchants who sold alcohol, and they specifically denied rights to African Americans. The statutes made it illegal for a dram shop keeper to "sell any intoxicating liquor or drink of any kind to any slave, without permission, in writing, from the master, owner, or overseer of such slave." The law also prohibited free black people from obtaining a license to sell intoxicating liquors. Another provision in the statute book forbade the sale of liquor to Indians.[24]

21. Thomas R. Pegram, *Battling Demon Rum: The Struggle for a Dry America, 1800–1933*, 17–19: Rorabaugh, *Alcoholic Republic*, 204–5, 212–13.

22. Pegram, *Battling Demon Rum*, 34–36.

23. Sanders, "Germans of Ste. Genevieve," 21; Folders 1319–1320, Ste. Genevieve Archives.

24. *Revised Statutes of the State of Missouri, 1845*, chap. 72, sec. 1, 7, and 9, and chap. 80, sec. 3.

By the 1850s, the first wave of temperance enthusiasm had waned, as Americans became embroiled in the controversy over slavery and the blood-bath of the Civil War. Attempts to press the antiliquor agenda on the national Democratic and Republican parties failed, as the parties descended into sectional strife. The brutality of the Civil War and the disappointment of Reconstruction undermined many Americans' belief that human society could be significantly improved by government action. In the postwar years, the movement's most dependable supporters were women, who could not vote and who therefore had little influence on the major parties.[25]

When Reconstruction ended and the bitterness of war began to fade, the temperance movement was once again revived. In 1873, the Woman's Christian Temperance Union (WCTU) set out to place the antiliquor crusade at the forefront of American reform movements. Throughout Missouri and the rest of the nation, middle-class women gave speeches to church groups, taught Sunday school lessons, used personal connections, circulated pamphlets, hung posters, sang songs, marched in parades, carried banners, and lobbied legislators and congressmen to push their agenda. During the final decades of the nineteenth century, temperance advocates turned from the tireless promotion of abstinence to a strident demand for the complete prohibition of the sale and consumption of alcoholic beverages.[26]

The temperance crusade underscored divisions in Missouri society. With a few exceptions (including Ste. Genevieve), rural areas and small towns supported the antiliquor movement. Antitemperance feeling ran high in St. Louis, where prosperity rested largely on the brewing industry. Members of the urban working class, many of whom depended on jobs in the breweries, resisted the antiliquor crusade. The strength of the movement flowed from the Baptist, Methodist, and evangelical Protestant churches. The Catholic and the Lutheran churches, which dominated Ste. Genevieve, generally opposed the antiliquor campaign.

Counties with large German American populations, including Ste.

---

25. Pegram, *Battling Demon Rum,* 43–45; G. K. Renner, "Prohibition Comes to Missouri, 1900–1919," 372–81.

26. Pegram, *Battling Demon Rum,* 44–45.

Genevieve County, held out against the antiliquor tide. But the push for reform grew stronger and stronger. Even in St. Louis, a weekly temperance newspaper appeared in the mid-1880s. In 1887, the state passed a local option law, allowing counties to decide if they would issue liquor licenses. By 1917, a few years before the enforcement of national Prohibition, ninety-six of Missouri's 114 counties had gone "dry." Ste. Genevieve would hold out as one of the last remaining "wet" counties.[27]

Henry Shaw, a lawyer and the publisher of the *Ste. Genevieve Fair Play* in the 1880s, tried to occupy the shrinking middle ground on the liquor issue. He favored temperance but opposed Prohibition. Shaw had married Katie Boverie, a local belle from a prominent family.[28] The *Fair Play*, a Democratic newspaper, was sharply critical of Ernst's flamboyance and the *Herald*'s stridency on this issue. Shaw conceded that there were too many taverns in Ste. Genevieve, but he made a distinction between beer and wine and the more "ardent" spirits. He opposed the high licensing fees that put breweries and wine merchants out of business.

In Shaw's opinion, which proved to be prophetic, Prohibition was a greater evil than the one it purported to cure. As a moralist, Shaw urged moderation and even abstention with regard to alcohol. As a realist, he predicted that Prohibition would not work. He opposed it "because it does not prevent what it prohibits—the sale and use of alcoholic stimulants—and because it tends to breed a race of spies and informers ten times more infamous and unendurable than the greatest drunkard on earth."[29]

Ste. Genevieve did not climb aboard the temperance bandwagon in the 1880s, partly because of its French heritage, partly because of its large German population, and partly because of its strong communal experience of joy and celebration. Resistance to the antiliquor crusade did not mean the town was anti-American. Nothing could be further from the truth. Ernst based his antitemperance position on the ideas of liberty embodied in the Declaration, the Constitution, and the Bill of Rights. Shaw rejected a form of repression that he believed would cause people to spy and inform on their neighbors. To avoid this, he was willing to put up with a few

27. Renner, "Prohibition Comes to Missouri," 365.
28. *Ste. Genevieve Herald,* April 28, 1883.
29. *Ste. Genevieve Fair Play,* January 17, 1885.

obnoxious drunkards. Both he and Ernst, raucous opponents on many issues, drew upon their experience in a tolerant community, accepted human weakness, and recognized limits on political power. Perhaps more than many small American towns, Ste. Genevieve clung to a tradition of personal liberty.

The town proclaimed its patriotism annually on Independence Day. In 1882 the *Herald* announced "a grand picnic on the 4th of July which shall eclipse everything that was offered in this line before." Organizer George Sexauer invited everyone to attend. The Ste. Genevieve Brass Band promised to play for a parade and a dance. In true Ste. Genevieve fashion, the *Herald* reported, "It is hardly necessary to mention that a bar kept by George Sexauer is first class and furnishes the best of everything."[30]

In 1885, Ste. Genevieve celebrated the centennial of *l'annee des grandes eaux* (year of the big waters), when the old French settlement moved to its new location on higher ground. A large crowd gathered in the square at 6:30 on the morning of July 21, when the St. Louis Cavalry and Artillery fired a twenty-one-gun salute. The local priest celebrated a high mass and preached a sermon about the lives of the pioneers. Three steamboats arrived, bringing passengers from St. Louis, Chester, and Kaskaskia. The Ste. Genevieve Cornet Band led a procession to the top of a hill, where the flags of France, Spain, and the United States were unfurled.[31]

Firmin Rozier delivered a lengthy oration on the town's history. His brother, Mayor Charles Rozier, had to silence the sweating and roiling crowd twice during the speech, which comprised most of the orator's not-yet-published book. In his rambling speech, Firmin touched upon a wide variety of topics, including early French explorers, Catholic missionaries, Indian tribes, pioneer life, floods, politics, and famous men.

Summing up the town's history, with a somewhat rose-colored view, he declared,

> The people of Ste. Genevieve, exactly since a century and a half, have lived under four different governments without encountering great disasters or bloody wars, in such remarkable changes, which are generally accompanied with great disorders and misfortunes. They first lived and

30. *Ste. Genevieve Herald,* June 17, 1882.
31. Rozier, *History of the Early Settlement of the Mississippi Valley,* 139–40.

were subjects of the great French nation to the year 1769; secondly they fell under the jurisdiction and dominion of Spain until 1800; again under the Napoleon dynasty, until 1804; and lastly, and thank God, under the flag of the United States of America.[32]

Rozier's picture of a peaceful community, blessedly free from strife or misfortune, was muddied when the day's events ended in turmoil. Tempers flared when the beer vendor on the riverboat *Will S. Hays* overcharged passengers and then set up an unlicensed liquor stand just outside the city limits. Local beer sellers booted him out. Appropriately enough, the celebration came to a climax when a severe rainstorm turned the river bottom into a soggy facsimile of the flooded lands of 1785.[33]

In its general outlines, Rozier's summation came close to the truth. When the people of Ste. Genevieve rebuilt their town on high ground, the United States had not yet written its Constitution, and the Mississippi River formed the new nation's far western border. For the next twenty years, while the new American republic created its national identity, the frontier community functioned under Spanish rule, based in French and Spanish customs and traditions. The Louisiana Purchase and American rule did not erase the community's cultural origins. When new people came, they took their places in a stable society with strong roots. Among the most important expressions of these roots were leisure activities and festivals, which helped to define the community, anchor it in the past, and prepare it for whatever the future might bring.

In the 1880s, the people of Ste. Genevieve ushered in each new year with the French colonial ritual of La Guillonee, but they also turned out for a Fourth of July parade and picnic. They held out against America's push for Prohibition, but they based their resistance on the Bill of Rights. Every year a predictable round of holidays and rituals helped them define their unique character and identity during the long and complex process of legal, social, and cultural change that transformed and reshaped an old French outpost into an American town.

32. Ibid., 135.
33. Naeger, Naeger, and Evans, *Ste. Genevieve: A Leisurely Stroll,* 20–21.

CONCLUSION

Ste. Genevieve in 1885

They first lived and were subjects of the great French nation . . . ; secondly they fell under the jurisdiction and dominion of Spain until 1800; again under the Napoleon dynasty, until 1804; and lastly, and thank God, under the flag of the United States of America, from the last period to the present time, and to be hoped for all future time.

Firmin Rozier, *History of the Early Settlement of the Mississippi Valley*

WHAT DOES IT MEAN to become American or to be Americanized? When Ste. Genevieve became an American town, did its society become more egalitarian? Did all or most of its citizens participate in the political life of the community? Did individuals have the ability to succeed or fail, rise or fall by their own efforts? Did they enjoy more personal freedom? The history of the community in the nineteenth century—from the Louisiana Purchase to the town's centennial celebration—suggests some answers to these questions.

It is important to remember that Americanization, or democratization, was not instantaneous. The abrupt change in government in 1804 did not, and could not, bring an immediate transformation of the circumstances under which people lived their lives, the laws that governed them, or the customs and habits that passed from generation to generation. In one respect, the new order entered dramatically. The old commandant stepped down and began to share his power with a group of less eminent citizens. All of the new political leaders were white males, and all of them had already acquired some wealth or stature in the community.

Equality had not developed to any high degree either in French colonial society or in the American republic that replaced it. Tocqueville argued that democracy could not thrive in the presence of a landed aristocracy. But in Ste. Genevieve, several of the old French families possessed large land-holdings. The new American regime required them to defend their claims in court, but, ultimately, the United States government confirmed nearly half of these claims, which often encompassed thousands of acres. In Ste. Genevieve, the Vallé family retained its position of prominence, based on its ownership of farms and mines, throughout the nineteenth century.

Anglo-Americans came to Ste. Genevieve in search of wealth and status. Entrepreneurs like Moses Austin and John Smith T tapped into the lead mining resources north of the town. Lawyers like John Scott came to profit from the long, drawn out battles of rich men to confirm land claims. Physicians like Lewis Linn and Ichabod Sargent came, in part, to practice their profession. Linn turned the affection of the people into the basis for a political career. Sargent supplemented his income as a landowner, speculator, and farmer. His daughters married into prominent French families.

German settlers, who arrived in large numbers after 1830, challenged the local elite on issue of slavery. Both the French and the Anglo-Americans made a practice of enslaving people of color. A few German immigrants adapted to the local customs and acquired slaves, but most of them resisted this temptation. In St. Louis, the German American press championed abolitionism. During the Civil War, Germans in Ste. Genevieve supported the Union. After the war, Joseph Ernst established a staunchly republican paper that stridently supported the Bill of Rights.

Loyalty to the national government developed slowly. Anglo-Americans seemed to have no more respect for the Constitution than their French neighbors did. For instance, the local sheriff, Henry Dodge, left town to take part in Burr's famous scheme to conquer Mexico. But this breach of decorum did not cost him his job. During the Civil War, elite French and Anglo-American citizens openly sided with the Confederacy. After the war, however, Felix Janis, descendant of one of the old French families, made an impassioned plea for loyalty to the republic.

The rule of law made halting progress in the town. Elite white men settled disputes by dueling. Intimidated juries let murderers go free. Local officials, prosecutors, and defense attorneys struggled to make sense of a hodgepodge of old French and Spanish traditions and new American codes of law. Nevertheless, in the midst of all this confusion, people—all kinds of people—went to court and demanded justice.

The courts offered a small opening for women and African Americans, who were not full citizens of the republic, to challenge the limits on their freedom. Even before the American takeover, a free black woman named Elizabeth D'Atchurut went to the commandant and sued a white family for support of her mixed-race children. Marie LaPorte, a French-speaking white woman, learned her way around the American court system. Pelagie Amoureux, a black woman in a mixed-race relationship, fought back when men insulted and abused her. These women assumed that justice belonged not only to white males but to everyone.

Even before the Civil War, African Americans found paths to freedom. There were free black people in Ste. Genevieve in the eighteenth century. After the American takeover, their numbers grew steadily, in spite of increasingly restrictive laws. Free black people exercised many of the normal rights of citizenship: they married, bought property, left wills and estates, and took their grievances to court. The turmoil of the 1850s brought new threats to their precarious legal status. Some of them left the community; others stayed through the war and Reconstruction. Some fought for freedom by joining the Union army, and some of these soldiers, such as John White and Paul Vallé, returned to Ste. Genevieve after the war. African American and mixed-race families maintained connections of affection and memory through many generations, sustaining each other through decades of stress. Slavery had ended, but the day-to-day struggle for dignity and freedom had not.

The American ethos tied human dignity to work. At every level of society, people strove to better themselves by engaging in professions, business endeavors, or paid labor. Ambitious young men like O. D. Harris saw opportunities in mining and banking. Harris could not climb the economic ladder without some help. He allied himself with powerful French families but in the end found only failure and disgrace. Decades after the Louisiana Purchase, men with French surnames dominated the businesses and professions. German Americans found niches in brewing, crafts, and trades. Many young men (French, German, and Anglo-American) had to hire out as wage laborers, and for many others there were no jobs at all. Black men and women often had to accept positions as servants. Women, in general, had few opportunities, although some inherited businesses from their husbands or fathers.

For most people in Ste. Genevieve, the key to success and economic survival was not individual ability or effort but family solidarity. At the upper levels of society, old families like the Vallés passed large landholdings down from generation to generation. Professional men like Dr. Hertich encouraged their sons to follow in their footsteps and to support them when they became infirm. Middle-class families worked together to operate taverns, grocery stores, and other enterprises. Widows often kept the businesses going and passed them along to daughters and sons. Farm families like the Kerns and the Ribaults depended on the labor of sons, daughters, and sons-in-law. Nontraditional families banded together for support: a household of unmarried or widowed sisters might pool the money they earned as seamstresses; or a group of nuns might function as a family and devote their lives to educating the young. For those without a family to depend on, the only option might be the poor house.

Individuals and families do not exist in a vacuum. Throughout the nineteenth century, the Catholic Church played an important role in bolstering family life in Ste. Genevieve. The church administered the sacraments of marriage, baptized children, and buried the dead. Recognizing the realities of life on the frontier, the local church blessed mixed-race unions and blended families. The church also gave its support to nonbiological families created by adoption. In the absence of a secular school system, local priests and nuns took on the task of educating the young. In the late nineteenth century, Felix Janis and Joseph Ernst had a hard time convincing parents to send their children to the public schools, where they might have learned more about life in a democratic republic. Black families sent their children to the segregated public school, but many white families preferred sending their children to parochial schools, which reinforced traditional religious values.

These values sustained them in a world that could bring death without warning or explanation. Children died as frequently as adults. Epidemics swept lives away by the dozens. Treatments could be as frightening as diseases. Doctors and priests who tended the sick could succumb to contagion. Religious processions cheered the ailing and celebrated the dead. Survivors carved family names on stone monuments, marking the loss of individuals and uniting the community through the generations.

Ste. Genevieve existed within the republic, but it also had a life apart from it. The United States absorbed the little town, but it did not create it. Customs like La Guillonee harked back to times before the nation existed, but they remained as part of the town's identity. Anglo-Americans and German Americans, who came to the town after the Louisiana Purchase, adopted these old French customs as part of their communal life. The Fourth of July became one more holiday in an annual round of celebrations that reinforced the town's communal bonds. In 1885, when residents celebrated the centennial of the French colonial community's deliverance from the flooded Mississippi River they did it in true Ste. Genevieve fashion—with beer and food and patriotic speeches.

What did America bring to Ste. Genevieve? Most important, it brought participatory government. The town responded by nurturing five United States senators.[1] Trial by jury was another innovation. The local commandant no longer passed judgment in cases at law. People pleaded their cases to their peers. Juries, of course, could succumb to pressure and fear, and the system did not work perfectly, but it was a step toward a just society. Another important step was the creation of a free press. Local publishers brought out dozens of newspapers. By 1885, the little town had two stridently competitive publications, the *Ste. Genevieve Fair Play* and the *Ste. Genevieve Herald,* which was published in both English and German. Just as significantly, Americanization brought with it a system of education. Public schools got off to a ragged start. But the Catholic Church and, in particular, a group of determined nuns provided basic education on a continuing and stable basis to young people growing up in the town. By the 1880s, both public and parochial schools had opened their doors to boys and to girls, both white and black—although the schools were racially segregated.

---

1. The five senators from Ste. Genevieve are Henry Dodge, Lewis F. Linn, George W. Jones, Augustus C. Dodge, Lewis V. Bogy (Rozier, *History of the Early Settlement of the Mississippi Valley,* 335).

Did America bring freedom? This is the most profound and difficult question. If freedom means toleration of people's differences, the answer is no. Initially, Americanization resulted in the forced removal of native people (the Peoria, Shawnee, Delaware, and Osage) from the town and its surrounding area. Americans continued the French colonial practice of enslaving black people. Under the new republic, white citizens rigidly enforced laws against fugitive slaves and vigorously assailed the status of free persons of color.

Did America bring freedom? If freedom means the equal participation of all citizens in the political life of the community, the answer is no. Old French names appeared continually on the lists of board members, judges, prosecutors, and other local officials. The German Americans and Anglo-Americans who participated in governing the town were an elite group, often benefiting from marital or personal connections with prominent French families. Women did not serve in political offices, with the occasional exception of a postmistress and a manager of the local poor house. African Americans were excluded from the town's political process. The twentieth century would bring changes in the legal status of blacks and women, but equal participation would remain an elusive ideal.

Did America bring freedom? If freedom means the right of the individual to appear in court and ask for justice, the answer is yes. Local records show that the people of Ste. Genevieve sued and defended themselves with gusto. Even those who lacked political power—women and black people—went to court to press their cases, collect their debts, claim their property, and defend their honor. The right to go to court does not guarantee that justice will prevail, but it does mean that justice is possible. The people of Ste. Genevieve seemed to be optimists, and this sort of optimism—the hope that justice will triumph—is the heart of democracy.

Did America bring freedom? If freedom means personal liberty, the answer is no—and yes. In the years following the Louisiana Purchase, many observers contrasted the free and easy ways of the old French population with the more rigid behavioral norms of the Anglo-Americans. Observance of the Sabbath was an issue. Despite their strong Catholicism, the French inhabitants felt free to conduct business, dance, drink wine and beer, play cards, and otherwise enjoy life on the Christians' day of rest. The Americans passed Sunday closing laws that limited people's ability to buy and sell merchandise, particularly alcohol, on that day. Newspaper editor Joseph Ernst regarded this as an unwarranted limitation on personal freedom, and so it was. Ernst did not hesitate to say so, quite rudely, in print. In doing this, without apology or shame, he exercised his right of free expression that was protected by the First Amendment to the United States Constitution. That right—the right to brazenly criticize the law and the government—that is the wellspring of democracy.

BIBLIOGRAPHY

Author's Note on Primary Sources

Many primary sources are available for the study of Ste. Genevieve's history. There are very few collections of personal papers, but there is a wealth of information in official records and church archives. Many important records are housed at the Ste. Genevieve County Courthouse: deeds and property records are located in the recorder's office, and probate documents, in the office of the circuit court. County record books, licenses, and, in particular, the free black registry are housed in the county clerk's office. For the past few decades, Missouri's Local Records Preservation Program has worked hard to organize, index, and microfilm important historical records at the county level. As a result of this effort, many local and county records are now available, and many more will be available in the future, from the Missouri State Archives.

In cooperation with the University of Missouri–Columbia, the State Historical Society of Missouri and the Western Historical Manuscripts Collection identified, microfilmed, and indexed a huge number of important documents, collectively called the Ste. Genevieve Archives. Reels of microfilm and printed indexes from this collection are housed in several locations, including the Ozark Regional Library in Ste. Genevieve.

Ste. Genevieve Catholic Church has maintained baptismal, marriage, and burial records since the eighteenth century. These are not public records, but the church secretary graciously provides information to researchers. There is a computerized index to many of the original records.

The Missouri Historical Society in St. Louis also houses important collections of records and papers relating to Ste. Genevieve.

Census records are essential to the study of local history. Every tenth year, the United States government counts the people in the nation and collects all sorts of data about them—name, age, race, occupation, and much more. The federal government publishes summaries of the data in statistical formats after every census. The original information collected by census takers remains confidential for seventy-two years. This information is arranged by state, county, and town on numbered reels of film, which are available at many libraries.

The research for this book involved the examination of the censuses for Ste. Genevieve City and Ste. Genevieve County in the years 1850, 1860, 1870, and 1880. For some census years, the federal government gathered information on mortality during the twelve month period preceding the census, and for others, there were special censuses, recording information on, for instance, surviving Civil War veterans. In general, the researchers who worked on this book used microfilm of the census on file at the Ozark Regional Library in Ste. Genevieve. The State Historical Society provided copies of the mortality schedules for Ste. Genevieve in 1849–1850, 1859–1860, and 1879–1880. The microfilmed census provides information on individuals and families, and it can be used, as it was in chapter 9 of this book, to obtain general information about such things as employment in communities, counties, and states. The microfilmed census data is available at many libraries and archives around the nation and is provided by the National Archives and Records Administration (NARA).

Collections and Papers

Library of Congress, Washington, D.C.

Born in Slavery: Slave Narratives from the Federal Writers' Project, 1936–1938. Manuscript and Prints and Photographs Division.
Overby, Osmund, and Toni Prawl. "Pierre Delassus De Luziere House." HABS No. MO-1283, January 1987. Historic American Buildings Survey Collection.

Missouri Historical Society, St. Louis

Amoureux-Bolduc Papers.
"Correspondence between Mr. Scott and Mr. Lucas, St. Louis, August 10–September 20, 1816." Pamphlet.
Delassus-St. Vrain Collection.
Ordinances Passed by the Trustees of the Town of Ste. Genevieve, Missouri, 1842.
Historic New Orleans Collection, New Orleans, Louisiana.
Spanish Census of Ste. Genevieve, Missouri, 1787. Census Collection, 1732–1980.
Statement of the Situation of the Estate of Camille Delassus, March 20, 1824, file 59–0084. Franz Papers.

Dissertations, Theses, and Unpublished Papers

Bibb, Debbie. "Lisette." Typescript, Southeast Missouri State University.
Farris, N. Renae. "French Roots, American Woman: Marie LaPorte of Ste. Genevieve, 1766–1849." Master's thesis, Southeast Missouri State University, 2002.

Hamilton, M. Colleen. "French Colonial Land Use: The Felix Valle House State Historic Site." Master's thesis, University of Missouri–St. Louis, 1990.

Kester, Greg. "They Carried a Heavy Burden: The Use of Slave Labor in the Lead Mines of Southeast Missouri." Master's thesis, Southeast Missouri State University, 2000.

Manning, Mary Christina. "Elizabeth Shannon: A Freed Slave and Her Family." Paper prepared for Dr. Bonnie Stepenoff, Southeast Missouri State University, 1999.

Sanders, Barbara. "The Germans of Ste. Genevieve, 1830–1890." Paper prepared for Dr. Susan Flader, University of Missouri–Columbia.

Federal and State records

American State Papers: 8, Public Lands. Vols. 2, 3, 4, and 6. Washington, D.C.: Gales and Seaton, 1834.

Biographical Directory of the American Congress, 1774–1971.

Congressional Globe. 46 vols. Washington, D.C. 1834–1873.

Laws of the State of Missouri, Fourteenth General Assembly, First Session, 1847.

Revised Statutes of the State of Missouri, 1845. St. Louis: J. W. Dougherty, 1845.

State of Missouri vs. Ambs. Supreme Court of Missouri, St. Louis, 20 Mo. 214, 1854, Mo. LEXIS 174, October 1854.

U.S. Bureau of the Census. *Compendium of the Tenth Census, 1880.*

———. *Eighth Census: 1860, Population Schedule: Ste. Genevieve County, Missouri.* NARA Microfilm, M653, Free Schedule, Reel n#645, Slave Schedule, Reel #424.

———. *Missouri Mortality Schedules, Ste. Genevieve, Missouri.*

———. *1890 Special Census to Enumerate the Union Civil War Veterans or Their Widows: Ste. Genevieve, Missouri.* NARA Microfilm, M123, Reel #28.

———. *Ninth Census: 1870, Population Schedule: Ste. Genevieve County, Missouri.* NARA Microfilm, M593, Reel #807.

———. *Seventh Census: 1850, Population Schedule: Ste. Genevieve County, Missouri.* NARA Microfilm, M432, Free Schedule, Reel #413, Slave Schedule, Reel #664.

———. *Sixth Census: 1840, Population Schedule, Ste. Genevieve County, Missouri.* NARA Microfilm, M704, Reel #230.

———. *Tenth Census of the United States: 1880, Ste. Genevieve County, Missouri.* NARA Microfilm, T9, Reel #715.

———. *Thirteen Census: 1910, Population Schedule: Ste. Genevieve County, Missouri.* NARA Microfilm, Reel #810.

———. *Twelfth Census: 1900, Population Schedule: Ste. Genevieve County, Missouri.* NARA Microfilm, T623, Reel #886.

Newspapers

Columbia Missouri Intelligencer. June-October 1833.
Franklin Missouri Intelligencer. November 1823.
Jefferson City Missouri State Times. September 8, 1865.
Missouri Citizen. May 13, 1859.
Ste. Genevieve Democrat. June 8, 1850.
Ste. Genevieve Fair Play. 1872–1885.
Ste. Genevieve Herald. 1882–1885.
Ste. Genevieve Independent. May 16-December 10, 1857.
Ste. Genevieve Pioneer. May 4, 1850.
Ste. Genevieve Plaindealer. June 9, 1855-April 11, 1862.
St. Louis Missouri Republican. 1828, 1845–1850.
St. Louis Republic. August 5, 1876.

Oral Sources

Amoureux, Phillippe, and Fran Barker. Interview with the author, January 13, 2005.
Kern, Shirley. Interviewed with Cathy Grove, summer field school, 2001.

References

Abernethy, Thomas Perkins. "Aaron Burr in Mississippi." *Journal of Southern History* 15, no. 1 (February 1949): 9–21.
Archibald, Robert R. "Honor and Family: The Career of Lt. Gov. Carlos de Hault de Lassus." *Gateway Heritage* 12, no. 4 (1992): 32–41.
Ashe, Thomas. *Travels in America Performed in 1806.* Newburyport, Mass.: Reprinted for W. Sawyer and Co. by E. M. Blunt, 1808.
Audubon, John James. *Delineations of American Scenery and Character.* New York: G. A. Baker, 1926.
Baker, Paula. "White Women's Separate Sphere and Their Political Role, 1780–1860." In *Major Problems in American Women's History,* edited by Mary Beth Norton, 108–15. Boston: Houghton Mifflin, 2003.
Baker, Vaughn B. "Cherchez les Femmes: Some Glimpses of Women in Early Eighteenth-Century Louisiana." *Louisiana History* 31, no. 1 (Winter 1990): 21–37.
Banner, Stuart. *Legal Systems in Conflict: Property and Sovereignty in Missouri, 1750–1860.* Norman: University of Oklahoma Press, 2000.
Bartels, Carolyn M. *The Forgotten Men: Missouri State Guard.* Independence, Mo.: Two Trails Publishing, 1995.

Basler, Lucile. *Pioneers of Old Ste. Genevieve.* Ste. Genevieve: Lucile Basler, 1983.

Bates, Frederick. *The Life and Papers of Frederick Bates.* Vol. 1. Edited by Thomas Maitland Marshall. St. Louis: Missouri Historical Society, 1926.

Beauford, Gertrude. "De Luziere, De Lassus, St. Vrain, and Derbigny." *Daughters of the American Revolution Magazine* (May 1980): 688–91.

Bellamy, Donnie D. "Free Blacks in Antebellum Missouri, 1820–1860." *Missouri Historical Review* 67 (January 1973): 198–226.

Bender, Thomas. *Community and Social Change in America.* Baltimore: Johns Hopkins University Press, 1978.

Berlin, Ira. *Slaves without Masters: The Free Negro in the Antebellum South.* New York: Pantheon Books, 1974.

Berthoff, Rowland. "Conventional Mentality: Free Blacks, Women, and Business Corporations as Unequal Persons, 1820–1870." *Journal of American History* 76 (December 1989): 753–73.

———. *An Unsettled People: Social Order and Disorder in American History.* New York: Harper and Row, 1971.

Boyle, Susan C. "Did She Generally Decide: Women in Ste. Genevieve, 1750–1805." *William and Mary Quarterly* 44, no. 4 (October 1987): 775–89.

Brackenridge, H. M. *Recollections of Persons and Places in the West.* Philadelphia: J. B. Lippincott, 1868.

———. *Views of Louisiana: Together with a Journal of a Voyage up the Missouri River, in 1811.* Chicago: Quadrangle Books, 1962.

Buckley, E. R., and H. A. Buehler. *The Quarrying Industry of Missouri.* Vol. 2, 2nd ser. Jefferson City: Missouri Bureau of Geology and Mines, 1904.

Burnett, Robyn, and Ken Luebbering. *German Settlement in Missouri: New Land, Old Ways.* Columbia: University of Missouri Press, 1983.

Chapman, Carl H., and Eleanor F. Chapman. *Indians and Archaeology of Missouri.* Columbia: University of Missouri Press, 1983.

Chidsey, Donald Barr. *The Great Conspiracy.* New York: Crown Publishers, 1967.

Clark, Emily, "By All the Conduct of Their Lives: A Laywomen's Confraternity in New Orleans, 1730–1744." *William and Mary Quarterly* 54, no. 4 (October 1997): 769–94.

Coffin, Margaret M. *Death in Early America.* New York: Thomas Nelson, 1976.

Cox, Isaac Joslin. "General Wilkinson and His Later Intrigues with the Spaniards." *American Historical Review* 19, no. 4 (July 1914): 794–812.

Delassus de Luzières, Pierre-Charles. *An Official Account of the Situation, Soil, Produce, and etc. of that Part of Louisiana Which Lies between the Mouth of the Missouri and New Madrid, or L'Anse à la Graise, and on the West Side of the Mississippi, Together with and Abstract of the Spanish Government, and etc.*

Lexington, Ky.: J. Bradford, [1796]. Reprinted by the Felix Valle State Historic Site, Ste. Genevieve, Mo.

Douglass, Frederick. *Narrative of the Life of Frederick Douglass, An American Slave.* New Haven: Yale University Press, 2001.

Drake, Daniel. *Malaria in the Interior Valley of North America,* a Selection by Norman D. Levine from *A Systematic Treatise, Historical, Etiological, and Practical, on the Principal Diseases of the Interior Valley of North America, as they Appear in the Caucasian, African, Indian, and Esquimaux Varieties of its Population.* Urbana: University of Illinois Press, 1964.

Duden, Gottfried. *Report on a Journey to the Western States of North America and a Stay of Several Years along the Missouri during the Years 1824, 1825, 1826, and 1827.* Columbia: State Historical Society of Missouri, 1980.

Durham, Jennifer. *Benjamin Franklin: A Biographical Companion.* Santa Barbara: ABC-CLIO, 1997.

Ekberg, Carl J. *Colonial Ste. Genevieve: An Adventure on the Mississippi Frontier.* Tucson: Patrice Press, 1996.

———. *François Vallé and His World: Upper Louisiana before Lewis and Clark.* Columbia: University of Missouri Press, 2002.

———. *French Roots in the Illinois Country: The Mississippi Frontier in Colonial Times.* Urbana: University of Illinois Press, 1998.

———. *Louis Bolduc: His Family and His House.* Tucson: Patrice Press, 2002.

Finiels, Nicolas de. *An Account of Upper Louisiana.* Edited by Carl J. Ekberg and William E. Foley. Columbia: University of Missouri Press, 1989.

Fisher, Linda A. "A Summer of Terror: Cholera in St. Louis, 1849." *Missouri Historical Review* 99, no. 3 (April 2005): 189–211.

Flint, Timothy. *Recollections of the Last Ten Years in the Valley of the Mississippi.* Carbondale: Southern Illinois University Press, 1968.

Foley, William E. "Friends and Partners: William Clark, Meriwether Lewis, and Mid-America's French Creoles." *Missouri Historical Review* 98 (July 2004): 270–82.

———. *A History of Missouri: Volume I, 1673–1820.* Columbia: University of Missouri Press, 1971.

Franklin, Benjamin. *Autobiography of Benjamin Franklin.* New York: Barnes and Noble, 1994.

———. *Benjamin Franklin: Writings.* New York: Penguin Putnam, 1987.

Franzwa, Gregory. *The Story of Old Ste. Genevieve.* 2nd ed. St. Louis: Patrice Press, 1973.

Frazier, Steve. "Lost History of Valles Mines." Park Hills, Mo.: Missouri Mines State Historic Site, n.d.

Garrison, George P., ed. "Moses Austin: the Journal." *American Historical Review* 5, no. 3 (1900).

Gillespie, Michael. *Come Hell or High Water: A Lively History of Steamboating on the Mississippi and Ohio Rivers.* Stoddard, Wis.: Heritage Press, 2001.

Goodspeed's History of Southeast Missouri. Cape Girardeau, Mo.: Ramfre Press, 1964.

Gracy, David B. *Moses Austin: His Life.* San Antonio: Trinity University Press, 1987.

Greene, Lorenzo, Gary R. Kremer, and Antonio F. Holland. *Missouri's Black Heritage.* Rev. ed. Columbia: University of Missouri Press, 1993.

Harr, John L. "Law and Lawlessness in the Lower Mississippi Valley." *Northwest Missouri State College Studies* 19 (June 1, 1955): 60–70.

Hoff, Joan. "The Negative Impact of the American Revolution on White Women." In *Major Problems in American Women's History,* edited by Mary Beth Norton, 76–77. Boston: Houghton Mifflin, 2003.

Houck, Louis. *History of Missouri.* Vol. 3. Chicago: R. R. Donnelly and Sons, 1908.

Husband, Michael B. "Senator Lewis F. Linn and the Oregon Question." *Missouri Historical Review* 66 (October 1971): 1–19.

Ingersoll, Thomas N. "Free Blacks in a Slave Society: New Orleans, 1718–1812." *William and Mary Quarterly* 48, no. 2 (April 1991): 173–200.

Jordan, Philip D. *Frontier Law and Order: Ten Essays.* Lincoln: University of Nebraska Press, 1970.

Journals of the Lewis and Clark Expedition. Vol. 2. Edited by Gary Moulton. Lincoln: University of Nebraska Press, 1986.

Kinnaird, Lawrence. "The Spanish Expedition against Fort St. Joseph in 1781, a New Interpretation." *Mississippi Valley Historical Review* 19, no. 2 (September 1932): 173–91.

La Guillonee: A French New Year's Eve Custom and Song, a Collection of Essays. Old Mines, Mo.: Old Mines Area Historical Society, 2004.

Linn, Elizabeth A. (Relfe), and N. Sargent. *The Life and Public Service of Dr. Lewis F. Linn.* New York: D. Appleton, 1857.

Linn, Lewis. "Cholera Remedies by a Missouri Physician." *Columbia Missouri Intelligencer,* June 29, 1833.

Litwack, Leon F. *Been in the Storm so Long: The Aftermath of Slavery.* New York: Knopf, 1979.

Lowrie, Walter, ed. *Early Settlers of Missouri as Taken from Land Claims in the Missouri Territory.* Easley, S.C.: Southern Historical Press, 1986.

McCandless, Perry. *A History of Missouri: Volume II, 1820–1860.* Columbia: University of Missouri Press, 2000.

McClure, Ethel. *More than a Roof: The Development of Minnesota Poor Farms and Homes for the Aged.* St. Paul: Minnesota Historical Society, 1968.

McIntyre, Charshee. *Criminalizing a Race: Free Blacks during Slavery.* Queens, N.Y.: Kayode, 1993.

McLear, Patrick E. "The St. Louis Cholera Epidemic of 1849." *Missouri Historical Review* 63, no. 2 (January 1969): 171–81.

Meirink, Dorothy. "From Carondelet down the Road a Piece to Ste. Genevieve." *Provincial News Notes* (of the Sisters of St. Joseph), April 1999, 24.

Morrow, Kristen Kalen, "Ste. Genevieve's First Family... A Chronicle of the Valles." *Gateway Heritage* (Fall 1987): 25–33.

Naeger, Bill, Patti Naeger, and Mark Evans. *Ste. Genevieve: A Leisurely Stroll through History.* Ste. Genevieve: Merchant Street Publishing, 1999.

Newlin, Claude Milton. *The Life and Writings of Hugh Henry Brackenridge.* Mamaroneck, N.Y.: Paul P. Appel, 1971.

Ohman, Marian M. *History of Missouri's Counties, County Seats, and Courthouse Squares.* Columbia: University of Missouri Extension Service, 1983.

———. "Missouri County Organization, 1812–1876." *Missouri Historical Review* 76 (April 1982): 253–81.

Pegram, Thomas R. *Battling Demon Rum: The Struggle for a Dry America, 1800–1933.* Chicago: Ivan R. Dee, 1998.

Pelzer, Louis. *Henry Dodge.* Iowa City: State Historical Society of Iowa, 1911.

Peterson, Charles E. "Early Ste. Genevieve and its Architecture." *Missouri Historical Review* 35 (January 1941): 207–32.

Peterson, Richard E., et al. *Sterling Price's Lieutenants: A Guide to the Officers and Organization of the Missouri State Guard, 1861–1865.* Jefferson City: Richard E. Peterson, 1995.

Primm, Wilson. "New Year's Day in the Olden Time of St. Louis," read before the first meeting of the Missouri Historical Society, St. Louis, January 5, 1867. In *La Guillonee: A French New Year's Eve Custom and Song—a Collection of Essays.* Old Mines, Mo.: Old Mines Area Historical Society, 2004.

Public Schools of the State of Missouri. *Thirty-First Report of the Public Schools of the State of Missouri.* Jefferson City: Tribune Printing, 1881.

Rees, Mark A., and Neal H. Lopinot. *Archaeological Survey and Testing of the De Lassus de Luzieres-Hecker Site (23SG176), Ste. Genevieve County, Missouri, CAR Project 1141.* Springfield: Southwest Missouri Center for Archaeological Research, March 2001.

Renner, G. K. "Prohibition Comes to Missouri, 1900–1919." *Missouri Historical Review* 62 (July 1968): 363–97.

Rorabaugh, W. J. *The Alcoholic Republic: An American Tradition.* New York: Oxford University Press, 1979.

Rosenberg, Charles E. *The Cholera Years: The United States in 1832, 1849, and 1866.* Chicago: University of Chicago Press, 1962.

Rothensteiner, John. "Earliest History of Mine La Motte." *Missouri Historical Review* 20 (January 1926): 199–213.

———. *History of the Archdiocese of St. Louis.* Vols. 1 and 2. St. Louis: Blackwell Wielandy, 1928.

Rowan, Steven. *Germans for a Free Missouri: Translations from the St. Louis Radical Press, 1857–1862.* Columbia: University of Missouri Press, 1983.

Rozier, Firmin A. *Rozier's History of the Early Settlement of the Mississippi Valley.* St. Louis: G. A. Pierrot and Son, 1890.

Savage, Mary Lucida. *The Congregation of Saint Joseph of Carondelet.* St. Louis: Congregation of St. Joseph of Carondelet, 1923.

Schaaf, Ida M. *Sainte Genevieve Marriages, Baptisms, and Burials from the Church Register, Some Marriages from the Courthouse Records, and a List of Inscriptions from the Protestant Burying Grounds.* St. Louis: Ida M. Schaaf, 1918.

Schmidt, Bob. *Boys of the Best Families in the State: Co. E 2nd Missouri Cavalry.* French Village, Mo.: Robert Schmidt, 2002.

———. *Civil War Veterans of Southeast Missouri for the Counties of St. Francois, Ste. Genevieve, and Washington.* French Village, Mo.: Robert Schmidt, 1999.

Schroeder, Adolf. "German Folklore and Traditional Practices in the Mississippi Valley." In *French and Germans in the Mississippi Valley: Landscape and Cultural Traditions,* edited by Michael Roark. Cape Girardeau, Mo.: Center for Regional History and Cultural Heritage, 1988.

Schroeder, Walter A. *Opening the Ozarks: A Historical Geography of Missouri's Ste. Genevieve District, 1760–1830.* Columbia: University of Missouri Press, 2002.

Schultz, Christian. *Travels on an Inland Voyage through the States of New-York, Pennsylvania, Virginia, Ohio, Kentucky, and Tennessee, and through the Territories of Indiana, Louisiana, Mississippi, and New-Orleans, performed in the years 1807 and 1808.* Vol. 2. Ridgewood, N.J.: Gregg Press, 1968.

Sharp, Mary Rozier, and Louis J. Sharp III. *Between the Gabouri: A History of Ferdinant Rozier and "Nearly" All His Descendants.* Ste. Genevieve: Histoire de Rozier, 1981.

Shoemaker, Floyd C. *Missouri and Missourians: Land of Contrasts and People of Achievements.* Vols. 1 and 2. Chicago: Lewis Publishing, 1943.

Smith, John David, ed. *Black Soldiers in Blue: African American Troops in the Civil War Era.* Chapel Hill: University of North Carolina Press, 2002.

Stepenoff, Bonnie, and Debbie Bibb. *Ste. Genevieve Historic Preservation Field School 2000 and 2001: The Delassus-Kern House.* Jefferson City: Missouri Department of Natural Resources Division of State Parks, 2004.

Steward, Dick. *Duels and the Roots of Violence in Missouri.* Columbia: University of Missouri Press, 2000.

―――. *Frontier Swashbuckler: The Life and Legend of John Smith T.* Columbia: University of Missouri Press, 2000.

Stiles, T. J. *Jesse James: Last Rebel of the Civil War.* New York: Alfred A. Knopf, 2002.

Stoddard, Amos. *Sketches Historical and Descriptive of Louisiana.* 1812. Reprint, New York: AMS Press, 1973.

Swallow, G. C. *First and Second Annual Reports of the Geological Survey of Missouri.* Jefferson City: James Lusk, Public Printer, 1855.

Swartzlow, Ruby Johnson, "The Early History of Lead Mining in Missouri, Part 4: The Austin Period, 1800–1820." *Missouri Historical Review* 29 (January 1935): 111–14.

Swift, James V. "Several Boats Were Lost at Ste. Genevieve." *Waterways Journal* 116, no. 32 (November 4, 2002): 14.

Thompson, Henry C. *Sam Hildebrand Rides Again.* Bonne Terre, Mo.: Steinbeck Publishing, 1950.

Thompson, M. Jeff. *The Civil War Reminiscences of General M. Jeff Thompson.* Edited by Donald J. Stanton, Goodwin F. Berquist, and Paul C. Bowers. Dayton, Ohio: Morningside, 1988.

Thurman, Melburn D. *Building a House in Eighteenth Century Ste. Genevieve.* Ste. Genevieve: Pendragon's Press, 1984.

Tocqueville, Alexis de. *Democracy in America.* Vols. 1 and 2. New York: Knopf, 1994.

Trexler, Harrison. *Slavery in Missouri, 1804–1865.* Baltimore: Johns Hopkins University Press, 1914.

Triplett, Frank. *The Life, Times, and Treacherous Death of Jesse James.* New York: Promontory Press, 1970.

Turner, Frederick Jackson. *The Frontier in American History.* New York: Holt, 1947.

Way, Frederick, Jr., comp. *Way's Packet Directory, 1848–1983: Passenger Steamboats of the Mississippi River System since the Advent of Photography in Mid-Continent America.* Athens: Ohio University Press, 1983.

Weiner, Alan S. "John Scott, Thomas Hart Benton, David Baron, and the 1824 Presidential Election: A Case Study in Pressure Politics." *Missouri Historical Review* 60: 4 (July 1966): 460–94.

Weller, Stuart, and Stuart St. Clair. *Geology of Ste. Genevieve County, Missouri.* Rolla: Missouri Bureau of Geology and Mines, 1928.

Wesler, Kit W., Bonnie Stepenoff, N. Renae Farris, and Carol A. Morrow. "Archaeological Test Excavations at the Delassus-Kern House, Ste. Genevieve, Missouri." *Ohio Valley Historical Archaeology* 14 (1999): 67–88.

Wish, Harvey, "The French of Old Missouri (1804–1821): A Study in Assimilation." *Mid-America: An Historical Review* 23, no. 3 (July 1941): 167–89.

Wood, Gordon. *The Americanization of Benjamin Franklin.* New York: Penguin Books, 2004.

Yealy, Francis Joseph. *Sainte Genevieve: The Story of Missouri's Oldest Settlement.* Ste. Genevieve: Bicentennial Historical Committee, 1935.

Women's Club of Ste. Genevieve. "Historical Highlights of Ste. Genevieve, 1735–1972." Ozark Regional Library, Ste. Genevieve, Mo.

INDEX

Burr, Aaron, 82–83, 93, 201
bushwhackers (guerillas), 102
Butler, Mann, 157
Byer, Ansehlm, 149–50

Cahokia (Prairie du Rocher), 13
Callaway, John, 79
Camp Jackson, 99
Cape Girardeau, Missouri, 65, 110
Cardondelet, Baron de, 28
Carlisle, Sallie, 167
Carr, William C., 79
Cassimere (free black), 127
Catholic Church. See Roman Catholic
    Church
Catholicism, conversion to, 157
Cavelier, Antoine, 127, 132–33
Cavelier, Israel, 132
Cavelier, Julienne Ricard, 132
Cavelier, Louis, 131–32
Cavelier, Mari Coton de Mahi ("Caterina
    Alemande"), 130, 131–32, 134
Cavelier, Philomena, 132
cemeteries: family plots in, 184; mainte-
    nance of, x; as record of causes of death,
    7, 174. See also Memorial Cemetery
    (Old Town Cemetery); Ste. Genevieve
    Catholic Cemetery; Valle Spring
    Cemetery
Chadwell, Amanda, 168
Charles (slave), 116–17
"child bed fever," 176
childbirth, 176
Chinese immigrants, prejudice against, 166
cholera, 7, 53, 87, 114, 172–74
cholera infantum, 176
Chouteau, Auguste, 36
Christmas celebrations, 193–94
church: and democratization, 7, 154;
    regular services established for, 156. See
    also Roman Catholic Church
Cincinnati (steamboat), 182
civil rights movement, 105
Civil War: and issue of slavery, 56–57, 88,
    89, 98, 105; proslavery sympathies dur-
    ing, 98; service by free blacks during, 7,
    100–101, 121, 133, 135, 202; treatment of
    returning veterans of, 101–2
Clark, Emily, 128
Clark, William, 3, 45
class. See social status
Clay, Henry, 46

clerk of the courts, responsibility of, 79
Code Noir (Black Code) of 1724, 122
Coffin, Margaret, 170, 172
colds, 174, 176, 180
Collet, Father Luke, 156
Columbia Missouri Intelligencer, 172
Cone Mills, 183
Congress, U.S., and land disputes, 32
constables, authority of, 79
Constitution, U.S.: development of
    democracy under, 75–76, 89–90, 197;
    influence on German American settlers,
    69, 72; loyalty to, 201
consumption, 71, 176, 180
Contancin, Mary Louise C., 171
convent school. See Academy of St.
    Francis de Sales
convulsions, 176, 179
Cook, Nathaniel, 79
copper mining, 142–43, 192
Corbett, Rev. Mother Gabriel, 164
Cornwell Copper Mines, 143
coroners, authority of, 80
Correspondent and Record, 86
Coton de Mahi, Antoine, 130
Coton de Mahi, Charles, 130
Coton de Mahi, Hyacinth, 130
Coton de Mahi, Louis, 130
Cotteux, Louis, 148
Courts of Common Pleas, 79
Courts of Oyer and Terminer, 94
Courts of Quarter Sessions, 37, 78–79,
    81, 85
Cox, Joseph, 184
cramps, 176
Crawford, William, 46
criminal law, handling of, 24
Crittenden, Thomas T., 94
Cromin, Frances, 116
croup, 174, 176
curfews, 98

Dahmen, Father Francis Xavier, 161–63
dancing: enjoyment of, 188; religious
    opposition to, 159
D'Atchurut, Elizabeth ("Lisette"): land
    occupied by, 31; lawsuit brought by, 24–
    25, 96, 108, 121, 202; occupation of, 126
De Mun, Auguste, 80, 94
DeAndreis, Father Felix, 160
death: causes of, 7, 114, 161, 170–83;
    reactions to, 7, 170, 203–4

About the Author

Photo by B. H. Rucker

Bonnie Stepenoff is Professor Emeritus of History at Southeast Missouri State University. She is the author of five other books, including *Working the Mississippi: Two Centuries of Life on the River* (University of Missouri Press). She lives in Chesterfield, Missouri.